14

WEAPON OF JIHAD

KAREN AND JAMES G. CRUMLEY

Although the author and publisher have made every effort to ensure the accuracy and completeness of information contained in this book, we assume no responsibility for errors, inaccuracies, omissions or any inconsistency herein. Any slights of people, places or organizations are unintentional. Beliefs or opinions expressed by characters in this book are not necessarily those of the authors or publishers.

ISBN Number 1-57087-493-X

Library of Congress Catalog Card Number 99-75762

Printed and bound in the United States of America.
99 00 01 02 03   10 9 8 7 6 5 4 3 2 1

ii

ACKNOWLEDGMENTS

Many thanks to Josh, Caleb and April and all of our friends and family members who have encouraged us in this project.

A special thanks goes to Aunt Irene and Uncle Marion.

We appreciate Connie Hartsfield for helping with the design of our cover.

Thank-you, Doreen Barnett, for editing the book and for hastening our progress.

Dedication

We dedicate this book to Josh, Caleb and April.

We also dedicate it to each other.
We managed to keep our love for each other, despite all the squabbles
and disagreements we had in seeing this project to completion.

PREFACE

President Clinton has said that the only thing that kept him from sleeping at night was the threat of biological terrorist attacks. Of course, he is right. This is a real concern. The President's apprehension mirrors the anxieties of many of us. It is a blind spot in our thinking. We are led to think that, even if terrorists were successful in using a biological weapon against us, it would be relatively minor. Yes, it would be horrible and possibly hundreds of people could be killed, but life would go on. We are, after all, the most powerful nation in the history of mankind. Any group or nation that visited such horrors on our people would face our full wrath. The nation would survive.

It is this presumed invincibility that masks our true vulnerability. *Weapon of Jihad* exposes this error. The real threat is annihilation...death unparalleled...total defeat.

Though the story and characters are fiction, the scientific facts presented are reality. Using the completely plausible plan in this story, a Third World power could successfully attack our nation.

We discussed the scenario described in our book with experts responsible for our defenses in these matters. When we asked them if it would actually work...THE ANSWER WAS ALWAYS...YES.

CHAPTER 1

Flying. No, perhaps floating. Drifting. Naked, but not cold. Below him, he saw the wrecked, bombed-out remains of a city he recognized as Berlin. Fighting raged only a few blocks away.

He hovered above the burned-out buildings as whiffs of smoke from their still-smoldering remains drifted past him. His mouth fell slightly agape as he peered down into a building where he saw the bodies of two individuals he immediately recognized as Adolf Hitler and Eva Braun.

Visible fumes began to rise up off of Hitler's body and the smell of burning flesh was so strong that the man could taste it. The fumes gathered like a black cloud and, coming upward in a reverse spiral like a cloud of many vultures, they came towards him. Voices came out of the cloud of fumes, speaking in a disturbing tongue that he did not recognize.

Coming closer, their forms began to be clearer and he saw their hideous contours. One of them loomed larger than all the rest of his followers. Terror surged through the man as the multitude of them, including the large one, soared past him. To his surprise, they ignored him. The creatures began to speak again, only this time he could understand them.

The man received some understanding of their nature. They were rebellious creatures...angry...hot...restless. Seen, but unseen. There, but not there.

Surrounded by their ephemeral forms, their red eyes darted back and forth, for they constantly sought whom they could devour with deceit and lies...lies blended with truth to yield a skillful deception. Lies that only the strongest, most vigilant and most prayerful could resist to see the truth. Even then, the truth could only be seen partially, like through an opaque glass.

The testimony of their existence poured from every news broadcast. They had names...Murder, Violence, Hate. Their power was one of persuasion as they hung on shoulders and whispered into receptive ears. Through this, the history of mankind had been painted.

The man became aware of a growing source of light coming from somewhere behind him. He rotated his suspended body in an effort to locate the source of the light. Its brilliance forced him to turn his head away and shield his eyes with one hand. A voice flowed from the radiance in waves of such strength that his intestines quivered violently, compelling him to fold his arms across his abdomen. The creatures threw their claws up in defense and hissed until the air vibrated.

"Leave. You are defeated." The voice sent shivers all over them and they retreated, looking back in fear at their powerful enemy.

The largest of the creatures spoke to the rest. "We will leave. But we will begin our search now and we will find the one that we can occupy. We will find the one with all the right conditions. The seed will be there. We will blind the ones that need blinding. We will deceive the ones needing deceiving and make all oblivious to his ways. He will work our purpose. We will control all that the Most High has created and we will ascend up to be like the Most High."

• • •

He got out of bed and groped his way to the bathroom to relieve himself. He shuffled to the basin and wet his face and his thin gray hair.

"Dreams...Why does he have to give me dreams?" He spoke through gritted teeth and glanced up at the ceiling. "Why don't you just talk to me, huh?" He shuffled back to the toilet and eased himself down on it.

"How about a big booming God-type voice...'Moses, Moses'...you know, Charlton Heston...Ten Commandment stuff...'General, General. Arise...wake thy rusty, old wrinkled ass from thy deep slumber and hearken thou unto me.' See? Then you could just spit out whatever the hell it is you want me to know. What would be wrong with explaining some of this crap to me, just once? But, no. I get some screwed-up nightmare that doesn't make any sense to me.

"Seems like if I told you I didn't understand dreams, you'd go 'Oh, O.K., no more dreams.' I could just go, 'Yeah, Lord. Thy humble, ignorant dip-shit doth listen'. Well, I just don't get it O.K.?

2

"I betcha you're thinking right now, 'Well, Elijah didn't give me half this much horse-shit.' You gotta admit, you did *talk* to all those Old Testament farts."

He rose abruptly from the toilet. "See? I hope you're happy...scared me shitless."

"Honey, are you all right?"

"I'm fine, Sarah. Go back to sleep."

Sarah sat up in bed. "Dick, were you talking to me, Hon?"

"Naw, just chewing on God's ass." He raised one eye up. "Just kidding," he whispered.

"You've got gas?"

"I said I was chewing on...go back to bed dear!" Sarah had grown quite hard of hearing. Besides, General Dick Herndon was renowned for talking to himself. "It's the only intelligent conversation I can get into," he often quipped.

Stepping into the shower, the General shook his finger in the air. "I know, being in the business that you're in, that you've noticed by now that I'm not your basic righteous and holy type." Sudsing with one hand and gesturing with the other, he added, "Now, I'm not trying to tell you how to run your business or anything like that, but you're bound to be able to find somebody else to show this crap to."

He toweled off and shook his head as he continued. "You know, I'm not exactly staying up late praying, 'Please, send me another weird-ass dream that will scare me shitless.' ...Dream, my ass! Dreams...dreams are fuzzy...gray, black and white sorta things. These things...even life seems like a dream compared to these things." He toweled his head off and then wrinkled his nose in disgust as he sniffed the towel. He rubbed his hand in his hair and whiffed the burnt flesh smell again. "Damn, shoulda shampooed. I just love these little souvenirs you always send back with me. How do you do that, that's what I wanna know...God stuff, huh?

"You know, I'm not exactly Mr. Popularity at that five-sided warehouse for remedial thinkers where I work. Can't you just see it? 'Hey, Mr. Joint Chief of Staff. Would you like to hear the latest tidbit that the Almighty has let me in on? What's that you say, Sir...? Why does he only see fit to confide in me, Sir...? I don't know, Sir, but I'll be sure to bring that point up to him, Sir.'

3

"And about that crap with flying around in the air as bare as a baby's bottom...Some kind of symbolic bullshit, no doubt...! Well, I can damn sure do without that. Anyway, I guess you heard me bitch enough. I'm sure you'll sort it all out for me somehow."

Amy

Spring, 1973, Lubbock, Texas

Malik Azar looked up from his pathogenic bacteriology text to glance at his roommate, Sadeq Nadim. The silence in the room demanded his attention. Outwardly, Sadeq stared at the same passage Malik studied. The test would be tomorrow.

But the furrow on Sadeq's brow belied his apparent studying. Malik had seen this expression many times on his roommate's face, mainly in quiet moments, in the two years since they had flown from Iran and been placed together in the dorm. He did not know what was haunting Sadeq, but it looked painful. Sadeq's dark eyes focused on some event deep within himself that contorted his face in concern and caused tears to well up, but not fall.

Sadeq noticed Malik's gaze and blinked, as usual, snapping his face into a nonchalant expression. Malik knew from experience that it was useless to question him about it. Sadeq never gave Malik any hint of what was hidden beneath that dark gaze.

And yet, Sadeq was Malik's closest friend in many ways. Their cultural heritage bonded them as they worked together in this strange American culture to earn a degree in microbiology and take the information back to their own country. The fact that they were both good students was the reason the Shah's government had selected them for overseas study.

They learned English together...real English...the kind spoken by the people of West Texas. This included the slang worlds made by dropping the jaw lower than necessary at each vowel. Each time someone said something that the boys could not understand, they looked at each other, hoping the other one got it. The person speaking usually tried again more slowly or

4

louder, but sometimes, even that did not help. People always smiled when the boys spoke.

Sadeq had shared his Texas vision with Malik on the plane. He had seen all of John Wayne's movies and was aware that everybody in Texas wore cowboy hats and boots...big boots...to protect them from all the rattlesnakes. They would, of course, have to learn to ride horses well. Maybe he could be in a rodeo. He would even master the cowboy slang. How did it go? Pardner? He was looking forward to meeting John Wayne in person.

Even though Malik shared all of this with Sadeq, the fact remained that they came from very different families. Malik hailed from a family swept up completely in the Shah's modernization movement. Malik's sisters received the same education as Malik. Sadeq's family, on the other hand, remained firmly rooted in the traditional Muslim model. Sadeq spoke very little about this. It seemed to depress him to talk about it.

"Hey...Is *E. coli* lactose positive or negative?" Mike Thompson stood leaning on the door, thumbing through a Difco Manual. "Man, this test is gonna kick my butt!"

"Positive, I think," Sadeq answered as he tried to find it in his notes. Mike lived in the adjoining room of their suite. His blond hair and fair skin were in contrast to his olive-skinned friends. But Mike had never let this bother him. Malik thought it was because Mike had been raised as an "Air force Brat," as Mike put it. Out of self-defense, he made friends easily. His endearing qualities included his strong accent and his ability to make people laugh. He did not do this on purpose. He just accidentally did things that people thought were funny. It went along with his long gangly appearance.

Mike always did his best to Americanize his Iranian friends. He helped them with the language and tried to explain things they did not understand. When the black-haired beauty in the dorm lobby stood up and lectured a young man, Mike tried to explain that the women here were a little different. Malik liked it. But, Sadeq stared at the girl, judgment written all over his face.

"How could that woman be so disrespectful?" Sadeq questioned. Malik and Mike just shook their heads and kept walking.

Mike took his friends home with him at Christmas and Thanksgiving because they could not go home. He taught them all of his favorite traditions, including the Silver Dollar.

The trip to the famous country-western nightclub was supposed to show them how Texans had fun. Instead, an inebriated drugstore cowboy, made bold by several beers, came up and picked a fight with Sadeq over a young lady wearing a lavender pair of hotpants. Just as Sadeq was about to meet with a Texas fist, Mike stepped into it.

"Hey, good buddy...let me buy you a beer," he said nodding and waving in the direction of a young lady with a tray in her hand. "Three beers over here, please."

His smiling gestures confused the drunken cowboy. The waitress pushed her way through the crowd to the tense scene.

"Here ya go, good buddy."

Mike reached to grab a beer to hand it to the cowboy, but he stumbled, hurling the waitress, her tray and the three beers onto the cowboy in a loud crash. Before the cowboy could swim out of the pool of beer, Mike quickly grabbed the Iranians and pulled them to the car to escape before the law showed up.

The boys always had a good laugh when they talked about the night of the mass "Streaking" in the courtyard between the three freshman dormitories. They awoke at two in the morning as Mike burst into their room. A loud commotion grew outside their window. Running to the window, Mike dawned a shocked expression.

"Oh, my God! Get a look at this!"

Malik stumbled over to the window, rubbing sleep from his eyes, and did not believe what he saw. Masses of students dashed across the courtyard with absolutely no clothes on their bodies. They all sang, chanted and yelled until the sirens of the Campus Cops began. Then, as suddenly as they had appeared, they disappeared, scampering into bushes and buildings.

Malik and Sadeq were working towards a degree in microbiology with a minor in chemistry. This required so much lab and study that they simply could not understand how these Americans could have so much time to play and party.

They arrived at the microbiology lab they had scheduled for that afternoon. Susan, one of their lab assistants, greeted them at the door.

"OK, Gentlemen. Pick up your supplies in those baskets and get started." She tossed her red, shoulder-length hair all around. Then she brushed it back out of her face and tied it in a neat ponytail. The boys did exactly as she said. They genuinely respected Susan. This was her last semester before graduation. Her intelligence and straight-forwardness complemented her friendliness and sweetness...as long as things were going her way. Everyone she worked with knew this, so they worked very hard not to cross her. She studied regularly with the more serious students like Malik, Sadeq, Mike and Tom. Tom was Mike's roommate. His longer-length, brown hair announced his laid-back attitude. He never looked like he was studying, but, then again, he did not need to do too much of it. He got it the first time.

That afternoon, the lab involved bacterial identification techniques. Bunsen burners glowed on all of the lab tables. Some of the students were inoculating beige, green or red bacterial media. Others prepared stained slides with green and navy blue stains.

A curious mixture of smells filled the room. The clean smell of alcohol mingled with the soupy smells of the media and the nauseating smell of bacterial-cultures. Susan moved around the room, going from table to table, checking the students' procedures and giving advice. The smells and sounds wafted down the hall from the lab.

Amy Williams hurried along the hallway towards the lab entrance. She was a well-built blonde and she wore her tight sweater proudly. The fact that she and Susan had been roommates for two years proved that opposites really did attract. Amy studied business management. She detested the ugly smells emanating from the lab and held her breath as she paced into the lab looking for Susan.

Susan looked up from across the room and smiled, surprised to see her roomie. Then she began wading her way through the students to get to the door. Amy's face grew increasingly red as she avoided breathing while she waited for Susan. Just as Susan arrived, Amy's roving eye caught a glimpse of Sadeq.

"Now, there's one you haven't told me about, Roomie!" she whispered as she indicated Sadeq with her eyes.

7

Amy pulled Susan outside the door and said, "Do you have your car keys? I left my project in the trunk last night and I have to take it to class in less than fifteen minutes."

She glanced at her watch nervously as Susan fumbled in her pocket for the keys. Susan gave Amy the keys and Amy trotted to the stairs.

As she reached the door to the stairwell, Amy called, "And I'll expect a full report on that one later today!" referring to Sadeq. Sadeq had also noticed her.

After supper, Susan went up to her room to study for that horrible mid-term final in Bacterial Physiology. The small room held everything in its rectangular shape. A thin bed hung on each sidewall.

The beds and desks were the only similar things on the opposite sides of the room. Susan had kept many of her books, so her bookcase bore many science reference materials. On her desk sat a picture of her parents and her brother. Her bulletin board above the bed held various five by seven electromicrographs made by the electron microscope. She studied them as she fell to sleep each night. Her favorite was the virus that looked like a lunar-lander on bent, spiky legs.

The simple blue bedspread contrasted with the complex black and white pictures. A white trash can with a big yellow smiley face on the side gave the room more color.

Amy's side of the room, by contrast, was splashed with many bright colors. Brilliant orange flowers mingled with green leaves and yellow buds on her bedspread. Her bookcase held mainly picture albums and one orange lava lamp, bubbling up strange globs every few seconds. A large poster advertising the movie Love Story dominated her bulletin board.

Susan noticed her car keys on her desk. "Well, she must have made it back."

She turned on the radio and sat down to get started on her notes. She had only been studying for a while when Amy charged into their room.

"Do you have to be so noisy?" Susan griped to Amy.

"What's eatin you, Roomie?"

"Oh, it's just this mid-term. You know...GPA... Grad school!"

Amy came a little closer. "If you'll tell me about that guy in your lab, I'll go away and won't bother you all night."

"It's a deal!" Susan had been dreading keeping Amy quiet long enough for a little studying. "So, what do you want to know?"

"Well, who is he? What's his name? What's he like? Is he rich? You know, stuff like that."

Susan grinned. "Oh, the usual stuff."

"Yeah," laughed Amy.

"Let's see—his name is Sadeq Nadim and he's from Iran. He is a very good student, which you probably don't care about, and he must be rich or he could not be over here. And to answer your next question, no he's not married or going with anyone. Is that all?"

In the background, the radio played *Midnight at the Oasis*, and Susan could see where Amy was getting some of this. Two of their friends were dating guys from the Middle East and this was something Amy, who considered herself an expert, had not yet experienced. As the radio blared out the seductive song about an American with a crush on a young sheik, Susan rolled her eyes and slowly shook her head in response to Amy's dreamy expression.

Amy continued, "He has the most gorgeous dark eyes, and that olive skin...MMM. He looks just like Omar Shariff."

"O.K.! Enough! I have to study!"

Amy took her cue, grabbed her book and exited the bear's den as quickly as she could.

The next week, Amy volunteered to help Susan with her job as lab assistant. "What a surprise," thought Susan. Amy certainly was entertaining. Susan knew better than to try to resist. She was resigned to the situation.

"Sure, you can help me grade some papers...or something."

Amy flitted into the lab, showing absolutely none of the previous disgust towards anything biological. *Selective squeamishness—interesting concept!* thought Susan.

Malik and Sadeq saw Amy moving around the room, trying not to look too obvious, but the effort was wasted. They knew the look of a woman on a hunt, and they could tell by the way she kept looking at Sadeq that he was the intended prey. Sadeq looked at Malik.

"Look at those green eyes!"

9

That was one of Sadeq's requirements for the perfect woman. They had discussed these requirements several times, so Malik knew this could be trouble. This girl was just too practiced at enticing young men. "Be careful, Sadeq. Do not you remember the warning old Muslih gave us concerning these American women?" Muslih, a member of the Shah's Council, had introduced the boys shortly before they had been given final instructions and sent to the United States.

"Old Muslih has never seen *this*."

As lab came to a close, Sadeq secured Amy's phone number and caught up with Malik down the hall. They walked over to the dorm, ate and cleaned up. The whole time, Sadeq chattered about his newfound love interest. Malik listened patiently as they strolled across the campus to the party.

Every few months, all the students from Iran got together to socialize. It brought them back together with their roots. They all exchanged notes about happenings in Iran.

This time, Ahmad Razavi reported that there was apparently some kind of economic slump going on in Iran. His parents had written of hardships and spoke of the restlessness of his neighbors. It sounded like trouble could be brewing at home. The Shah's troops had now put down several riots. One of the government buildings had been bombed. Seeing the disbelief on their faces, Ahmad decided to read the letter aloud to them. Silence befell the group when he stopped talking and sat down. Amir Azimi tried to lighten the mood by interjecting small joke.

"Yes, and I can just picture that old Muslih running around trying to put out all those political fires!" Nobody laughed. Ahmad looked down and replied that he had heard that Muslih had been arrested.

Malik could see that this party was not going to last much longer. With all that news, everyone wanted to go home and mull over what the consequences could mean for him or her. This report made all of them very unsettled. Would this mean that they would have to go back home? What kind of political unrest could be happening there? When they had last checked, the Shah had things well in command. Everyone was happy and the ties of the Iranian government with the U.S. were strong.

Malik could not help noticing how Nima, Ahmad's wife, was so emotionally supportive to Ahmad. With all this uncertainty, Malik felt the need of an educated, understanding wife like Nima. He wondered what life would have been like if he had been married before he came to the United States. True, it would be more complicated, but at times like this, married life would be worth the trouble.

As Malik and Sadeq returned slowly to their dorm, Malik turned to Sadeq. "Do you ever wish you had brought a wife with you?"

"Are you telling a joke? I am only now beginning to enjoy the life of a bachelor! I plan on calling Amy when we get to the room."

"I thought you did not like the way the American women think."

Sadeq grinned. "OK, maybe I can give it a try."

• • •

A groomed, smiling Sadeq, wearing a white-on-white shirt, opened the glass door of the dorm that Amy and Susan called home. He had picked the white colors of the shirt because they contrasted with his skin and eyes so well. He knew American women liked Omar Shariff and he tried to imitate that look.

He called her just as he was leaving his room and asked her to meet him downstairs. As he walked in, she stepped out of the elevator. He had never seen such a beautiful sight. Her shoulder-length blond hair was curled at the ends and it bounced lightly as she swept into the room. Her green eyes sparkled seductively to Sadeq as her mouth formed into a slight smile.

Even though several other students stood in the room, Amy was all Sadeq saw from that point on. Her tight sweater blended perfectly with her very short, straight skirt and fishnet hose. He was looking forward to exploring those later! Her enticing eyes wore a hint of green eyes-shadow that brought out her emerald-colored eyes. There she stood—his perfect woman, and she was going to be with *him* that night.

Amy surveyed the room for Sadeq as she exited the elevator. She collected all the interested glances of the young men in the room as she waltzed over to Sadeq. He was so handsome with his olive skin and dark eyes, set off by that shirt. So, he had a good taste in clothes, too! She intended to find out everything she could about him that night. The thought

11

of being with a sheik sent her hormones racing even faster than they usually did. Being on the pill had not slowed them down for even a second. If anything, they had sped up...at least, she had used them more. She loved this new age of freedom.

Sadeq opened the door of the car he had borrowed from Mike and let Amy slide into the passenger seat. Her thighs filled out the hose and the skirt rode even higher as she scooted into the seat. Sadeq almost gasped at the sight. She peeked back out of the car and gave him a wink and said "Thank-you" in a voice that made him hold his breath. When he got into the driver's seat, Amy slid over and slipped her arms around his arm. He was not sure he could drive. His gaze kept shifting to those legs and then to her breasts, moving ever so slightly every time the car hit a bump in the road. He could hardly eat, watching the curvature of her lips as they surrounded her fork. He pretended to watch the movie, but his body demanded that he pay full attention to Amy's form draped on his shoulder and her leg that kept lightly brushing up against his. The smell of her soft hair made his mind work feverishly to figure out a way or a place to go where they could be left alone. He made a call to Malik after the movie was over. Malik agreed to go to the library so everything was set. Amy walked to his bed and sat down, running her hands lightly over his bedspread. He turned and locked the door.

The following morning, Sadeq hurried to call Amy. Malik shook his head as he watched.

"Hello." Amy's sleepy voice made Sadeq wish he were there.

"Good Morning, Beautiful."

"MMM...Sadeq. Good morning."

"I wish I was with you right now."

"Me, too."

"How about tonight?"

"MMM...Yes."

Malik could see that he was going to have to find some other place to live for a while.

As the day continued, every time he looked around, Sadeq was gazing into Amy's eyes...at meals...between class...all the time. And every night. Malik camped in Mike's room so much that he began to feel like he belonged there. Still, the thin dorm walls could not diminish the impact of the sound effects in the next room.

The next month in microbiology lab, Susan saw Malik walk out the door to get some water. She nonchalantly followed and caught up with him. "Malik, I need to talk to you."

"Sure," said Malik, looking at her curiously.

"I want to warn you about Amy. She came back to the dorm after her date with Sadeq and she was floating on her usual cloud."

"Usual cloud?"

"Yes, usual cloud...Look, she's my roomie and everything, but I've always hated her ways with boys. It's like she has to keep trying new types all the time. She falls completely in love, totally dedicated...at least for three months. The love luster begins to fade from her eyes and she looks around for someone else to love. They never last long and she never cares who she hurts. She puts on a real good love start, then dumps the guy fast and hard, never looking back."

Malik stopped walking and turned to face Susan. "Do you tell me she does this all the time?"

"Yes. Tell Sadeq not to fall too hard for her. It won't last."

"It is too late! You should have seen him when he came home that night. That is all I hear from him—Amy this, Amy that—sometimes I leave the room just to avoid hearing that name again for a few minutes. He is about to take me out of my mind. And worse, he does not now study. Do you know that lab test next Tuesday?"

"Yeah?"

"Well, he is not looking at it yet. He is not like him now. I am worried concerning him. He has their first five sons named already."

"Uh-oh, that's bad. What can I do to help?"

"I do not know, but I knew Amy was bad the first time I see her. I told Sadeq to wait for his woman waiting in Iran but he wants to take Amy home instead."

"His woman in Iran?"

"Yes, Arya has been pledged to him since he was a child."

Malik looked off and shook his head slowly. His stomach rose to his heart as the dreaded reality set in. Poor Sadeq!

13

"Do you want me to talk to him?" Susan asked.

Susan saw the degree of his concern and she wished she had taken the time, before now, to warn Sadeq. Just then Sadeq rounded the corner, looking for Malik. Susan and Malik exchanged glances and Malik walked forward to meet Sadeq.

"Sadeq, Susan desires to speak with you."

Susan hated this. She felt responsible. What could she say? How could she make this easier for Sadeq? "I just wanted to talk to you about Amy."

At the very mention of Amy's name, Sadeq grinned happily.

"Oh, thank-you for showing me to her! She is so perfect! Why did you not show me to her for so long?"

Susan's heart sank as she realized the pitiful situation. "Look, Sadeq. She is not what you think. I know right now you think she's the perfect girl, but believe me, she's not. I live with her and I'm telling you it won't last. Don't let her hurt you."

Sadeq was confused. Why would Susan say such cruel things about Amy? Maybe Susan was jealous of Amy.

"Why do you say those things? That is not true!"

Susan tried again. "I've seen her do this lots of times. She is playing a role, apparently a very convincing role. She will grow tired of it before long. Don't get hurt. Be careful. Please listen to me, Sadeq."

Sadeq grew angry now. He brought his thick brows together and down. He did not believe Susan. He did not know why Susan was lying like this, but he did not believe it. And, he would not listen to it any more.

Mike and Tom came out of the lab door just in time to see Sadeq turn quickly away from Susan and Malik and push past them back into the lab. There, he grabbed his books and lab supplies and sped angrily out the door. He did not wait for the elevator. He stormed down the stairs loudly instead.

"What was that about?" asked Mike as he reached Malik and Susan. "He looked like he was ready to explode."

"Yeah, and it's my fault," explained Susan. "I'm sorry, Malik. Is he going to be all right?"

"I do not know. Leave him by himself for a while. Maybe he will see what we are talking about. He can be so stubborn. Come on, Mike. I'll tell you all about it."

Malik and Mike walked back into the lab, followed by Tom and Susan. She had stopped to glance back at the door to the stairwell, concerned.

It was well past ten PM when Sadeq wandered back into the dorm where Malik had been waiting for him. Sadeq scowled at Malik. He had gone to see Amy and his visit convinced him, even more, that they were all wrong about her.

"I spoke to her. You are wrong. Amy loves me and is going to be my wife," Sadeq said, mostly to himself. Malik just looked at him.

"I hope to see you are right, Sadeq."

And Sadeq was right...for a while. Then, one evening when Malik went to his room, Sadeq sat brooding and studying at his desk.

"I don't believe what I'm seeing! I do have a roommate."

Sadeq set his jaw. "Stop it, Malik. Amy had to study."

Malik gave Sadeq a knowing look. "Oh...O.K." He did not know that Amy ever studied.

Sadeq could not help himself. He kept looking at the phone until finally, he picked it up and dialed Amy's number.

"Hello." The fact that Susan answered the phone told him that Amy was not there. Amy always answered the phone if she was there.

"Oh, Hi...Is Amy there?"

Susan recognized Sadeq's voice. "No, Sadeq, I'm sorry."

"Do you know where she is?"

Susan started to say that she had thought that Amy was with him. She had gotten all dressed up before she left. She thought better of telling him that.

"Uh...No, sorry."

"Could you get her to call me when she gets in?"

"Sure."

Sadeq stared at the phone for a while after he put it down. Malik pretended not to notice. Then, the old, dark expression appeared on Sadeq's face again. The phone rang at about twelve o'clock. Malik let Sadeq answer it.

"Amy, where were you. I tried to call...Oh...O.K. ...I love you too."

"Well?" Malik asked.

"She went to the library...is that OK?"

"Sure." Malik saw that it was a touchy subject.

The next morning, Malik and Sadeq walked across the campus to their eight-o'clock class. Malik had been very careful not to bring up Amy, but he noticed that Amy did not get up to eat breakfast with Sadeq. He looked to the left to watch the traffic as they crossed the street. His eyes caught a sight that sent his breakfast to his throat. Amy was across the block, walking along the other street...with her arms wrapped around another boy's arm.

She must have felt Malik's shocked gaze. As quickly as she saw the boys, she dropped the young man's arm and distanced herself from him. Sadeq caught sight of her.

"Amy!" he called and ran toward her.

"Oh...Hi, Sadeq." She started walking toward them. "I stayed up so late studying last night that I overslept."

"It's OK. We can eat together at lunch."

"Yeah...Uh...Sadeq. I can't today."

"Why not?"

"There's a study group meeting at lunch."

"Oh, OK." They walked silently until Amy had to turn off to her class.

"It is good that Amy has learned to study...don't you think?" Sadeq said.

"Yeah...Sure." Malik looked straight ahead.

But, that night Malik opened his room door and found Amy lovingly wrapped around Sadeq once again, as if nothing had happened. She smiled up at Malik, then planted a big one on Sadeq. Sadeq was obviously enjoying himself, so Malik gathered his stuff and headed off to Mike's room...again.

A few days later it happened again...only this time Sadeq saw Amy holding onto another boy. Sadeq's jaw dropped and he stopped midstep in reaction to the sight. To Malik's surprise, Amy did not try to hide it this time.

"Hi, Boys!" she called, ignoring the fact that Sadeq had not taken a breath since he saw her. Neither boy said anything.

"Oh, I forgot to introduce you. This is Stan. Stan, this is Malik and this is Sadeq." Malik saw Sadeq's hand shaking. "Oh, yeah," she continued, "He's my cousin from New Mexico. I haven't seen him in a year." Sadeq blinked and took a breath.

Amy saw his reaction and laughed. "Oh, I bet you thought it was something else. Sorry!" She ran to Sadeq and slid her arms around his waist. "You know I could never love anybody else!"

Sadeq smiled an insecure grin. "Oh, Amy...you scared me. Don't ever do that again."

As they kissed, Stan stood by, wearing a curious expression and a slight smile. Malik only knew one thing...his eyes had locked with Amy's and he did not trust her, even if Sadeq did. He tried to tell Sadeq many times, with no success.

Sadeq managed to deny every report of Amy's wanderings. He would not be convinced. Still, something inside him pulled at him. He reacted by trying to be closer to her...more often. But the more he strove for a deeper relationship with Amy, the more she pulled away.

"I need more space, Sadeq. You're smothering me," she told him. Amy suddenly required more time...to study. Sadeq caught her walking with other boys and confronted her about it. "Oh, they're just friends," was her reply.

Malik asked Mike about it. "But does she still love Sadeq? She doesn't call him anymore. The more she hurts him, the more he wants her."

"Yeah...and the thing is that if he'd be mean to her, she'd come begging back to him."

"Oh, Sadeq will never be mean to Amy."

"I know. Amy's such a witch. She's trash...she needs somebody to beat her or she won't love him. As long as Sadeq chases her like some lovesick puppy, she's just going to walk all over him. He might as well throw himself on the floor and volunteer to be her door mat."

Finally, Amy called Sadeq and asked to see him. "Look, Sadeq. I don't mean to hurt you, but...I just don't think it's working out. I used to love you, but I'm not so sure now. Maybe we need some time away...you know...we can just be friends for a while." She ignored the hurt on Sadeq's face. "Anyway...I've got to go study now." She purposely kept from meeting his tortured eyes. "See you around, Sadeq."

Even with this final announcement from Amy, Sadeq refused to believe that it was over. He was sure that she would come back to him after she thought it over.

Someone told him that they had seen Amy with another boy. At first, he flatly refused to believe it. But the picture of Amy holding on to another man kept popping up in his brain. Finally, the curiosity got to him so he carefully waited outside the glass walls of the ground floor entrance and watched to see if there was any truth to the rumor.

Amy surveyed the room for Bill as she exited the elevator. She collected all the interested glances of the young men in the room as she waltzed over to Bill. He was so handsome with his blond hair and blue eyes, set off by his navy blue shirt. So, he had good taste in clothes, too! She intended to find out everything she could about him that night. The thought of being with a future Congressman sent her hormones racing even faster than they usually did. She loved this new age of freedom!

Susan looked up from her notes when the phone rang. Malik's voice sounded worried.

"Susan, do you have some time?"

"Sure," she lied, "What's up?"

"Sadeq is up. It's really bad. He watched Amy go out with another boy. I think he believes us now. Anyway, can you come over?"

"Give me a minute. I'll be right there."

Susan arrived at Sadeq's room where Malik, Mike and Tom had been trying to talk to a drunk Sadeq. The room smelled of vomit and alcohol, then disinfectant. Sadeq had reacted to his discovery by finding someone to buy him a good supply of booze. Sadeq sat on the edge of his bed blubbering about life.

"How could she *do* this to me...? I loved her. I was going to marry her. Now...I HATE her. My father was so right. He tried to warn me," he sobbed, "Why didn't I listen to him?" In the background, the stereo sang the song, *American Woman*. The words mirrored Sadeq's ugly mood exactly as it crooned about how bad American women were.

Sadeq laughed a hysterical laugh, "See? Even the record tried to warn me. Everybody told me and I was too stupid to listen. OK. You are right, I am wrong. I hope you are happy!"

Susan felt so bad for him. She had seen Amy do this before, but she had not realized the emotional havoc that her roomie was bringing to her victims. All she could say was, "I'm sorry, Sadeq. Amy doesn't know what

18

she does. I know it doesn't help you to know this, but it's not personal. It's Amy. She's sick or something."

They all tried to comfort him, but there was little that could be said or done. Everyone just stood around, frowning and watching Sadeq. Malik felt embarrassed for him, so he sent them all home, promising to take good care of Sadeq.

When the room emptied and grew quiet, Sadeq's expression changed, donning the familiar dark stare. Malik waited, thinking that Sadeq would come around like he usually did. But, Sadeq's face contorted in agony as he began to blubber, sobbing inconsolably.

"My moth...mother." More sobbing followed. "I never knew why...why he...he hit her...I thought he was just mean to demand her obedience...her arm...it was broken once...I hated him. I thought he was wrong to treat her so..." He laid his head back and put his arm over his eyes, convulsing over something that must have been horrible in his memory. He wiped his nose.

"She just wanted more freedom...that's all. I thought it would be OK, bu...but not my father...so cruel." He shuddered again, staring off into the distance. "Maybe he was...right...Amy has freedom...and look what..." He broke down again, sobbing as he lay curled in a fetal position on his bed.

Finally, Sadeq fell to sleep and Malik pulled the covers over him.

The next morning, Sadeq woke up with quite a headache. Malik prescribed aspirin and juice to help his head but nothing could be done for his mood.

"These women here are no good," Sadeq observed as he rubbed his eyes.

"You cannot judge all American women by Amy, Sadeq."

"Amy is the only one I liked, and look at her."

"But what about Susan?"

"She is an exception and you know it, Malik."

"I know many American women who are not like Amy at all."

"Well, I do not. And I will never trust another one. My father tried to warn me as we were leaving Iran, but I was stupid and did not listen to him. He knew the whole time how it would be here."

"My father also warned me, but I have not found any women besides Amy that fit his description. I enjoy their spirit. These women are interesting because they have freedom."

"If you ask me, Malik, freedom gives them the wrong attitude. They have no respect for men like the women at home. American men are weak for allowing their women to have so much power over them. This is an evil society."

"Maybe the American men like their women to have some spirit like I do. I want my women to be intelligent."

Sadeq's face hardened. "Then you are weak, too, Malik. You have been here too long! This evil society has begun to become a part of you."

CALCUTTA

CALCUTTA, INDIA—FALL, 1974

Ramin and Saeed stood on the dock, testing their legs after being on the boat. They gladly accepted the mysterious assignment offered by the emerging underground political group in Iran. The hardest part of the trip, so far, had been avoiding the attention of the Savak; the Shah's hated secret police that were famous for ingenious atrocities performed on their victims.

Ramin's cousin had been one of those victims and this was a major factor in Ramin's hatred for the Shah. The Shah was indeed an evil dictator and Ramin had vowed to aid in his downfall. Ramin's cousin had grasped his arm as he left, and looked at him with fire in his eyes. They were bound in the spirit of rebellion now, each doing whatever they could to rid Iran of the evil influence of America. The Shah, to them, personified that evil influence and the end of their traditional values.

So far, Allah had protected them. They had boarded the boat in Bandar Abbas and sailed out of the Gulf of Oman to the Arabian Sea. After docking at Bombay for supplies and cargo, the boat had continued on to the southern tip of India, where the weather had gotten a bit rough. The smell of the salty spray that was tossed each time a large wave slammed the boat was something Ramin would not soon forget. It mixed with the diesel fumes to make a nauseating combination. Saeed had been sick from the moment they boarded the boat. Now, Ramin could commiserate with him. The higher the waves tossed the boat, the higher Ramin's stomach had risen towards his throat.

They had skirted around the island of Ceylon and headed north in the Bay of Bengal. Finally, they had disembarked in Calcutta, slowly regaining their normal balance. Bangladesh was just a few miles to the west, so they had been instructed to walk along the shore to get there. Their target destination was Bhola, a small island just off the coast of Bangladesh. Ramin loved the feel of the warm sand flying up into his sandals as they walked along to the chorus of the breaking waves. Anyone who saw them would assume that they were simply tourists visiting the coast.

That had been an important part of their instructions. They were not to be noticed. It made Ramin nervous to think about it. It was going to be hard to avoid drawing attention, doing what their leader had asked them to do.

They hired a fishing boat to take them to the small island of Bhola. Saeed paid the fisherman as Ramin jumped off the boat into the knee-deep seawater and waded up to the beach. He fingered the long glass tubes in his pocket. The wrappers on the sterile swabs crinkled against his hand and reminded him of the scientific nature of his assignment.

He and Saeed had not been chosen because of any particular scientific knowledge or abilities. They had been picked for this assignment for two reasons. The first reason was their loyalty to the Ayatollah's government in absentia. The Ayatollah had been in exile in France since 1968. He still managed to greatly affect affairs in Iran.

The second reason was readily obvious if a person looked at Ramin and Saeed. The scars on their bodies identified them as survivors of one of the most deadly plagues ever to wander the world. Ramin's dark face, arms and legs were blemished with the lighter-colored pox scars of the disease. Yet, they were the lucky ones. Many had died, including Saeed's brother. Other survivors had been left blind, deaf or insane from the dreaded disease.

Walking in the sun along the path to the village, Saeed questioned Ramin. "Are you sure we will not get it again?" He was uneasy at the thought of suffering through the disease again.

"No, you and I can not have it anymore. Stop worrying," answered Ramin, secretly dreading the same thing. He almost convinced himself, too. Though he had been told this, he was not sure at all.

Saeed had not been briefed as Ramin had. "What do we do when we get to the village? Just walk up and ask someone for a sample?"

"No. We will go in as visiting healers. We will ask if there is any sickness in the village and offer to help. When we find it, we will know it."

As they approached the village through the trees along the path, the smells of the evening meals being prepared made their stomachs grumble in hungry protest. But the thought of what they had to do made Ramin queasy, so the hunger quickly left him.

The giggling of chasing children warned them just in time to avoid colliding with the boy in the lead. He was running as fast as he could, but he was looking back at his pursuers instead of looking where he was going.

"Ah!" yelled Saeed. "Watch out!"

The boy barely missed him and kept on running right past him.

"Come here!" fussed his mother who was approaching from another direction and had not gotten his attention. She smiled up at Saeed and Ramin as she caught her balance.

"I am sorry. My son does not know how to be polite to visitors."

"We understand," said Ramin. "Could you answer a question for us?"

"Of course. What do you want to know?"

"We are healers from Jamsheddar. We have heard that you have sickness here and we have come to help."

The woman looked at him curiously. His accent sounded strange, but she did not give it a second thought—anyone who was willing to help against this sickness was welcome.

"The other doctors are here, also. Would you like me to take you to them?"

Ramin's heart jumped in panic but he kept his smile. "No, we would like to work alone. We are not used to working with white doctors."

The woman understood and nodded. "Come with me."

She led them around a circle of huts and slowed as she walked up to certain hut. A red rag hung on the door to keep people out and safe from the sickness. She called into the hut and a weak voice answered her. She turned and motioned Saeed and Ramin into the tiny hut.

Ramin recognized the smell of the sickness immediately. It turned his stomach, but he carefully smiled at the ailing young woman lying on the grass mat on the hard-packed dirt floor. The woman did not smile back. She did not care about what went on around her because of her high fever. The blisters had just begun to form on her arms and face. Their red raised centers contained clear fluid. Ramin smiled as he realized that he had just found the kind of victim that they had been sent to find. She was in the precise stage of the disease that they needed. Now, he must convince her to let him have some of the liquid in those blisters.

"We are healers. Do you mind if we help you?"

Ramin knew exactly how she felt right now and it did not surprise him that she did not respond to his question. He began his procedure by pulling the sterile swabs and blood sample tubes from his pocket and handing them to Saeed to hold.

He took one of the packages containing two sterile swabs and opened it aseptically, the way he had been shown. He carefully knelt down and pulled out one swab. Touching the swab to one of larger blisters on the woman's arm, he rubbed it until the thin covering allowed the clear liquid to leak out. He dabbed the swab on all sides in the liquid, then carefully opened the long test tube. After dropping the swab into it, he replaced the stopper. He did the same thing with another blister, using the other swab and a different tube. Then he carefully wrapped the tubes in his handkerchief and put them back into his pocket as the woman moaned and rolled over away from them.

Ramin smiled and nodded at Saeed. Saeed looked like he had been holding his breath the whole time and his eyes were wide in apprehension. Apparently, he had not enjoyed his encounter with the illness either.

As they quickly left the hut and disappeared down the path to the shore, they did not talk to each other, or to anyone else. They wanted to get away without being noticed. They would get the sample back to Iran in preparation for the Ayatollah's return to power. Their mission would be complete.

23

In another hut across the village, the woman who had showed Ramin to the sick woman spoke to the white doctor. "Other healers from north of Calcutta have come to help."

Dr. Pete Wilson, who had been sent there by the World Health Organization, looked up at the woman. "Really? Where are they?'

He hoped that the help he had summoned had finally arrived. Just a few months ago, the WHO had been ready to declare that this disease had been eradicated. Then, the floods had come and these cases in Bangladesh had surfaced. It was certainly a virulent strain of the virus. Maybe these would be the last victims. He followed her to the woman's hut, but there was no trace of the two men.

"That's strange," he muttered to himself. He turned and went back to the task of immunizing the remaining villagers.

GRADUATION

LUBBOCK, TEXAS—MAY, 1977

The morning sun shone down on the sea of black graduation caps arranged in rows across the first fifty yards of the football field. Malik sat within the third row of the graduates, wearing the collar that identified him as a candidate for his Master's Degree. Next to him, sat Sadeq.

As soon as the ceremony ended, the graduates milled around the area, visiting. Malik looked at Sadeq and the weightiness of the moment mirrored on his face.

"So that is it." He paused. "We have been here so long that Iran seems like some dream I had a long time ago."

Sadeq turned and studied Malik. "I don't need to tell you how I feel about it, do I?"

Malik shook his head. "Uh, no.... You've made that very clear."

"I have been wanting to go home for so long...it's all I can think of. I can't believe you have any feelings for this place."

"Maybe it's not the place...maybe I just know I will miss our friends."

"These Americans are so different...I don't know how you can call them friends."

Malik dropped his eyes. Sadeq had still not learned to accept people for who they were. He looked back up at Sadeq.

"Don't you appreciate anything they've done for us? What about all the times Mike took us home with him on the holidays?...and besides that...it's not just leaving friends. Aren't you worried about how things are in Iran? It's been six years and it's different now. I don't even know what to believe...all the rumors. Nobody knows who is in charge over there."

Sadeq smiled. "The Shah is on his way out...the Ayatollah is so powerful that he's basically pulling the strings, even from his exile in France. There is no question...the clergy will take control...as they should."

Malik swallowed hard at the thought. His family had eagerly accepted the progressive changes that the Shah had instituted. It would not be easy for them to go back to the old ways. Malik tried to change the subject.

"I wonder what the others are doing now." All of the other Iranian students had been suddenly called back to Iran. "Didn't you think it was strange that they let us stay...? Really, I guess I'm happy they told us to go into virology. There is so much to learn. Do you remember the coffee pot?"

Sadeq raised his eyes to the ceiling and shook his head. He hated this story, and he knew he would have to suffer through it one more time. "Oh, no...not again..."

"You all thought you had it all under control.... All under control. You said that over and over."

"Yes, yes, we were wrong and you were right." He hoped conceding this point would spare him the rest of the story. It did not work.

"I can't believe you thought it was O.K. to have the coffee pot in the virus lab."

"Malik, I told you before...I did not put it there...and I am still sure that it was just a coincidence."

Malik laughed. "...just a coincidence that all of you grew fever blisters exactly three weeks after they started working on simplex in that lab."

Sadeq caught Susan out of the corner of his eye. She strolled towards them, and Sadeq smiled to see her. Her arrival would stop Malik's story. She grabbed each one of them and gave them a big hug.

25

"Congratulations...I knew you could do it." Mike came out of the crowd, and she added loudly, "though I had my doubts when I saw that you were running with Mike, here."

Mike dropped his mouth open and put on his best hurt look. "Wha...What do you mean?"

Susan laughed at Mike as she continued. "My personal favorite was the day the lab mouse scampered up your arm."

"Oh, now, come on..."

"You jumped back like this..." she threw her arms out in a mimic of Mike and lost her balance, landing in the middle of another group of people.

Mike kept objecting. "I only broke a few beakers...."

"Yeah, but it took all of us to pull you down off the lab table."

"I...I can't help it if I have a small problem with critters."

"Problem?...I'd say more of a hysteria."

"What are you going to do for entertainment when nobody at your new job at the CDC has any 'hysteria'?"

"You're right...it could get boring."

As Mike and Susan bantered back and forth, Malik noticed that Sadeq's attention had drifted elsewhere. Sadeq's face transmitted a hateful glare to some location off in the distance. Malik followed the white-hot line of his fierce stare and found Amy directly in the line of fire. She successfully avoided looking back.

Malik knew it had been a very deep cut. Sadeq had not "fallen" for another girl since Amy's little experiment with his heart. True, he had gone out with many girls, but he had never let one get to him again. In fact, he sought girls that he could never really be interested in. They were pretty enough, but they lacked a certain quality that Sadeq had outlined in his description of the perfect woman. He never got serious. He simply took what they would give him and went on before any emotional ties could be made.

The moment Sadeq saw Malik looking at him, he changed his expression immediately.

"Malik...Malik...where are you, buddy?" Mike had been trying to talk to him. Now Malik cleared his thoughts.

"Oh...sorry. I uh wish I could be at your wedding."

26

"It's O.K., I understand. You have to go back. You know I'm going to miss you. Keep in touch, man." Somehow Mike knew he would never see Malik again. They were going their different directions now. He planned to begin his third year in medical school and his first year of marriage, after the wedding in the last week of June.

Malik felt the same feeling. His life was about to change. He feared that he would be stepping back in time as he stepped off the plane in Tehran. He did not know if he would ever see Mike again. He had never known such a loyal friend. He gripped Mike's hand and patted him on the back. He knew that his friendship with Mike would have to be through the mail only.

As the group gathered up and walked to the parking lot on their way to a celebration meal, Malik hung back from the group and watched. He wore a dark expression underneath his smile. It matched the uncertain dread that filled the pit of his stomach.

Horn Ranch

East of Del Rio, Texas

"Fun...if he thinks this is fun, he can kiss my lily white cheeks," fumed Joshua. His Dad was always rattling on about how people from the city would pay money to get to do the things that he and his brother, Caleb, just took for granted.

Caleb rode just to the right of his older brother. It was probably an hour to first daylight and, in the darkness, Caleb's horse had just taken him off the stock trail on which they had been riding single file to pull him right through a thorny mott of blackbrush.

After cussing his horse for what he considered to be an appropriate amount, Caleb turned his attentions to letting his father know what he thought about the whole situation.

"What in the name of God Above are we doing out here in the middle of the night? You know, if you weren't so tight-assed, we could get this done by helicopter. The Wardlaws gather their whole outfit by helicopter. Look

Pops, we wouldn't have to gather the whole ranch. We could just gather the worst part...like this rough SOB."

Their Dad just shook his head in the dark and did not even bother to respond. Some of his neighbors were resorting to helicopters due to the labor shortage, but most had found that doing it the same way it had been done for the past two hundred years was still the best. Besides, like he told his sons, "That helicopter isn't much help once you've got the livestock in the pens...when the real work begins. It won't brand a calf and it won't vaccinate or deworm a sheep."

The work had been the same since they were little boys. Of course, back then they would beg to go with him and the Mexican Cowboys. Back then, it was legal to give the vaqueros from Mexico work. Ranching in the Southwest Texas brush country was also more profitable in those days. It bothered him when he had to turn down men who had worked for him for years. The fines and threats of jail time by the Border Patrol were just too great.

"All right, y'all know where to go. Whoop and holler when you're there and we'll start. Hustle it up. It will be daylight before long, you know the stock won't gather good once it starts to heat up." The griping and grumbling continued as they rode up the hill, but he knew his sons would do the job just like they always did. He did not blame them though. *Just the three of them rounding up this huge pasture...what a joke.* He used to employ six or seven men to gather this same pasture.

Daylight came, but he could not hear either of his sons whooping in the distance. *No wind, I should be able to hear them easily.*

"Pheweet," a shrill whistle sounded. "Dad! Over here!" shouted Caleb. About a quarter of a mile away on a small caliche knoll, Josh and Caleb were standing up in their stirrups, motioning with their hats for their Dad to come to them. They were in such a tall stand of Cenizo that he could just barely make them out.

He hooked his sorrel horse in the flank and headed straight for them. It was not like them to waste the cool early morning on fooling around. Every minute they delayed meant rising temperatures. When it got hot, all the stock, sheep, cattle, goats would seek the nearest shade. Getting them to move would be difficult. Even if they could be moved, they would usually travel only as far as the next shade. He had told his boys several times, "Every time I'm out here on horse back in the cool of morning, I thank the Good Lord for letting me do this just one more time. As the day wears on and the sun heats up, I'm a lot less thankful."

Before he even caught up, Josh and Caleb reined their horses around and headed off away from him. "Come on, Dad. You've gotta see this."

They reined up to a hill overlooking a small mesquite-covered draw. "Good Lord, how many are there?"

"Sixty five" Josh said in a matter of fact manner as the line of wetbacks disappeared into the mesquite trees. Like any good cowboy, Josh had learned to get quick head counts of fleeing livestock. The skill worked equally well on fast moving illegal aliens.

A group of four or five was about the standard size. *Sixty-five wets in one bunch...telling that story at the coffee shop is a good way to be branded a liar or at least a gross exaggerator* mused Dad.

"A bunch that size won't stand much chance getting past the *chasers*," Dad observed.

'Chasers' was the local name for the Border Patrol. They also referred to them as the Border Taxi Service, stemming from the fact that it was commonplace for illegal aliens to turn themselves in once they were ready to return to home to Mexico. It was a good deal for the wets. They got a free ride home. It was a good deal for the Border Patrol because they could report them as apprehended illegal aliens.

Wetbacks seeking work in the U.S. had a regular gauntlet to run. The Rio Grande River itself presented the first obstacle. If the river was up, drowning routinely occurred. Once safely on U.S. banks, the fun really began. The Border Patrol used all sorts of high tech gadgetry like motion detectors, surveillance cameras, and night vision devices. Helicopters and small, fixed-wing aircraft constantly transected the Southwest Texas brushland. They would locate the wets and Patrolmen on the ground would move in.

Then, there was the old fashioned way...cutting sign. Many of the old hands in the Border Patrol could trail a group of men, rivaling the Indian scouts from days of yore. Despite all of this, more wets made it past the "Border Zone" than were apprehended. This zone was a twenty-five mile wide strip along the Rio Grande where the Border Patrol concentrated its activities.

Guides led most groups. The guides were paid pros, or perhaps experienced relatives or friends. Most guides strove to get their cargoes through this zone before daylight.

Once past this area, the heat lessened. Usually, a group of wetbacks that made it that far sought the services of a "coyote" to transport them the remainder of their journey.

"Dad, we'll have to back track that bunch all the way to where they first came on the ranch," Caleb said waving his hand toward the south end of the ranch. "Tell our neighbors too, I guess."

He was right. A band of wets of this number could mean a lot of damage and a lot of work. A few wetbacks cutting across country would generally just crawl over all the fences they encountered. The bigger the number, the more apt they were to cut a fence. Even if they did not cut the fence, a big group would physically smash a fence down to the ground by the repetitive action of so many crawling over a fence in the same spot.

The same results happened whether the fence had been cut or smashed down. Livestock would get out and the ranchers would have to invest considerable time trying to put them back where they belonged.

Josh's particular intolerance of wetbacks had led him to get rough with them. Wetbacks commonly caught and cooked a kid goat or lamb. One time, Josh happened upon two wets having a little a cookout under a clump of oak trees. They broke and ran as soon as they saw Josh. Josh worked his horse under the oak trees to investigate such suspicious behavior.

What he saw made his blood boil. It did not take him long to overtake one of the running men and knock him down with his charging horse. He piled into the dazed man and proceeded to work him over. His Dad caught up and pulled him off the poor man. "Dad, he barbecued Fat One."

Sure enough, a second inspection under the Oaks yielded the hide and head of the pet goat. His distinctive ear tag made him easy to identify. The boys had bottle-raised him. He had gotten to be such a nuisance around the house that they moved him to the backside of the ranch. He had no fear of humans and, doubtlessly, had run right up to the men hoping for a handout.

"Son, we'd be doing the same thing if we were in their shoes. They're just looking for work over here to feed their families. They cross this country with nothing on them but the clothes on their back. They get hungry," he said, hoping to soften his son's anger.

Such a large group traveling in the daylight this close to the border. Most wets managed to put a lot more miles between them and the border before this time of day. They'll leave a lot of sign...easy for the Border Patrol to get a line of travel on them...strange, Dad thought.

"Let's hook and spur...get out in front of them...check it out."

Dad and the boys reined the horses to a distance that he considered safe, directly in front of the group of men. Normally, wetbacks did not concern him in the least, but he sensed something different about the group, besides its size. He wished he had the security of his saddle gun. He seldom carried it when rounding up livestock. It was just something else to have sticking out of the saddle while you're trying to work your way through the brush.

Caleb's horse pawed the ground nervously. Dad's horse kept turning, causing him to have to rein him around in a circle in order to face the group. He was already questioning his wisdom for confronting these men. *By God, it's my ranch,* he thought.

They did not greet him like normal wetbacks. Most wets would immediately make some sort of disarming conversation. These said nothing, just stared tensely. They looked like wets, but something about them... perhaps their mannerisms...hinted of something different.

Two of the men spoke quietly to the man Dad had sized up as the leader or the guide for the group. The leader stared at one tall wet who was carrying a large, woven shopping sack, the kind that was commonly used in Mexico. He gave a small shake of his head toward this man. This signal did not go unnoticed by Dad and it served to increase his apprehension.

Finally, the leader broke the staring contest. "¿Hont' sta Compda?"

It was a familiar question, one that Dad and the boys had heard many times. The Border slang actually said, "¿A donde esta Campdale?" or "Where or which direction is Campdale?"

Campdale was a common destination for illegal aliens. Border Patrol-men referred to it as the international Coyote capital. Several members of the little community made their entire livelihood by transporting wetbacks.

"Direcho P'Ya," Dad replied pointing to the Northeast.

"Ah, Sí, Gracias."

"De nada," nodded Dad.

The group picked up all their plastic milk jugs filled with water, small clothes packs and shopping bags and headed off in the indicated direction. Dad and the boys rode a short distance and turned to watch the wets as they walked out of the mesquite-covered draw and headed up into the Cenizo.

Josh and Caleb turned to their father with quizzical looks on their faces. Without waiting for his son to mouth a question, Dad answered, "Guatema-lans maybe...I don't know."

The group of men traveled for approximately ten minutes before they stopped. The leader did what he always did after any noteworthy event when crossing men into the U.S. He paused and committed the event care-fully to memory.

"What do you think Farid?" the tall one said to the leader.

"I think two things," he said in almost a growl. "The first thing I think is speak only in Espanol or English. You know this. The second thing I think is that no one will be ever be allowed to carry a weapon on these missions again. What were you thinking about doing, you idiot. You were ready to pull it out."

"Farid, I was afraid that they..."

"And that's another thing, you can not call me Farid...Hector Sanchez...remember?"

"What are you worried about?...the bush has ears, huh? No one can hear us."

"My friend, you do not understand. The Border Patrol will find us. I expect them to find us. One could be walking toward us as we speak...he could hear you."

Farid Hashemi was accustomed to having absolute authority over his missions. His authority came from the Ayatollah himself. Having someone along who could question his actions was something he would not tolerate for long. In fact, he had basically decided to "scrub the mission" and had been purposely making it easy for the Border Patrol. As far as Farid was concerned, the insistence of his "visitor" on carrying a weapon forced this decision. However, it did afford a unique opportunity. *I will be able observe the reaction of the authorities to finding a weapon...useful information.*

He half hoped that the Border Patrol would treat his "visitor" roughly when they found his weapon. It would be easy enough for Farid and his to men deny any knowledge that one of their numbers was concealing a gun. *Senior, how could we know that this one had a gun in his bag?* practiced Farid. His current mission did not include smuggling weapons into the U.S. Actually, smuggling men into America was not his mission, per se.

The Ayatollah had told him, "One day, my son, we will be a united people and have the opportunity to strike America, the Great Satan. What you learn may help us strike."

Farid did not understand many things. When would they attack? How many men? He assumed thousands, but even with thousands smuggled in, it would still be suicide type missions. And Weapons...how would they be obtained? When he asked his superiors about these things they answered, "You are regularly taken into custody in America. It is better if you know little."

His job included learning the art of crossing men from Mexico to America and all its nuances. What was the most efficient and safe method to accomplish this plan? How would it be possible to house these men undetected near a military objective? He must learn the Border Patrol's methods and procedures and learn how to deal with Mexican Federales. It was important to make Mexico a safe staging area.

Part of it was easy. For one thing, all Mexican officials universally spoke bribery. Also, with very little effort, an Iranian could be made to look the part of a Mexican national. Of course, it took careful selection of the right men with the right features. The quality of recruits they sent to Farid amazed him and, once dressed to play the role of a wetback, they were indistinguishable from the real thing.

Ultimately, this decided his basic method of crossing men into the U.S. He tried other techniques, but none proved satisfactory. The beauty of the plan was that, if his men were caught, the Border Patrol gave them a ride back to the border. Farid discovered early that the one critical issue was to have authentic enough I.D. to convince any American Law Officer that he had just taken another Mexican National into custody.

"Except for a few specialized instances, I do not bother with trying to obtain or forge any kind of American documentation of identification. The Mexican National is the perfect cover with the least risk of drawing close scrutiny. Invariably, American authorities will check on just one thing...does the man they have in custody have a criminal record in the United States or possibly aboard? If the answer is 'no', they then assume that his Mexican I.D. is valid and merely deport him," reported Farid in one of his many briefings to his superiors.

"Silencio!" Farid barked. "Helicopter." In the distance, he heard the faint but familiar whop of helicopter blades. "OK, do not make it too easy for them. Remember your training. I expect everyone to report back as soon as they are deported."

Proving Ground

Iran, 1980—Close to the Iraqi Border

Mohammed shoved the old woman so hard that his desert-camouflaged hat flew off his head. She had charged out of the simpering, huddled mass, falling at his knees and pleading up at him. She had already lost most of her front teeth, so she looked grotesque to him as she contorted her face in deep sobs. Now, she wiped the blood from the corner of her mouth with her veil and sat there rocking and convulsing in utter despair.

"Murderer!" she spat at him.

"Get back, old woman!" he ordered.

He did not have time for this. He was *not* a murderer. And these were not people.

"Now?" His wide-eyed subordinate came up from behind him.

"Yes. Get them as close as possible."

The old woman was not the only one crying loudly. Many of the other women wailed in chorus with her. They clutched onto their children, who also sobbed. The men in their turbans stood there looking hatefully at Mohammed and his men. One middle-aged man with a full beard spit in their direction in defiance of his situation.

A stocky young man, who appeared to be about twenty-five years old, attacked an unsuspecting soldier. The Baha'i wrestled the soldier to the ground and punched him in the face hard twice before the other soldiers could pull the rebellious man off the beaten Iranian. The soldiers pushed the struggling rebel next to the old man that had spit. The soldiers fired on them immediately until they struggled no more.

Behind the frightened, huddled group, the bodies of the biowarfare victims lay on the woven mats on which they had been carried out of the ragged tents. They no longer moved. The few who were still alive after the disease had been dispatched efficiently as their screaming families watched from a distance.

Most of the bodies bore huge seeping whelps covering their bodies. Some of them still had their eyes open. They stared vacantly. Big, bruise-like areas covered the bodies. Blood trickled out of their ears and eyes.

He walked over to the gruesome pile to make sure they were dead. Even though Sadeq had told the soldiers that their vaccinations would protect them, Mohammed wanted to avoid the contagion as much as possible. He held a rag over his nose and mouth.

The experimental weapon had proven its worth on this group of Baha'is. The Shi'ite Muslims in power routinely persecuted these isolated groups. They would eventually all be exterminated anyway. Mohammed had been involved in many of the raids against them, but this was different.

Mohammed's required two years of service in the military had not broken his spirit like it had others. He had, instead, learned to close his eyes, mind and soul and simply put his duties out of his mind. At first, the imploring dark eyes of the children and women had caused him to hesitate. He had watched as another new soldier was executed on the spot when he resisted his orders. Then, the soldier's family at home had also suffered the consequences. So, Mohammed had shut it all out and performed his duties admirably for Allah. In a week, he planned to go home for a rest. He always trembled some as he held his children tight.

Now, the soldiers coerced the remaining Baha'is to go over to the chosen location by the bodies. They knew what was coming. The dirty little children cried in confusion and terror and held tightly onto their mothers' robes. Somehow they sensed what was happening. They tore their young eyes from the terrifying soldiers and buried their faces into their mother's robes, refusing to look at the death before them. The adults looked at each other for the last time through their tears. One mother turned her back to the guns in the vain hope of protecting her baby with her own body.

Then, the troops opened fire.

Soon, the dust settled and the barrage of gunfire mixed with screams of agony shifted to the pitiful moans of the dying Baha'is. One Baha'is toddler was not hit. He jumped up from the pile of fallen bodies and ran off to the right, screaming. The soldiers laughed and took good aim. He would run no more. The troops, who would, under normal circumstances, now begin to loot the victims, cautiously stayed away from them. They put their rags to their faces, unconsciously trying to elude the disease. They had received immunizations also in preparation for their assignment. Still, they did not want to touch the dead.

A few of the Baha'is managed to survive the onslaught, being shot in the arms or legs. They groaned as they writhed in pain. The soldiers walked up to them, pointed their pistols to the survivors' heads and pulled the trigger.

Now, in the quiet, the grisly scene even nauseated Mohammed. The bloody carcasses had fallen on top of each other and they had huge gushing gapes, many on each corpse. Some of them had been hit in the abdomen. Shiny, pale intestines slithered out of the ragged bullet holes and lay casually draped across the bodies they had fallen on top of, oozing their foul contents. The smell overwhelmed even Mohammed.

Others had been shot in the head. Cream-colored portions of brain lay spattered nearby. One of the heads lost an eye, which hung on by the thin, shimmering white thread of the optic nerve.

The soldiers quickly gathered up all the meager tents and belongings of their victims and piled them on top of their bloody corpses. Sadeq had insisted that it all must be burned. The military now had a proven weapon that was cheap and easy to produce. But it had to be kept completely secret, or the other governments would simply vaccinate their troops.

The smell of burned human flesh enveloped the area as the gray ashes drifted down from the heavens to which they had been lifted by the roaring fire. The charred corpses and their possessions were pushed into a large pit and buried, leaving no trace of the Baha'is people or the horrible disease they had been subjected to. Large trucks drove over the sand to smooth it. Within a few days of blowing sand, the fateful patch of desert would show no sign of the terrible experiment that had been carried out on this forsaken spot in the Iranian terrain.

The world would never have an inkling of the mournful tragedy that had occurred...Or of the peril that lurked somewhere in a secluded freezer.

NASSER GHANE

1991, SOMEWHERE IN THE IRAQI DESERT

Sand buried the bunker and any evidence of its existence. Thick, reinforced concrete formed the walls. Men crowded together so close in the bunker that it was impossible to lie down and sleep. It didn't matter. Nobody could sleep. No one had slept for days.

The poor venting concentrated the smell of so many sand-covered, sweating bodies in the bunker. Despite the numbers, almost no one spoke. The men now lacked any of their earlier fear. Fear took energy. Exhaustion had taken the place of fear.

"They're coming back. I feel it...I hear it." Silenced followed as all ears strained to hear.

"I hear nothing. Let them come. We're safe here." Nasser Ghane's voice had the force of a commander. The men respected him. Rumors of other CO's abandoning their troops were common. Everyone knew Nasser Ghane would not abandon his men. However, few agreed with his confidence in their safety.

"No, he's right. I feel it, too." Gradually, the distant *whump* and vibration became apparent to all as the debris sprinkled onto the floor. Each blast walked closer until the men knew that their bunker had been located. The bombs began falling in clusters. Hidden fear manifested itself, but the screams went unheard. The sand and the concrete only muffled the explosive noise. Shards of concrete shot out from one corner of the bunker. The broken pieces knifed into their flesh as efficiently as any shrapnel. Fine dust filled the bunker making breathing difficult. The blasts did not slowly fade into the distance as before. This time, the bombs closed in on the bunker. More broken pieces of concrete blew down from the ceiling.

It stopped. The men coughed and struggled to breathe. Tons of dirt and sand now covered the air vents.

"Open it up," commanded Ghane.

"Trailers...spotters, Sir."

"Now," sputtered and coughed Ghane. "They have already located us. It will be dark soon."

The men filed out of the bunker. The wounded that could walk struggled out, but others had to be carried. Ghane's eyes searched in all directions.

"Get them all out...go to all the bunkers. We need to reposition all tanks...vehicles...everything, and cover them again." Ghane nodded toward two tanks that had been flipped out of the sand. "Salvage what you can...keep the men busy...get them fed too."

One man ran up and stood nervously in front of Ghane, waiting to be recognized. He waited patiently as Ghane stood in a blank stare. Finally, Ghane shifted his gaze slowly toward him. He already had a good idea what the man wanted. About five hundred meters away, he saw men working feverishly in the sand.

"Tell them I'm coming...find someone...tell them to bring a bulldozer."

When he got there, he saw exactly what he had expected. The first rain of bombs from the B-52's had moved enough sand to expose a very small area of the top of one of the bunkers. The men inside would have probably only experienced some minor injuries. Except that the bombing had continued. In the middle of the rain of bombs, the bunker took a direct hit on the exposed bit of concrete. The delayed fuse allowed it to achieve maximum penetration. It breached a hole in the bunker and did not explode until it hit the concrete floor below.

Now, Ghane stared briefly at the hole. He knew what grisly horrors lay below. "Fill it in...cover it."

As he walked away, he looked briefly at one man wailing and rocking in the sand near the gaping hole in the concrete. His ranting was almost incoherent. His brother had been in that bunker. He rushed toward Ghane as others grabbed and restrained him.

"Sir, please! Perhaps he is only injured...please...at least let us look," he choked. Ghane set his jaw and continued to walk, not responding. *A blast of that magnitude inside a solid concrete bunker...no place for the explosion pressure to escape...no need to let anybody see that mess. It's hard enough for them to deal with their fear.*

Nothing in his battle experience prepared him for what he was now facing. His men had seen nothing like this when fighting the Iranians. That kind of fighting was a job, of sorts. You would shell each other for while, then both sides would for break for tea. Then you would fight for while longer and break for lunch. But, death was the only break in this war, and death from the air lurked constantly.

Uncle Saddam, himself, had made it clear that because of his distinguished battlefield command in the Iranian War, Ghane could have virtually any command that he wanted. Saddam was not really his uncle. He was more like a distant cousin. Even Ghane was not sure of his true blood relation to Saddam Hussein. He had requested a battlefield command because he despised the notion of using his relation to Hussein to obtain a safer, non-combat duty.

Ghane particularly despised the practice that Saddam had started of handing military positions to family and friends and sons of friends without merit. This one practice had caused all sorts of command problems. Desertions from his untried officers were a major concern.

Ghane hated deserters. Officers who deserted especially enraged him. One of his deserting officers had nearly made it back to Baghdad before he was apprehended. Ghane ordered him to be brought back. Men from the deserter's own unit comprised the firing squad. No one really believed the young officer would be put to death. He had come from a privileged family and all of Ghane's troops knew it.

Ghane had gone to the bunker that was serving as the stockade for various offenders where the young man was being held. As soon as the young officer saw Nasser Ghane standing before him, he angrily shot out, "You might as well release me. One call from Father will have all this nonsense stopped."

"He had better hurry, then," said Ghane in a quiet voice as he motioned to the guards.

As the guards led the young officer out, he saw the assembled men and firing squad. He realized, for once in his arrogant young life, that Daddy somehow had not been able to fix things. His legs lost strength. He could not stand before the squad. They brought him a chair. He began to cry pitifully, calling out the names of soldiers he could remember on the firing squad and begging them not to shoot. Not one member of the squad hesitated.

For the common soldier, this execution actually served as a morale booster. But, here was a commander who had suffered what they suffered, living or dying in the same bunker with his men. If the favorite son of a member of the privileged class deserted, he received the same treatment as the most common deserter. This was very different from the other elitist officers under whom the men had served. Huddling in the same bunkers with the common soldier rather than the comparative safety of the officer bunker further bonded Ghane's men to him. It also gave him additional incentive to be concerned with the well being of his men.

Ghane knew that the allies had a fix on his positions. Once discovered, such a concentration of bunkers, men, tanks and equipment would draw even more intense bombing runs. Aerial reconnaissance or satellite imagery had probably already picked up all this daylight activity around the bunkers. *Give them something to shoot at,* he thought.

He gave the order to his Senior Officers. "I want every piece of equipment moved tonight...to here. Dig in...sand bag bunkers," he said pointing to a spot a map. "If it's damaged and can't be moved, pull it out...make it look hit. Tomorrow at first light assign all deserters and disciplinary problems to cover them up again." *That should attract plenty of attention...solves two problems...deals with deserters and creates a diversion.*

The lessons of fighting a modern force without air cover were literally being pounded into his brain. *If I can just keep my tanks and men intact until the ground offensive begins, the advantage will be mine.* At least, that is what he had repeatedly been told. Privately, he had doubts. Win or lose, he knew that, once the ground fighting did begin, the world would gain respect for them and fear them as a fighting force, especially the Americans. Ghane visualized his divisions running rampant through the Americans' untested ground forces. He knew he would have large loses due to lack of air cover, but the whole world would still have to sit up and take notice.

Desperation led to this last maneuver. If the enemy discovered their new positions, the sandbag bunkers would not offer much protection against a sky full of B-52's. It would buy them time and that was what he needed...days...just days. The allies would start the ground offensive any day now.

Dark at last...moving the all tanks can begin in earnest. Ghane signed. He really had expected another raid. A junior officer ran up and stood at attention directly in front him, waiting to be recognized.

"What it is it?"

"Sir, the ground offensive has begun. They have blown past all forward positions. The main thrust is coming straight for us."

Finally, thought Ghane. He strode toward a tank that had just been uncovered from the sand. Two of his senior officers stood near the tank. The tank commander had the turret hatch open. He stood up in the opening as it churned its way out of the sands. He jerked his head around and looked up at something in the night sky. Ghane had nearly reached the tank when the tank commander yelled a warning, as he tried to jump out of the hatch.

Everything went white. Ghane knew he was lying on the ground. He did not know how or why. His mind was confused. Fire surrounded him and he thought he heard several explosions. His body was being dragged through the sand. He tried to move his hands and legs but nothing seemed to work. His eyes focused long enough to see that his uniform smoldered and smoked. Blood soaked his uniform shirtsleeve. Someone's face hovered close to his face, shouting his name. He tried to answer, but his mouth would not work.

The white overtook his mind. He heard whoever was shouting his name. Then, the dark absorbed his mind and the shouting faded away.

• • •

Ghane's eyes would not focus. Intense pain radiated from his right arm. Slowly, he gained some ability to see. Gauze covered his arm and head. A large, unbandaged burn covered the back of his hand and wrist. Confusion still muddled his thoughts. Finally, he realized that some kind of incoming fire must have hit him. He had obviously been unconscious for some time. In the broad daylight, he could tell that he was resting in the back of a personnel transport. A loud whirring sound vibrated the air around him. A number of wounded troops filled the transport. It surprised him to find that his men had put him in a transport with common soldiers. He could move now, but the pain nearly caused him to pass out when he sat up. *By now, the ground battle must be in full swing. I must talk to my officers.*

The pain nearly overwhelmed him. He struggled out of the back of the personnel carrier on wobbly feet. To his left, he saw an American Abram tank with a totally bored soldier manning the machine gun atop the turret. An Apache Attack Helicopter circled overhead. Directly in front of him, two American soldiers tried to get a group of ragtag Iraqi soldiers up off their knees. Another American soldier videoed them. Ghane's hazy mind finally sorted out that he had become a Prisoner of War.

Surely, none of these could be his men. They were not proud warriors. They were pitiful, groveling, crying men prostrating themselves in front of their captors. Ghane, with his American education, understood every word the Americans said to the Iraqi soldiers.

Instead of giving terse commands, they told the captives that they would be OK as they handed them packets of food. Any other commander would have felt some relief at seeing his men well treated. These were not his men...they could not be. It enraged Ghane... *These Iraqi soldiers were defeated by such soft-acting Americans. Wait until they run into his men.* Ghane wobbled back to what he now realized was an American personnel carrier. He lacked the strength to get back into it, passing out after several attempts.

Days went by before Ghane began to fully realize the total rout that his own troops had suffered and how little of the American blood had been spilled. With Ghane gone, the command structure of his unit broke down quickly. As a result, surrender quickly followed and a senseless slaughter was averted.

Soon, Ghane was sent home from the allied POW sites to recover from his wounds. Because of his privileged family status, he had the luxury of satellite TV. Watching the account simmered his humiliation into something much deeper. The whole world watched and *laughed*. The whole world watched on TV as one of the largest tank forces ever assembled dwindled to nothing in hours. The "Mother of All Wars" had turned into the "Mother of all Defeats," as one commentator noted.

In the months that Ghane lay sulking in recovery at home, he vowed many things. His eyes narrowed as his hands gripped the arm of the chair. *Soon...the bleeding will begin again.*

BUSINESS AS USUAL

WASHINGTON, D.C.

Senator Daniel Catshell stood at the large window of his plush office and looked out at the menacing cloud forming in the distance. The office had been brightly lit until a creeping darkness slid over the mahogany desk and bookcases. Senator Catshell stretched his shoulders as he watched the wind beginning to blow.

All the time he spent bent over the budget was beginning to make his shoulders ache. He pushed his thin fingers through the gray hair on his temples. It contrasted with his dark hair and gave him an air of dignity. He had no intention of covering it. It made his blue eyes even more piercing.

After all his years of service, he felt like he had complete control of this governmental machine. The feeling of power seduced him entirely. In a recent poll, his name had ranked the most recognized of all the Senators. He basked in a compelling perception of authority as he contemplated the governed masses of people walking below on the sidewalk or driving nearby on their way home from work.

Behind him, momentos of the things he held closest to his heart adorned his desk. Pictures of his auburn-haired wife, Rachel and their two sons, Justin and Brian, smiled out of a shiny, gold, three-part frame. Next to them sat an antique-gold five by seven frame displaying his parents. They were standing outside their two-story house. His father had his arm over his mother's shoulders and they were both smiling.

Next to the frames sat the only other item on his perfectionist's desk. The proposed budget claimed the most prominent, central part of the desk-top like some sort of trophy.

The intercom buzzed. "Senator Briggs is on line one, Senator Catshell," toned Anna, his secretary. He took the phone and smiled as he punched the button.

Senator Jim Briggs' seventy-two years made his voice low and gravelly. After being here in Washington for over twenty years, Jim did not get excited easily over coming legislation, but this was different.

Jim had seen many budgets, through many legislatures and many Presidents. None of them had worried him like this one did. He liked Daniel, personally, and he and Daniel agreed on almost every other aspect of running the government. They *never* agreed on the budget.

The country's budget seemed to swing like some giant pendulum. He had witnessed the public trend carry the budget to the extreme of ridiculous spending, with no thought of having to pay for it. Now, he watched as the public demanded a lean-spending government. Many of the big-spenders had been voted out of office by the responsible young voters of the baby-boomer generation as they grew older. Someone was going to have to pay for all these programs.

He knew the over-spending had to stop. However, he also knew why some of the programs, now deemed expendable, had been put there in the first place. All these youngsters now running Congress had not been there to hear the arguments for the implementations of these aspects of government. They did not know why their predecessors had instituted these programs and they simply did not care why. All the youngsters could say was, "Cut, cut, cut" as they blindly slashed through all the tapestry woven by past legislatures. The particular item that had been cut by Daniel's proposed budget and had grabbed Jim's attention was in the defense budget.

"Say, Daniel, why are you proposing to cut so much out of the defense spending?" Being a veteran himself, Jim prided himself in guarding the rights and privileges of servicemen.

"Every bit helps, Jim." Daniel had expected this. Jim always nit-picked his budget proposals.

"But this time you've gone too far. My God, you even axed some of the vaccinations. How much could that possibly save us? What about all of the bio weapons in the Middle East?"

"Look, it's not just the cost of the vaccine that we don't need. Some of those vaccines also cause serious side effects. Side effects cost money, Jim. Do you have any idea how much money we've spent on litigation from vaccination liability? Don't you remember the Swine Flu vaccine fiasco back in '76? We're still paying for that one. And what about the tie between vaccinations and the Gulf War Syndrome?"

"But what about the danger from Biowarfare? You cut that portion of the defense budget to the bare bone."

"You know as well as I do that any bio attack on the United States is going to be either on our troops, who have been vaccinated, or some small time terrorist attack here in the U.S. That's small shit. Come off it."

"I just feel that we are letting down our guard. What about Saddam? And just what makes you so all damned sure that they couldn't mount a big offensive with it?"

"Go read the literature for yourself. Every secret study done by our own guys has shown how hard it is to get everything just right, especially for an aerosol of...say...Anthrax. The mechanics of such an intentional infection are impossible...or somebody would have already done it. Don't you think Saddam would have already done it? Right now, Jim, we're in more danger because of our own deficit, and you know it!" laughed Daniel.

"I'll tell you what..." Jim knew Daniel's tone of voice all too well. It meant that Jim would not get his way...completely. He might as well get something out of it. "Maybe some of these things could be tolerated a little better if you'll help me out a little on the vote tomorrow."

Daniel smiled. Now this game interested him a bit more.

45

The whole matter escaped Daniel's mind the minute he stepped out of his office to go to a press conference. He eagerly announced how much money he had saved the taxpayers in his proposed budget. The public was happy and nothing else mattered.

INSIGHT

PENTAGON

"**T**hen Job answered the Lord, and said,
'I know that Thou canst do all things.
And that no purpose of Thine can be thwarted.
Who is this that hides counsel without knowledge?
Therefore I have declared that about which
I do not understand.
Things too wonderful for me which I did not know.'"

General Herndon gave a half snort. "Sounds like the poordumb bastard was as confused as I am." "General Herndon, Sir. It's time for us to leave," sounded a voice outside the door.

The knocking at the door did not even register to the General. In a sarcastic tone he continued, "You know I really like this part.

'Then Thou dost frighten me with dreams;
And terrify me by visions;
Death rather than my pains.
I waste away; I will not live forever,
Leave me alone for my days are but a breath'

"Son of a Bitch...! By God it's amazing...truly amazing." He shook his gray head.

Captain Goodloe stood outside the General's door wondering what to do. Should he interrupt his conversation? As his Aide, he had seen this man scold Congressmen, higher-ranking brass and even the Secretary of State like so many misbehaving children. The incredible thing was not that he did it, but that he got away with it...no reprisals.

Even those who could not stand his intolerant, arrogant, over-bearing ways sought out his insight. Goodloe's mind wandered back to the time when he had actually met Collin Paxton. To his surprise, General Paxton knew who he was, even though he was a lowly Captain. The whole scene was vivid in his mind. It was one of those classic, formal, stuffed shirt Washington affairs and a regular Who's Who of Desert Storm Brass.

Paxton had explained while shaking his head, "We've called this man out of retirement three times...can't find a replacement for him. He has one profound ability...he can cut through all the tripe and see the fundamental flaw or wisdom in any military action. And believe me, he has no problem telling anyone exactly what he thinks."

"Captain, let me tell you one story that will do more than anything else to explain the value of this man," continued Paxton. By then, a number of notables had gathered around. Goodloe had managed a nervous glance about the group, and spied the smiling, round-faced features of General Frank Malinovski bobbing knowingly in agreement.

"We had just finished with our plans for the Desert Storm Offensive and I wanted to get in one dress rehearsal before we presented it to the President. Herndon was already in an uproar because he had been assigned to oversight. Each Commander got up with his charts and maps and explained his phase of the operation. Finally, we finished and I turned to Herndon and said, 'Hey, whatcha think, Dick?' Remember what he said, Frank?"

Malinovski chuckled, "Yes Sir, I do." He gave his best deep, gravelly-voiced imitation of Herndon, "'I think it's the biggest steaming pile of horse shit I've ever seen.'" Chuckles followed, along with comments of agreement with the General's recollection of the event.

"I, personally, thought it was a heck of a plan. The staff had worked their butts off...night and day...non-stop," said Paxton gesturing with his hand. "He jumped up, grabbed a marker and shook it in my face." Paxton gave his

Herndon imitation, "'Damn it! If you'll just listen to me, we can kick this bunch of Sand Niggers' asses and lose damn few of our kids out in that God-forsaken pile of sand!' Herndon never was one to let political correctness get in his way when communicating. We're careful not let him out of the closet very often."

Laughter followed and, with a few additional comments, the gist of the conversation drifted, but Goodloe wanted to know more. What was the outcome? He worked up the courage to stammer out a question.

"Sir, what did you do, I mean, what did you do with General Herndon's suggestions?" The whole group roared and laughed like it was the funniest thing they had heard in years. Paxton wiped tears out of his eyes and wheezed out the word, "suggestions."

"We did everything that old man told us to do," Paxton said in an amused tone that indicated that there should not have been any question about it.

Paxton's voice turned more serious. "Brian, we scoured the woods for you, son. You see, we've got a problem. We have computer gurus by the sack-full. They can model this scenario and model that contingency, but they just don't...well, let's just say that Herndon is unique. We looked carefully for someone with your aptitude. Learn all you can from him."

Goodloe's mind came back to the job at hand and he drew in a deep breath. *God only knows which "big dog" he's talking to now.* He tapped on the door once more and then stuck in his head. "General, Sir...Sir. We need to leave right away."

"Brian, come in, Son...come in," Herndon said motioning with his hand.

"Good morning, Sir." He tried to cover his mild surprise at finding the General by himself. He was sure he had heard talking. "Uhmm, reading the Bible, Sir?" Brian had often noted the book as it always sat on the right corner of the General's desk.

"Yeah," chuckled Herndon, "The Book of Job...you ever read it?"

"Yes, Sir, I have."

"That poor miserable asshole...poor bastard, he did catch hell, didn't he?'

Goodloe mused to himself. *How can this man have such beliefs and yet, even when discussing the Bible, he is incapable of completing a sentence without profanity.* Lots of riddles surrounded this man...riddles... ha! A mere conversation with the man was often like a riddle. Half the time he spoke in riddles. Then, while you were trying to figure out what on earth he was talking about, he switched to some ridiculous subject.

"Yes Sir, as I recall, he was a man of great afflictions." He held the door open for the General. "Sir, we must hurry or we'll be late for the Sub-Committee meeting."

The general followed Captain Goodloe out into the hall. "Yeah, we don't want to keep Senator Cat Shit Breath waiting, do we?"

"It's Catshell, Sir...Senator Catshell. Remember, Sir, you told me to remind you to watch your language today."

"Yeah, well, I'm working on my mnemonic devices. That's how I remember his name. Ever smell that man's breath? There's nothing that smells quite like that...and I tell you, that man has gotta eat cat shit for breakfast."

As they strolled down the hall and Herndon continued to prattle on about the Senator, Goodloe could not help thinking that this was not the way he had visualized his job. He was supposed to somehow absorb the vast reservoir of military knowledge that this man housed. And yet, here he was, walking down the halls of the Pentagon with a man reputed to have the most brilliant military mind in modern history...and all he could talk about was a Senator's bad case of halitosis. *Utterly absurd,* he thought as he tried to feign interest in the General's rattlings.

Maybe everybody is right about me, Goodloe thought. *I'm just too serious about everything.*

Senate Intelligence Subcommittee

"O.K., Well let's move on. General, it was my understanding that the main reason you're here today before our Subcommittee is to go over some intelligence information as it relates to our pending resumption of oil trade with the Iran-Iraqi Coalition." Senator Catshell monotoned.

"Yes Sir, that's correct...I uhmm, I...I apologize for my previous..." General Herndon fumbled with uncharacteristic humility.

"Forget it, let's get down to the issue at hand. General, I've read your report and, for the life of me, I can not see anything that would negate our plans to resume trade with these people. The bottom line is that they've been good boys and it's my intention to see that we let them out of the doghouse. We need to reward their good behavior by letting them back into the world community," Senator Catshell fired with a caustic tone.

"Well, Son of a Bitch...Hell, yes they've been good," bellowed Herndon. The veins bulged on his neck. "If you consider developing and testing bio-logical agents on human subjects good. Well, shit yes...they're regular can-didates for the Nobel Peace Prize."

"You have not been able to confirm that."

Goodloe could see that the General was beginning to boil over. "Sir, remember to watch your temper and your language," he whispered.

"We believe that the reports we have received are accurate, Senator," offered the General in a more moderate tone.

"But, you can't confirm that, can you," squeaked Catshell as he shook his finger belligerently at the General.

"No, we can't...because some little chicken shit persuaded the Presi-dent to pull all of our operatives out of there," the General countered while pointing his finger back at the Senator. "Dumb-Ass, our spy satellites can't see that crap."

Goodloe covered his eyes with both hands and shook his head. It was really against everyone's better judgment, and only after considerable kiss-ing-up, that Herndon had been allowed to reappear before the Subcommit-tee. By now, both men were standing and engaged in a full-blown shouting match.

"That's it! I'm not taking anymore of this! Meeting adjourned!" Catshell wheeled and stormed out.

The redness in the General's face remained as he took rapid breaths, trying to calm down. "Let's get outta here, Son. I have a favorite little waterhole not far from here."

The General fumed all the way over to the bar and spoke very little. Mostly, he muttered to himself while looking out the car window. At the bar, it took vigorous chomping on an unlit cigar and several drinks before he was in the mood to talk again.

"I can't stand that little chicken-shit. Brian, it amazes me...truly amazes me. How does somebody like that man get elected in the first place? Let them back in the world community! Reward their good behavior! Kiss my ass! They are nothing but a bunch of barbarians...public beheadings, infecting their own people just to test the crap they come up with. I shouldn't have held back. I should have told the little pervert what a Dumb-ass I really thought he was."

"Uhh, Sir. You did tell him that...several times, Sir."

"Eh, well, I don't have much patience with people like him. I guess I've been around too long...seen too much. Ignorant politicians and brass can kill a lot of people." The alcohol, coupled with his state of mind, started him rambling.

"Now you take Ike. There was a good SOB. He would listen to what you had to say. He was a good man in a desperate time. I pray to God that when the whole world gets its collective asses in a crack like we were in back then that another good man like Ike can be found.

"Hell, I can remember it like it was yesterday. I was just a kid with a talent for logistics on his planning staff. Everybody was on the poor bastard's ass, pressuring him to invade Europe before we were ready. The Nazi's would have clobbered us. They were still too strong. We would have never gotten off the beaches. We'd been working like hell on the Normandy invasion plans.

"That man went through each planning group and wanted to know what every swinging dick thought. He just showed up...wasn't announced. I thought my CO was going to piss in his pants. They were so busy kissing his ass and telling him just what they thought he wanted to hear. Brian, you know what he did?"

"No Sir, I don't." It was not the truth. In fact, Brian had heard this same story several times. At least the General had lost his anger and the history interested him. He was a walking piece of military history, spanning more than fifty years. Besides, he had discovered it was easiest to pick the General's brains while he was reminiscing.

"I don't know why he did this...maybe it was just the look I had on my face...who knows," continued Herndon. "But he looked right at me and said, 'Son, what do you think?' Well, I might have been still wet behind the ears but, hell, the man was looking for answers. It was heavy on him. You could see it in his eyes. I told him if we went now, we would get the living dog crap kicked out of us...lose God only knows how many kids. I spent the next ten minutes telling the man the basic flaws with our plan.

"Ike never said one word...not one damn word the whole time I was talking. When I was finished, he didn't say 'thank-you very much...kiss my ass'...nothing...just got up, turned and walked out. My CO looked like he could have shit a brick. He told me, 'I'm going to kick your young tender ass up between your shoulders.' Two days later Eisenhower called me to his HQ. By the time Operation Overlord was committed to, I was the CO...just a snot-nosed kid. That took balls for that man to do that.

"Yes Sir, he was a damn good man, but he didn't listen to me every time." He paused and drew a breath. While he was looking up at the ceiling, Brian could see his eyelids fluttering rapidly. "All those kids floating in the surf. They started stacking up like so much driftwood. The waves washed them back and forth...pulling them back from the beach and then rolling them back up on it. That's when you could see their faces...that's what I hated seeing the most...their faces."

Brian tried to think of something to say. He had never seen the General with such a painful expression on his face. This was one of the few stories he had not heard repeatedly. *Omaha,* Brian thought. *He must have made an inspection right after the beachhead was secured.*

The General sat in a blank stare, and spoke so softly that Brian did not catch every word. "You didn't have to show me that...well, that was the first time you showed me things. I told Ike that beach was a death trap...didn't listen. Still, he was a good man." Herndon remained in his stare for several moments. When he broke it, he resumed talking in his normal gravelly tone.

"Now, I gotta believe that McNamara had to be the most ignorant fool I've ever met. Fired my ass so fast it made my head spin. He got a lot of kids killed...for nothing...for bull-shit...by God I just can't..."

"General, Sir...please forgive me for interrupting." Brian spoke in a more assertive manner than usual. "Sir, I've got to ask you something, if you don't mind."

"O.K. Captain, go ahead." Brian knew interrupting his story must have irritated him. He only addressed him as Captain when he was displeased with him.

"Sir, I'm sorry. I just can't get over this morning. Sir, you were ready to go to war with Senator Catshell. Sir, if I might say so, from what I have learned about you, if you are that adamant about something, it's got to be important."

"The little bastard is a traitor," Herndon said in a low, somber tone. "And he is not as stupid as he looks...but I don't think he, or anybody else, realizes what they've done...hell, I'm not sure I understand it. It's basically influence peddling taken to a new high. The Coalition has passed the money through lots of hands. It's damned near impossible to track. Hell, there's a chance it goes right to the White House. In all fairness, he has no idea of the consequences of his actions."

"Sir, foreign government influence peddling is..."

"...is pretty damn common. Do you think I give a fat rat's ass if those rag heads cut a trade deal with us?"

"Well, Sir, to be frank, you've gone to great lengths to repeatedly make your case against the Coalition. And Sir...well, I just don't understand."

"Brian, I have access to uhmm...to some intelligence that no one else has."

Ah, so that was why he was so angry. He had a special operative that was pulled out of the Coalition, thought Brian.

"Let me see. How should I put this? Uh...a few nights back I went on a naked fly-over to Tehran." Herndon motioned with his cigar in his hand.

Finally, thought Brian. *Now I'm learning the real inside stuff...'naked fly-over'...must be some kind of intelligence jargon.*

"Heh," snorted and chuckled Herndon. "I must have been a hell'va sight...my old, wrinkled pecker flapping around in the wind...heh, heh. I wish you could have seen what I saw. But I damn sure didn't like what I saw. That big, ugly son of a bitch. I do believe that big, ugly bastard I saw coming off Mr. Hitler has found himself a home. Looks like he's found somebody...just like he said he'd do." Herndon sighed and shook his head.

I don't know if he's losing his mind, or if he's just speaking in riddles again, thought Goodloe. "Sir, I'm sorry, but you have lost me...I just don't follow you."

"Huh, yeah, I imagine so. Look, Son, don't ask me to explain all that crap I was babbling about. Brian, just let me bottom-line it for you. The

United States is fixing to get the horse manure kicked out of it. We're going to get hit hard...perhaps death of proportions never seen before in the history of Mankind."

"The Coalition?...Who, Sir?...Nukes?...How is it going to happen?"

"Yeah, the Coalition...no nukes...they got 'em alright...Soviet Block busted up...they were strapped for cash...Nukes to the highest bidder, Good God...what a helluva mess. We bought all we could just to keep them off the market...still they got a few, but that's not how they're gonna do it...haven't got enough.

'Look, Son...I admit I'm telling you things that I...that I...I can't independently confirm. Damn, I've tried to. I've called in a lot of favors—twisted a hell of a lot of arms chasing this thing. It eats on me night and day. It's all I think about. About the only thing we've been able to get a confirmation on is that they're training a hell of a special forces unit...lots of em...real bad asses...make our Navy Seals look like Girl Scouts. I've taken it to the big brass...they just laugh at me."

"Sir, I can hardly imagine them laughing at you."

"Well...not to my face, but I bet they're making coo-coo signs behind my back. Hell, you know yourself that they let me go to the Subcommittee just to pacify me."

"Sir, how are they going to hit us?"

"When Yamamoto hit us at Pearl, it was inconceivable. I've tried to get our smart-ass computer-modeling boys to give me some insight. They came up with every conceivable model of them hitting us. I told them...that's the problem...conceivable. You know, that's something I've never understood."

"Never understood what, Sir?"

"Yamamoto...he hit us with the inconceivable...he had us...he really caught us with our drawers down. The man was brilliant. He knew us...traveled around a lot over here. He didn't want a damn thing to do with going to war with us. He told his own people that he could kick our butts for eighteen months. After that, our superior war production capabilities would catch up to him...He knew the end would be inevitable. The one best chance he had was a total surprise attack. He knew all this was true...so why didn't he finish us off at Pearl, huh?

"Brian, it's going to be something new...something we're not expecting...not prepared...I just don't know how they're going to do it...but they're damn sure going to do it. Soon, too. I've been shown that plainly. Uh...my intelligence source can be rather tight-lipped, but he's damn sure graphic. I'll say that for him."

Goodloe's mind raced through the myriad of "General Herndon Stories" he had heard, especially all those that ended with "That's exactly what Herndon said would happen" or "That old fart was right again." It had been drilled into his head to overlook the General's eccentricities and take him seriously, but Goodloe was not prepared for the strangeness of this conversation.

"Son, a lot of this is baffling to me too, but I have it on the highest authority that when all this goes down, you will be a major player...no...don't ask me...it beats the shit out of me, too."

WARNING

SAN ANTONIO, TEXAS

Antlers lined the high ceiling of the famous, old bar as the ceiling fans slowly rotated, sending the cool breeze down on the men at the table in the corner. But the cool air failed to moderate the hot words flowing from Eric as he sat staring with glazed-over eyes into the beer in his mug. Mike and Tom could do little to change his mood, which got darker with each beer.

They had stopped for a few cool ones after the last meeting of the convention adjourned. The members of the American Association of Tropical Medicine and Hygiene had chosen San Antonio for their annual convention this year. Mike was glad for the chance to visit with Tom and Eric in his own hometown. But Eric's obvious depression had dominated their time together. Mike attempted to steer the conversation in a more positive direction.

"Tom, what have you heard from Susan? I really wish she could have been here."

"I spoke to her before we came. She's wrapped up in her job at the CDC. She is responsible for the maintenance of vaccines there."

Eric pulled himself away from his beer and attempted to speak, even though the alcohol had numbed his tongue. "I bet that's a fun little job. It must be hard to keep all those seed stocks fresh at what...-20°C without allowing too much mutation. I read that DNA studies showed that current vaccine strains differ from the originals. Makes you wonder if they'll even work after a while."

"I'm sure Susan knows how to maintain them, Eric." Tom was quick to defend Susan.

"Yeah. But didn't you hear what they said in the meeting? They are actually considering destroying that Vaccinia strain because a birulent... viru...virulent recombinant virus could be made with it. Seems to me that if somebody has a desire and a few thousand dollars worth of equipment, they could even recreate something like Smallpox. The whole nucleotide sequence of the virus will be published soon. All they have to do is put it into another Pox virus."

Mike threw a glance at Tom as he tried to change the subject. "I got a letter from Malik at Christmas. He always remembers that holiday. Anyway, he said that they are fine. He did not say much about his work but he sent me a picture of his family."

"How many kids?" Tom was in awe over anyone who decided to have more than one child. His only child, a daughter, now lived with his ex-wife and her new husband. He barely tolerated the hassle on her twice-a-year visits.

"Three boys and two girls now. Two of them are teenagers." Mike understood having teenagers in the house. His eighteen-year-old daughter, Melissa, shared many of his own interests. But, Jacob, his son, at seventeen, was every bit into being a royal senior. His severe independence sometimes led him into skirmishes with Mike. Chris, the baby, was already thirteen years old, and he looked like Mike. Mike had survived well through all his years of service in the Air Force to pay off his medical school debts, but he had never lived through any wars like the ones at his own house in the past few years. He blamed his gray hair on it all.

"And Sadeq?"

"Yeah. The poor guy has one son and *six* daughters. Geez. Anyway, they're both doing some sort of lab work. He didn't specify."

Eric came alive out of his beer again. "You know it's people just like Malik and Sadeq that I worry about. What do you thuppose...suppose their government has them doing? Hmmm? Haven't you ever wondered? I bet they're over there right now bioeng... bioeng...making some sort of little surprise for us as we speak!"

Mike's anger rose. He did not care if Eric was drunk. He did not have to talk about Malik that way. "Oh, quit being so damned paranoid! You know they would not intentionally do something against us."

"I do? Really? We're wide open to attack."

"Oh, come off it. The Feds would stop any biowarfare attack before it could do any real damage, and you know it."

"Really?" Eric slurred. "I work there, remember? It was bad enough before the DOD cutbacks in '91. I know households that have more operating funds than we do. You saw what the Hono...Hono...Honolulu War Games showed. Eight hundred of our best tropical disease experts showed that, despite their best efforts, a massive pandemic could occur. Now it's worse!" Mike sat back to avoid the sudden spray of Eric's last word. "Since the hiring freeze, some of our lab work is contracted out to private labs with no quality control at all. And, in '93, an epidemic of Yellow Fever got completely out of hand in Kenya because the international labs failed to identify it. WHO can't help either. Their annual budget is a whopping twenty-five thousand dollars. That would be gone in the first fifteen minutes of an actual pandemic...if anyone could recognize it, that is."

Tom could not accept that. "What about the WHO plan to mobilize rapid-response teams for 24-hour arrival at any hot spot? Didn't I read that the Chief of Emerging Diseases in Geneva planned to send equipment to areas in the world to set up quick diagnosis capabilities, along with electronic computer links to make them easier to report?"

"Sure, nice plan. But...no money. Every nation involved is biting budget bullets. Even the U.S. stalled on about two hundred million dollars it owes WHO. That's a fourth of WHO's budget."

"Well, you're talking about world-wide preparedness. The U.S. is much better prepared." Mike was hoping.

This time, Tom shook his head. "The Pentagon only has two portable biological containment facilities and they would be used for military protection first. The CDC only has one for use by civilians."

Eric yelled across the room to the waitress, waving his empty glass around above his head. "Hey! Another cold one here!"

Mike and Tom exchanged glances and tried to act inconspicuous. Eric's outburst had attracted the stares of the other patrons. The waitress brought his beer. He continued to rant.

"We can't even keep a supply of vaccines anymore since the Swine Flu fiasco. The government paid millions of dollars in damages after there was only one confirmed case of Swine Flu and thousands of cases of Guillian-Barre Syndrome from the vaccine. Nobody wants the responsibility. We barely have enough to immunize a few troops. The American public is on its own!"

Mike and Tom had heard enough. They decided that it was time to get out of there before Eric's voice got any louder. But it was too late. Eric raised his voice a little and continued.

"I tell you, I've had it! Some of our people moved to Pakistan to get away from all this crap. They spend their time training the locals. I wonder if there's room for one more?" He slammed down his mug, slinging beer all around the table. Then, he stood up and swaggered. Mike caught him. It was time to leave.

MALIK

IRAN

Malik looked up at the small bulletin board above his desk. He scanned across meeting announcements and calendars until he came to the pictures he had thumbtacked onto the board. He looked at the pictures and, in his mind, he could almost feel himself standing there in San Antonio next to Mike's family.

Mike's daughter, Melissa, was nineteen years old just like his own firstborn son, Reza. Even in the midst of the upheaval against the Shah, Malik had decided to honor him by naming his son after him. He knew well how much the Shah had done for him by sending him overseas for his education. Because of it, he now held a certain global insight.

He studied the smiles on the faces of Mike's children and unconsciously smiled in response. Those smiles held the same friendliness he had grown to appreciate in Mike. It was a friendliness he did not experience much in Iran. Malik's mind wandered back to the time when he and Sadeq returned to Iran.

Iran had been a pot of boiling turmoil ever since he and Sadeq had stepped off that return flight in Tehran. The tension had been visible almost immediately. It had taken an hour to leave the airport because of the demonstration being staged there. Angry mobs, carrying signs against the Shah, shouted chants loudly and pressed into the entrance of the airport. The airport apparently symbolized the Shah's modernization campaign.

Before Malik and Sadeq left with their families, the Shah's troops arrived to handle the crowd. It did not help much because some of the troops agreed with the protesters. They were, at least, sympathetic to their cause. The confusion only increased. Finally, the car they rode in broke free and got on an outward-bound street. Only then were they able to relax enough to really take in the happiness of their families.

Malik's mother wept with big, happy tears as she held him closely. He had missed her more than he had realized. In his arms, her body felt frail. She had aged considerably more than she should have in the six years he had been gone. Her normally carefree expression was now lined with the worry she quietly bore. She had not complained about things in her letters, but Malik now saw that there was much she had not mentioned to him.

He looked inquiringly at his father as they rode in the car. His father gave him an expression that told him that it would all be discussed later. Still, Malik knew, by that look, that his father would soon confirm his worst fears about the state of affairs in Iran.

His sisters were much more mature now, but they were also much too quiet. They eagerly hugged him but they were too conservative to be the same giggling little girls he had left at home. Something had changed.

As the next days had gone by, Malik began to appreciate the situation more. Massive transformation was under way in Iran. Two years later, the

Shah left Iran for medical treatments. The Ayatollah returned from exile in France to take the reins of the new religiously based government.

Malik and Sadeq worked in government labs. They also taught at the University. This pleased Malik completely.

Within one month of their return, Sadeq married Arya, who had been waiting for his return. They were very busy raising a family, and it was a very traditional family,

The new hard-line order completely absorbed Sadeq. He wore a long curly beard like many of the religious leaders. His wife was never seen without her head covering, and his daughters were learning how to run a proper religious household. They did not have time to learn about other matters.

Sadeq carefully monitored the proper education of his only son, Yousef, who was now eighteen years of age. Sadeq constantly talked about Yousef at work. Yousef looked just like Sadeq, except that Yousef's more rounded face hinted of his mother's face. He carried the same no-nonsense attitude as Sadeq and fit easily into the strict religious upbringing to which he was subjected.

Malik fell in love with one of the students in the first class he taught. Yahya had caught his eye with her curiosity and her determination. She showed some of the same qualities that Malik had seen in Susan. However, she did not look anything like Susan. Her long, black hair was soft and silky, and her dark eyes pulled at Malik's very soul. She was tall for a woman, but not too tall to go perfectly with Malik.

Malik enjoyed the spirited debates with which Yahya countered him. Even in her youth, she knew how to argue well, since she had been brought up in a very open family. She loved Malik completely. She knew he enjoyed her spirit, so she showed it regularly, but she never let him get angry. She always ended her playing with plenty of cuddles and kisses. Malik could never be angry with her.

She made a beautiful, loving mother for his children. She played with them and taught them as much as she could. She was forced, after the revolution, to wear her head covering in public, but she never quit teaching her daughters in secret. Yahya made sure that they were as well educated as her sons were. They all knew how to use those curious, dark eyes, just like their mother did.

At first, Malik relished his teaching assignment. For the first three years, he enjoyed the freedom of teaching whatever he thought needed to be taught. He grew a short professional-looking beard.

Then, the Iran-Iraqi war put a severe financial strain on the people of Iran in 1980. By 1982, a complete system of Islamic government was instituted. The Supreme Court invalidated all previous laws that did not conform to Islamic dictate.

The Judicial system, under the authority of the Fagih, now had a harsh system of punishment. It included flogging, stoning and amputation. The air of relative freedom that Malik had enjoyed was gone.

The Universities were forced to teach only Islamic curriculums. Although many of the facts and skills that Malik and Sadeq were teaching were not in the realm of Islam, they had strangely been allowed to continue teaching them. Malik avoided any political comments because of the severe punishment and the watchful atmosphere.

Malik had noticed, however, that Sadeq was in his element now. He fared extremely well in the new order after the formation of the new Iranian/Iraqi Coalition, finding favor from government leaders at every turn. He had acquired real prestige and power. Malik did not understand all of this, and he had a feeling that Sadeq kept secrets involving possible deals with their superiors.

Sadeq disappeared for days at a time. Malik wondered why he was allowed to be gone so much like that. Sadeq never spoke about his time away. Somehow, Malik knew better than to ask about it. Whatever it was, it must have been something that Sadeq did not want to brag about because he always seemed so distant after his return from his mysterious deeds. He was suddenly appointed to be a counselor to the President of the country, and he regularly met with the powerful Nasser Ghane of the Coalition.

Malik, on the other hand, fell into the disfavor of the religious leaders. His first mistake was being born a member of his family, which was widely known for its moderate beliefs. His family members were in great danger of elimination because they had associated so closely with powerful members of the Shah's regime. Muslih, who had helped Malik so much earlier in life, was jailed on a trumped-up charge of embezzlement. He was also sentenced to sixty lashes. Finally, the Ayatollah ordered him to be publicly be-headed as a show of intolerance for support of the Shah.

Malik's father tread lightly afterwards to avoid becoming the next vic-tim. He never openly supported the new, non-traditional movement that had somehow gotten some public officials into office. Their success was short-lived, as the opposing party managed to come up with false charges against them. They were removed from office and actually jailed.

Malik's mother stopped her volunteer activities and, at least in public, tried to show obedience to the new laws. She wore her head covering to protect her family.

Malik asked Sadeq to help the new leadership loose interest in the persecution of his family. The severe scrutiny died down some afterwards. Still, the family was careful.

Other things about Malik caused the government leaders to be suspi-cious of him. He insisted that he could write letters to Americans, which was seen as a sure sign that he remained loyal to the outcast modernization movement. Under the new Islamic rule, Americans were seen as evil and their society was to be shunned.

The letters were bad enough, but the pictures from Mike on the bulle-tin board really bothered them. Americans were not be seen as human. The religious leaders approached Sadeq about this to see what he could do. Sadeq saw Malik's desires as a form of weakness, similar to the weakness of the Americans. Still, he remembered that Malik had helped him through so many bad times and he had every intention of protecting him, if he could. But he would have appreciated it if Malik would have cooperated. Periodi-cally, Sadeq would remove the pictures and slide them into Malik's desk drawer. It only served to make Malik more determined to have them openly displayed.

The government officials had people routinely scanning Malik's mail. He was not allowed to write, in detail, about his work. He knew that if he said too much, they simply confiscated the letter and it never reached its destina-tion. So, he took care in his letter writing.

They tolerated Malik and all of his weaknesses only because they needed him. He did not know exactly what magical protective skill he held that made them put up with his slight rebellions. They needed him for something. He just did not know what, but he knew he would not like it.

His work involved production of vaccine. He had read that most other countries had stopped vaccinating against Smallpox, but Iran was seemingly using huge quantities of the vaccine. Sadeq had told him that they were selling it to other countries, like Israel, that still vaccinated their troops. Malik could not see where there could be a market for his product.

Many times, after work, Malik went over his children's lessons with them. The teaching materials all the way down to Kindergarten were totally based on Islam. It bothered Malik, and he daily tried to impart added wisdom to his sons. Over and over, he assured them that the United States was not evil, the U.S. president was not a devil and the United States was not the enemy. Many of the teaching materials laid the blame for every problem Iran experienced directly on America. He did his best to discount these myths.

Then, he cautioned his sons not to speak of their daily discussions.

He and Yahya understood well that their position was precarious. Yahya held Malik close.

"Sadeq is so unpredictable, Malik. I know he's your friend, but I worry about him."

"You're right...and we're too dependent on him for our safety." Malik paused and looked into Yahya's concerned face. "Maybe we should make alternate plans for the children in case...in case Sadeq..."

"Yes, but what can we do for them?"

"We must make plans."

POWER

IRAN

Nasser Ghane waited patiently. He had waited patiently for a very long time now. It was critical for the Iranian President to think that he governed the Iranian portion of the newly formed Iranian-Iraqi Coalition. Even from Iraq, Nasser had carefully herded this man into office. And he was perfect for all of the plans. His apparent air of authority had served as the necessary screen for Nasser as he directed and prodded the man into every action he took.

Nasser smiled as he thought of how much he had achieved already. His transition from military to politics had been an easy one since his heroic actions in the Gulf War were widely known. He had positioned himself into a place of subtle, yet immense power. Then, the sudden death of Saddam Hussein had accomplished a major portion of his plan, without drawing any of the deserved suspicion to himself. The unexpected death of its leader had left the Iraqi government vulnerable and without direction. Nasser had easily convinced them of the need to join Iran in the "Coalition" to stand firm against the great, evil United States.

Everything was set and ready and it would not be long now. Nasser would soon be able to remove the Iranian President, his last obstacle, and assume true command of the Coalition himself. He took a deep breath and calmly continued to watch the President, as a cat watches its intended prey.

The President mulled over the major problems that had just been presented to him. The drop in oil prices dominated them. If he could just keep those up, everything else would fall into place. The political arena kept shifting like the sand, sending the prices lower at each turn.

This, coupled with the poor economic management of the nation's resources and continually increasing U.S. sanctions against the Coalition, resulted in declining agricultural output and forty percent inflation. The people were as restless as they had ever been. Something was bound to break. The President rubbed his throbbing temples in frustration.

Nasser saw his opportunity. "Now is the time, Mr. President."

"Yes, you've said that before Nasser. I'm just not sure it is what we need."

"Your Council of Guardians and Council of Ministers have met. We feel it is time. Everything will soon be ready."

"Their spies have not noticed our defenses?"

"No. We have been calling our troops and men in two or three at a time. Of course, it is slow this way, but they have not noticed. They stopped protecting their troops nearly ten years ago."

"They spend so much time monitoring our nuclear weapon capabilities. The diversion has worked exactly as planned. As far as they can see, we are behaving ourselves. The portable bioreactors have not even been noticed. The enemy has no concept of their danger. This has been so very inexpensive. And they never suspect the University."

"Our Army, Air Force and Navy have been almost completely protected. The second stage is also ready."

They had quietly sent the men to Cuba, across the Yucatan Peninsula to the border. The Mexican government believed that they were only Cuban immigrants.

"What about the mechanisms?"

"They are nearing preparation in Acuna. Sadeq has assured us that it will be effective in weakening the nation's defenses. Then, the second stage can begin."

"Are you sure that they will not be able to stop it?"

"It will be too late. The volunteers will have already reached their targets. Sadeq has sent some of the agent to Omid in Acuna to prepare them."

"And our people here in Iran?"

"We have been protecting our men in order of their importance. We should have plenty of time." Nasser stopped short of the complete truth with the President. Sometimes, even the President could not be told everything.

"I hope you are right, Nasser. Now could be the time. Wait until our people are protected, then we will begin. We will unite the Coalition in a Holy War against the Great Evil."

JAIME

MEXICO CITY SLUMS

Jaime Pacheco sat on the grimy curb, listening to the deafening drone of the city traffic. His young face held none of the hope of youth. A glaze settled over his somber eyes, caused partly by the smell of the exhaust, and partly by the ingrained sadness of his desperate situation. His seventeen years of life had been hard before, but now, since the death of his younger sister, Alicia, it hardly seemed worth the struggle.

Alicia had died of a simple infection in a cut on her leg. Even after Jaime had managed to scrape up money for the medicine, the ugly contagion had continued to pump toxins into Alicia's weakened body until it killed her. She had always lit up his life with her smile and her constant groundless optimism. Now, he was deep in despair. His father had disappeared a long time ago, and his mother had died of TB five years after that.

Luis Hidalgo rounded the corner and, relieved, plopped his thin seat down next to Jaime. He swiped the strand of hair from its favorite place in his eye and looked deep into Jaime's face. He smiled his wide smile that made his eyes look slanted. For once, he had good news for his friend.

"Jaime, come home quickly. We are being moved!"

Jaime jumped out of his depression as he grabbed his friend's shoulders. He had always thought that things would be better anywhere else.

"What? What did you say?"

"We are moving. North. To the U.S. border. The army is taking us...to get us out of these slums!"

"When?"

"Now! Come on! We must hurry or we'll miss the truck."

Jaime could not believe this turn in his life that had only a few minutes before seemed like a straight line to a slow, impoverished death.

They reached home to be greeted by a scene of pure chaos. Eight army-green trucks blocked the road, under the gloomy shadows of the run-down buildings the boys had been calling home. The buildings were essentially gutted-out shells. They had no functional plumbing or running water, and all the windows had been broken long before Jaime could even remember.

Jaime saw his two younger brothers and his three younger sisters running up and down the stairs, responding to the barking orders of his grandmother. She was only forty-eight years old, but she looked like she was at least sixty. Her solid gray hair was twisted into a braid and deep lines withered her brown face. She had lost most of her teeth, and her shoulders were hunched over, permanently bent by arthritis. But, she could still yell orders, and her colorless shift dress shook all around her as she did.

Not that there was much to load onto the truck anyway. The soldiers hurried them as they brought out the old "tortilla" mattress. They called it that because it folded so easily. It had large irregular holes in it where the large rats had borrowed its materials to build nests.

Each child brought his own clothing out in one hand. Since there was no water to wash with, dirt and other sorts of unknown grime were smeared across various parts of their bodies, and their hair was so dusty that it took on a lighter, more brown hue. Their sad eyes were much too big for their tiny faces. A simple glance into them told the whole hard, sad trauma of their brief lives. There were no real children in this place.

Grandmother ordered them to bring out her trunk. In it, she had two towels, three cooking pots, four plates, a knife and six forks and spoons of bent aluminum. Her faded picture of Jesus and the Last Supper and her candle were placed carefully on top of the other things in the trunk.

In her hand, she firmly gripped the only food they had left in the world, a small bag of dried pinto beans and a stack of seven tortillas she had prepared that morning. It was the end of the manteca and the flour, so she did not have any of that to bring with her.

And that was all there was. Everything else had been sold for food a long time ago.

Still, they had been more fortunate than Luis and his family. Luis did not even have the luxury of the single, filthy room that Jaime's family had lived in. They lived on the crowded streets, so all they needed to put on the truck was the ripped tarp they huddled under on cold nights. Luis only had one surviving brother and his mother, who was blind.

The excitement of the moment made the time go quickly. To Jaime, the loading only took fifteen minutes. Then, they were on their way. The rumors bounced through the people in the truck, just like the people bounced, as the truck slammed into one rut after another in the road. They knew nothing about any other places than the one they had lived in all their lives. That had been the whole world. They had no education, no television and no picture books. All they had were the repeated stories of those few who had traveled some.

Now, they were all traveling to a place that they knew nothing about. The soldiers just told them that they were going to Ciudad Acuna, on the Mexico-U.S. border. Each family was to receive a parcel of land that they could pay for later. Land! Surely, this was a dream, thought Jaime.

They were vaulted violently in the cloth-covered truck for the rest of the day. The smell of aged sweat permeated their noses as they were constantly thrown into each other with the force of each rut. They did not even stop to relieve themselves. The men and boys had no problems with this, but the women quickly learned to pass around an old coffee can that someone brought. The weary travelers thought that they would stop for the night. To their surprise, the soldiers merely changed drivers and kept driving through the night. Now, each bump transferred pain to their weary bodies. Still, they did not complain.

In the morning, the soldiers stopped the truck on the outskirts of a small town. The men dipped a near-rotten bucket into an old well to give everyone water. The women portioned out pieces of tortillas to their families as soon as they were loaded back onto the trucks.

In the middle of the next day, the cruel sun beat down on the truck. A young woman, named Gloria, moaned and fell to the bed of the truck. There, she gave birth to an underweight baby boy.

Jaime and Luis looked at each other in surprise. Gloria had lived one floor above Jaime in Mexico City. The thirteen-year-old looked so thin that nobody guessed that she was pregnant. As far as Jaime knew, Gloria had not been seeing anyone. She was far too shy. A sad, knowing look came over them as they realized how this had happened. Two of Gloria's sisters had borne children to their own father.

The ashen-blue infant did not even cry as the older women wiped the blood and afterbirth off his tiny face and thick, black hair. His miniature fingers jerked spasmodically, giving the only indication of his actual life. The older women tried to help, but the weak baby only survived for six hours. His mother was not conscious when he died. She had lost too much blood, and she died two hours later.

Jaime and Luis were not untouched by all of this, but their rough lives had left them callused to such common place events as death in childbirth. Still, they knew exactly how the girl's family felt. They simply avoided looking down at the dried pool of blood that marked the enigmatic events of birth and death in the same day. Perhaps, it was more merciful that way.

When the truck finally stopped for fuel, the passengers lowered the two bodies off of the truck. They did not know if they were buried. The soldiers hurried the passengers back onto the truck and drove off as fast as possible.

During the next night, an old man apparently died of a heart attack. The morning light found him wearing a frozen grimace on his face. His right hand clutched tightly onto his left arm. He wore a stubble of a beard, which matched his undershirt, and the greasy pants stretched over his swollen belly. His children and grandchildren, in the same truck, cried only for a little while. They left his body at the next stop.

Finally, after five days of brutal travel, the migrants arrived at their destination. And it was a pitiful destination.

The truck stopped, and the soldiers yelled the order to the group to get off of the truck. It was mid-morning in the Colonias of Ciudad Acuna. The scorching sun was intensified by its reflection off the near-white caliche earth. The hard-packed "land" bore cracks and loads of caliche rocks. Low mesquite bushes and prickly-pear cactus provided the only green in the area.

Nearby, stood a pathetic cluster of shelters made of cardboard boxes. The walls looked like advertisement signs: "Whirlpool Washing Machine" in sideways print, "Northern Toilet Paper" in blue print running diagonally in front of the other. Black and white-colored plastic trash bags covered some of the cardboard pieces. They fluttered in the hot, dry wind.

Jaime could not tell just how all of this was anchored down. Silver tape kept it from blowing away.

Curious people slowly emerged from the shelters to see what the trucks were leaving. As they saw the travelers unloading from the vehicle, several of the ragged onlookers frowned and slowly shook their heads. This only meant more hardships for them. The children, dressed in only underwear, hung onto their mother's faded skirts and rubbed the backs of their dusty hands against their cheeks. One little girl with long, brown uncombed hair stared at Jaime. When Jaime smiled, she ran behind her mother, peeking out every few seconds to see if he was still looking.

Jaime helped his grandmother out of the truck. As she stood and rubbed her lower back, he reached in for her beloved trunk, and laid it on the parched ground. The watching people eagerly evaluated the trunk as it was lowered. Jaime knew the look. It was a little too eager, and it probably meant trouble.

He would have to find a way to guard his grandmother's only belongings. He patted the top of the trunk.

"Sit here, Grandmother. I will talk to the Federales."

He stood in the line and scanned his new home. The parcels of land were smaller than the room they had occupied in Mexico City. He wondered where he could find cardboard.

"Where do we get cardboard?" Jaime asked a nearby boy.

Miguel pulled his thin hand out of his too-tight pocket and waved off to the east. "In the city, behind the stores."

"How far is the city?"

"Four miles. If you have money, you can ride the bus."

Jaime looked down at his dirt-stained bare feet.

"No. No money."

Miguel, at age eighteen, was already a hardened veteran of the war for survival here. It had not been long since he had been in exactly the same situation as Jaime was now. He pulled the bottom of his grayed-white T-shirt and it flopped loosely over his broad, bony shoulders. He gave Jaime an understanding smile.

"Tomorrow, I will walk with you and show you the best places. My house is that one over there, with the red label on the top. I will come get you."

As Miguel walked back to his house, Jaime studied his new surroundings. A mere fifteen feet separated the shacks. If they had a door, it was made of faded, shredding cotton material that danced in the hot wind, partially hypnotizing the disenchanted young man.

A rusted fifty-five gallon drum sat outside each hovel. Different colors of stubborn paint patches remained on the outside. Parts of the names of various American chemical companies decorated these barrels in a patchwork pattern. These had been previously used to transport compounds toxic enough to be regulated by the government.

A little way down the trenched road, a truck wearing a large capsule-shaped tank slowly rocked its way to each barrel. Someone came out of each domicile and carefully handed over two coins to the driver. The driver jumped out of the truck, filled the rusty barrel with water and drove on to the next house.

70

The hordes of flies retreated until the truck drove off. Then, they returned, buzzing furiously above the water surface. There was no lid for the barrel. Frustrated mothers swatted unsuccessfully at the fly armies. Sometimes, flies were hit hard enough to crash-land into the water. Filthy hands reached in and unceremoniously scooped them out.

But the enormous number of flies never lessened. The dead flies were quickly replaced by the breeding supply from two separate places. A twelve-inch ditch ran along both sides of the road. A slow-moving, unknown mixture of whatever drained out of the huts and off the neighboring land filled the ditch. It was thick brown and it fed the flies bountifully.

The public restroom was a few steps down the trail into the bushes. The whole population of the Colonias went to this location to relieve themselves. The small piles stayed where they were put, but the meager wads of paper blew with every puff of the wind. There had not been enough rain to partially bury or disintegrate them. They were everywhere.

Less than a mile away, a crowded herd of cattle waded in a continuous sea of their own aromatic manure. This served as the source of both the horrendous smell and a multitude of the flies.

A cooling darkness enveloped the Colonias. Jaime returned to his grandmother and siblings and did his best to bed them down for the night. They slept, huddled together around the old trunk on the plot of land that was assigned to them. After the eternal trip to this heaven, exhaustion quickly led to sleep, despite the rock-hard ground. At least, it was not bouncing.

The next morning, a more determined Jaime set out with Miguel and Luis to find cardboard for their shelters. As they walked past rows and rows of huts, Jaime saw that the closer they got to the highway, the more civilized their plight appeared.

Some of the people who had been there for a month or more had begun to make their own bricks to use in building a house. Jaime saw them laid out in lines in the small yards. The scorching sun baked them well. Closer to the highway, houses had actually been built using similar bricks. Most of them wore roofs of thatched brush, but some sported rusted pieces of tin, brightly reflecting the sun. Miguel filled Jaime and Luis in on how to make the bricks as they walked.

They passed the communally built structure that served as the church. The Church members had made the mud bricks and carefully smoothed them over with a layer of hardened mud. A piece of corrugated tin served as a roof, gleaming in the sun. A cross of wood branches hung above the doorway, which was a simple opening in the front of the twelve by twelve construction. There was no door. A single opening, containing no glass, marked the middle of each of the two-side walls...

Stacks of mud bricks supported scarcely—found wood planks in four neat rows on both sides in the room. The floor was caliche, swept dust-free. Another branch cross-hung over the pulpit area, which contained only an old card table.

Finally, they reached the ragged highway. They turned to the right and walked past the cattle feeding pens. The smell rose up and assaulted their noses, so they walked a little faster to get up-wind of it. The bony cattle watched them as they passed.

Many pedestrians walked to the city that morning. Miguel explained that these were mainly the lucky ones that had found work in the city as manual workers or maids. Others were on their way to the open market to buy beans and rice. Some slowly walked to the clinic.

Jaime, Luis and Miguel stayed far away from the shoulderless road to avoid being hit by the passing traffic. Jaime saw by the well-worn path that many tired feet had passed this way. A similar path ran along the other side of the road.

Most of the cars passing them were older models that had been put back together many times. They carried six to eight passengers each, as their mufflers, in need of repair, loudly announced their passing. Some of the metal panels were not the same color as the others on the car. Some had patches that had been sanded, but not repainted yet. The gasoline fumes were familiar to Jaime. They had the same strong smell in Mexico City.

They passed three Macquiladora twin plants along the highway. A few parked cars and tall chain-link fences surrounded the enormous buildings. Workers, dressed in relatively nice clothes, reported to work for the day. Miguel announced that he hoped to get a job at one of these someday.

They began to pass wooden stands of fruits as they neared the city. Jaime's grumbling stomach reminded him of his lack of food. Still, he must build some sort of shelter for his family before he could worry about finding food. He hoped that his grandmother was going to cook some of their beans for tonight's meal.

Some of the women from established huts had given them water that morning from their barrels. As hard as the life was in this place, people still had some compassion for each other. Besides, they were still interested in her trunk's mystery contents.

Miguel announced that they were nearly in town. Buildings, with people clustered around the doors, closed in together until they ran together completely. The only way to tell one from the other was the sudden change in colors of each adobe structure. Many were white, but others of chartreuse, bright pink and blue intermeshed into the mix. They were all two-storied. Some carried on businesses downstairs and served as homes on top with flowerbeds decorating upper windows.

They passed the busy market. Inside, Jaime saw the venders trading. Rows and rows of tables held goods for sale. Jaime had never seen so much in one place. There were foods, alcoholic beverages, and openly displayed jewelry of turquoise and silver, and even piñatas and wrapped goats-milk candy.

The boys went to the narrow alley behind the market. Miguel smiled as they rounded the corner. Three good-sized boxes waited for them there. The boys gathered the bulky cartons and continued on, looking for more. The loads they carried made it difficult to get past all the piles of trash in the alley. Still, they felt fortunate to find them.

When they had all they could carry, they began the journey back along the highway. Because it was only mid-day, fewer people traveled back than the number going to town earlier that morning. The sun had already efficiently heated the air to 101°. Jaime longed for some of the water his grandmother had been given.

They passed a small-sized Macquiladora on their returning side of the road. Many poorer people worked at this factory.

"Maybe, I can get a job here. It doesn't look like nice clothes are required." Jaime was always hopeful.

Miguel stopped short and looked directly at Jaime.
"You must never go to work there. It is a factory of death."

MACQUILADORA

THE COLONIAS, CIUDAD ACUNA, MEXICO, ONE YEAR LATER

J amie, at the young age of eighteen, now carried the responsibilities of the world on his fatigued shoulders. In the year that had passed since their relocation from Mexico City, he had aged a lifetime.

He was proud of the house that he had built. Three separate trips to Acuna resulted in enough precious cardboard to begin a shelter for his family. His brothers, Refugio and Rudolpho, steadied the structure as he fastened it together with wire as well as he could. A generous neighbor donated a black plastic trash bag, which was carefully tied over the top of the pasteboard fabrication.

Before he could get more plastic; the rains came and soaked the uncovered cardboard, making it weak and stained. Trips to Acuna resulted in replacement cardboard.

He began to build a few bricks in the yard. This required digging by hand into the stubborn caliche for the soil. Foraging trips to the brush areas surrounding the Colonias resulted in paltry strands of stiff grasses and weeds to mix with the caliche. After the bricks were formed, they were allowed to dry.

His grandmother wisely opened her trunk and allowed her new neighbors to peer into it. This lessened the curiosity about the family's concealed wealth and brought suggestions from the neighboring women that the faded Last Supper picture and the candle could be sold up the road at the Flea Market. His grandmother, with tears in her yellowed eyes, sent him to the market with her most prized possessions. Jaime brought back only five hundred pesos, but that was enough to keep them eating a meal of rice and beans long enough for him to possibly find work.

74

They bought a corroded water barrel that only had holes worn through at the top. All of its paint had rusted off. Then, they paid the necessary two coins the next time the water truck came. Now they had food and water, at least for a little while.

At the daily mealtime, the old trunk served as a table. The longer-legged boys stood around it as the girls and their grandmother sat closer to it, with their legs curled up under them. After the meal was cleared, the trunk transformed to Grandmother's chair.

Jamie's sisters, Maria, Lucinda, and Theresa, with their braids held tight with rubber bands, searched the encompassing brush and found a rough mesquite branch about four feet long. They stripped off as much of the loose bark as they could and rubbed it down with a little water. Then, they went out and returned with a bundle of dried grasses and more limber twigs to bind onto one end of the stick. Now, they had a broom to use in sweeping the hard caliche floor of the hut.

They used the largest cooking pot to wash dishes and clothes. Precious water from the barrel half-filled it. Sand was used to scrub the pot since there was no soap. They threw the wash water into the ditch running along the road.

The girls scrubbed the few clothes over a large, rough rock. Then carefully draped them over the thin, frayed cord they had strung between the two cedar posts that marked the territory of the lot behind their home. Hand-made mesquite pegs attached the tattered clothes to the line.

In the evenings, the girls searched the nearby brush area for cooking fuel. With the demand for wood, twigs and sprigs made up most of their haul. Then, the girls resorted to finding the low dry piles left by cattle and other animals. If they were dry enough, they would burn and could be used for cooking.

Jaime's brother, Refugio walked into town with some new friends. His angry face reflected his utter frustration. He saw no hope, and surrounded himself with others of the same persuasion.

His hopelessness led him to wander into the market. His hungry eyes saw the sparkle of the silver jewelry on one of the tables, and he waited until a group of tourists came up to distract the eagle-eyed vendor. As soon as he thought the busy man was not paying attention, he stealthily stuffed a handful of rings from the display into his pants pocket.

But the vendor had experienced this ploy many times before. The middle-aged woman he had placed across the aisle to watch the table instantly grabbed the youth and started yelling.

"Thief!"

Refugio struggled and managed to free all but a piece of his shirt from the woman. But it was too late. Other vendors had already surrounded him, and they gripped his arms tightly, brutally shaking him when he tried to free himself.

Jaime only knew that the Federales had scooped up his fighting brother and hauled him off in the direction of the jail. He went to the jail to find Refugio, but nobody there would even acknowledge the boy's existence. He feared the very worst for his brother. As he walked the path back to the Colonias, he could only imagine the horror of his brother's life now, and he was powerless to do anything about it. What was he going to tell his grandmother?

Jaime's youngest brother, Rudolpho, was eight years old. His thick, straight black hair fell abundantly around his curious eyes. After Refugio's arrest, Rudolpho went to town with a man who led many boys to the tourista streets of the city. Rudolpho was instructed in begging techniques.

On some days, he would run repeatedly up to the Gringos, pushing cellophane-wrapped packages of flat, candy-coated gum into their faces. He would look deeply into their eyes, looking for a twinge of compassion. Many times, the men started to walk away, so Rudolpho switched his hungry gaze to the women in the group.

"Oh, give him some money!" the women would say.

The men would reach into their pockets and give Rudolpho some pocket change, hand the gum to the women and smile at them. Rudolpho would smile his happy grin.

"Gracias, Thank-you, Senor!"

It was an act that Rudolpho had perfected easily.

At the end of the day, the old man collected half of what the young beggars had collected. Rudolpho carefully pocketed his share and scurried home to proudly present his scant pesos to his grandmother.

As he grew older, Rudolpho would be assigned to *car guarding* services. The nervous tourists drove over the bridge in a nice car. As soon as they parked, older boys ran out and offered to *guard* the car while the tourist went into the shops. Most of the time, the visitors handed the boy some coins and walked off, feeling a little more secure about the safety of their vehicle.

The fact that his younger brother begged for a living did not bother Jaime. Jaime had done his share of it in Mexico City. He knew the time was coming that Rudolpho would be too old to beg.

What bothered him more was the way the men came looking for young girls, like his sisters, in the Colonias. A car, carrying one or two men, drove down the rutted road. The men were in no hurry. They searched the barren yards for the young girls, and pointed out possibilities to each other. Jaime knew the seedy look on their faces. It always made his blood rise to his ears in anger.

He had to make more money for them. He did not want his sisters working for those men. He had seen the light in the young eyes of other girls who had gone with them be replaced with a sickening self-hate.

An excited Miguel came searching for Jaime and Luis. "Hurry! There is work in the city!"

Jaime and Luis did not even question the nature of the work. Miguel rushed them towards Acuna in more of a trot than a walk.

"They are digging ditches. They will pay us well to dig."

The three eager young men turned the corner and saw the group of men gathered at the city offices. They joined the group shoving hopefully towards the jobs they needed. An hour later, they were signed up for work to start early the next morning. Their jubilant moods carried them home in no time, to spread the happy news to their hungry families.

The city officials had decided to repair the water lines and the sewer lines in the middle of town. Jaime and his friends arrived the next morning just after daybreak. A short, fat official with a brushy mustache led them two streets over with their shovels. There, they were instructed to start digging just below the curb on the road.

The road was not paved, but it was packed very hard. They splashed a bucket of water onto the starting point of the dig. Jaime scraped the surface with the dull edge of the shovel and let the tip land hard on the road. Gradually, he was able to begin to dig into the softer dirt under the top layer.

The sun came up in its full heat by 9:30 and began to beat down on his aching back. His emaciated arms were not used to such a drastic workout, and they protested painfully in response to the work. His hands wore blisters and collected splinters from the shovel. Still, he did not complain. Every hour he toiled meant more time his sisters would be free from temptation to leave with the evil men.

Then, a shower started. He welcomed the cooling rivulets running down his hair and into his eyes. It gave him more energy and more hope, but it also made the clay in the soil more slippery. As he gave the needed force to break the road, his foot slipped back in the mire.

Finally, they reached the level of the first pipe. It was white and had an eighteen-inch diameter. It was the sewer pipe. And it was leaking. That was why the city wanted it replaced. A steady stream of raw sewage ran down into the soil, making aromatic puddles that now mixed with the rainwater. Each time Jaime struck down the shovel, thick, brown splashes flew in every direction, bathing and coating Jaime's legs. He tried not to think about it. He just kept digging.

Then, they reached the next pipe. It looked just like the other pipe, but it was the water supply pipe. It was also broken. Small streams ran from the sewer pipe to the water pipe, where they diluted in the clear water and entered the water supply for the city. Even Jaime understood the meaning of this. He was glad his family was not on the city water supply.

The city did not close the roads while they worked on them. The incessant file of crawling cars and trucks was less than two feet away from the working men. Most of the drivers were agitated because they were being slowed down. Their annoyed expressions had plenty of time to sink in the backs of the hard-working men as they passed. Horns honked in impatience. Motors raced in response to heavy, hurried feet. The caustic exhaust hung close to the ground, making the young men's' lungs cough in rebellion.

One green car got too close. Its threadbare tires slipped easily into the ditch, stranding the vehicle on its chassis. All the digging stopped, while the workers skidded together in an attempt to pull the car out. Finally, the rectified car spun out as it left the scene, sending globs of fetid ooze back at the workers in gratitude.

As the pipes were replaced, Jaime and the other workers refilled the holes with the mounds of dirt they had built before. This was much easier work, but it signaled the approaching end of the job...and of the pay. In the duration of the month-long job, Jaime brought his money home to his grandmother. He had purchased a piece of tin to serve as a roof for the hut and bought two sheets of plastic for waterproofing. There would also be enough money for rice, beans and even flour and manteca for several more months.

Jaime had stopped at the market and bought a special treat for his grandmother. She beamed her toothless smile when she saw the small paper bag containing a handful of coffee for her to boil.

It was not long before the accumulated wealth was gone. Theresa, his youngest sister became ill with dysentery. She ran high fever and had diarrhea that looked more like water. Her skin became like paper, and her eyes sunk into her thin face. Jaime paid the bus fare to take her to the clinic in Acuna. Then, he paid the doctor and paid for the medicines she needed. Everything cost so much money.

He needed to find more work. Other young men simply left the work-barren Colonias with men called coyotes to find work. Most took their chances crossing the Rio Grande River to work at ranches or factories in big cities in the U.S.A. They would give it a try. If they succeeded in the crossing, they would be gone for months, working and saving money to bring back home. If the Border Patrol caught them, the illegal immigrants would be returned fairly shortly, to try again later.

The wives, babies and small children stayed in the Colonias, battling for survival. They never knew if they would ever see their men again. They did their daily living chores, not knowing what they would do if their providers did not return soon. The women took care of each other as well as they could. Still, Jaime could not bear the thought of leaving his family there, helpless and possibly allowing the men to entice his sisters. He did not know what he was going to do.

Luis and his friend, Juan Gonzalez, joined Jaime as he sat thoughtlessly forming bricks in his yard one evening. Juan's medium-sized build was not thin like that of Luis and Jaime. He had a nice appearance, except for his acne-scarred face, which he tried to hide beneath purposely-long hair.

"Jaime, Juan says he knows where we can get work."

Jaime looked up hopefully to Luis. "Where?"

Juan's voice was cautious. He did not know Jaime well. Jaime had shot him a threatening glance once last week, after Juan had smiled at his sister, Maria.

"There is a Macquiladora on the highway where paper goods are prepared for shipment. A Senor Ramon Terrazas runs it. He will hire you. I have been working there for two weeks."

"Which Macquiladora?" Jaime did not recall seeing such a factory.

"It is the first one on the left side of the road."

Jaime shot a guarded gaze at Luis. "Isn't that the one that Miguel warned us about, Luis?"

"Yes, I think so, but Juan, here, says it's perfectly safe. He has not seen any heavy machinery or dangerous chemicals."

"I wonder what Miguel was talking about. Where is he?

"The last time I saw him, he was at the Salinas' house."

"Let's go find him."

They walked down the dusty road and turned left for two streets. The corner hut with the chicken-wire fence belonged to the Salinas family. There, they found Miguel and questioned his warning.

"I told you not to go there," Miguel said in a raised voice. "Who told you it was safe?"

"I did." Juan did not appreciate being doubted.

"You just don't know yet, Juan. People disappear from there. And then their families vanish also. Something is wrong. It is not safe."

"I have been working there, and I have seen none of that."

Juan turned to Jaime. "You must listen to me, Jaime. Senor Terrazas is nice to his workers. He hires us from the Colonias."

Jaime spoke to Miguel. "Miguel, maybe Juan is right. Besides, I need the money. There is no other work besides the work across the border. I can't leave my family now. Grandmother can't do this by herself, and care for Theresa. She is not well yet. And, if I work there, I can get free medicines for her from the factory clinic. I have no choice."

"Si, Jaime, I understand, but you must be careful."

As Jaime, Juan and Luis returned in the dark to their huts, Miguel watched them slowly disappear. He had grown to like Jaime and Luis and he knew he was going to miss them.

RAMON

CIUDAD ACUNA, MEXICO

Omid Farrahi, or Ramon Terrazas as he was known in Acuna, smiled as he thought of the good work he had done. He had been chosen partly because of his Hispanic appearance. He had always kept a trim figure so, even though he was short, he still looked well proportioned. His olive skin, green eyes and thinner eyebrows made it possible for him to fit easily into the Acuna population.

He had hurriedly learned to speak Spanish, but he thought he spoke it well. The people in Acuna who worked for him, however, thought his accent was strange and his language a bit too formal.

The Coalition had provided all the finances needed for Ramon to purchase the Macquiladora plant. The large, corrugated metal building sat on the right side of the highway that led south out of Ciudad Acuna.

"Santos, check the expected date for the next shipment. It should be here by now."

Ramon watched as his assistant, Eamen Nabavi, known to his workers as Santos Villarreal, turned on one foot to enter the office of the plant. The sealed packets had been produced in Iran under Sadeq's watchful eye. The production was reported to international authorities to be a clean room production of computer equipment.

But Sadeq had not been producing computer chips, or anything to do with computer chips. The "free samples" were small, thin white postcards with scratch and sniff squares of Variola major virus. The virus could withstand drying for months at room temperature, and it resisted heating at 212°F for five to ten minutes. Sadeq had chosen a hardy ally.

The white samples were dosed with a pleasant fragrance that exuded when the square was scratched. It was packed into an airtight, cellophane wrapper with little zigzagged edges. The closed packages were then sent through a chamber of virucidal gas for sterilization of the outer surface. This made it safe for the Iranians to handle. The virus was not a danger until the sealed package was opened. This was the reason for applying the mailing labels by hand. An accidental tear by machine could ruin the whole plan. Secrecy was imperative.

He strode confidently down the concrete main aisle of the plant. On both sides of him, the stocks of packaged postcards bragged of his hard and successful work. He would be ready in plenty of time. In fact, he was slightly ahead of schedule, despite the problems that had surfaced. He had handled them quickly and efficiently.

Santos returned from the office. "It is scheduled to arrive tomorrow, Senor Terrazas."

Santos always had to force himself to remember to address Ramon with his proper title. "How many do we have ready?"

"We have prepared close to twenty-six million parcels, Senor."

"Have you put the mailing labels on them yet?"

"Of course, Senor, all except the names we purchased from the small catalog companies. We are still making those labels, but they will be ready by tomorrow."

"Good. This is the last shipment. Santos, what is that in the corner?" Ramon pointed accusingly in the direction of a small pile of debris left by a hurried sweeper. Ramon, being a perfectionist, insisted that his plant be perfectly neat.

"It will be cleaned up immediately! Juan, get the broom and take care of that right now."

Juan looked up from his workstation and saw the offending mess. He quickly jumped up from his wood stool, grabbed an old broom and swept up the mess. He did not want to get behind on his work quota, so he returned to the bench hastily. He efficiently picked up the next postcard and placed the address label in its appropriate spot. Printed on one side of the card were the words: "New! Fresh Scent!" in bold, red print. The words: "Free Sample" stood out in bright blue print on the other side of the card.

Then, because the person who was supposed to work next to him did not come to work that day, Juan was forced to do the work of his absent friend also. He placed the labeled post card onto the stack in the cardboard box meant to hold the stacks steady.

Ramon passed two rows of young, Mexican men and women, who were suddenly very engrossed in their tasks. He stopped, and watched their work intensely, making them very nervous. Then, he entered the other part of the factory. On one side of the aisle were the filled boxes. Busy workers stacked boxes of free samples into the storage area.

Watching carefully, Ramon proceeded down the line of workers until he came to one voluptuous young lady. "Cecilia, come with me. I would like to discuss your hours."

Cecilia Benevides rose carefully from her workstation. She balanced easily on her black high-heels. Still, she could not keep up with Ramon because the bottom of her red, floral-print skirt was too tight to allow big steps. Her hair was shiny-black, and it had a naturally tight curl to it. It bounced below her shoulders, sending its perfumed scent all around as she walked. She bit her full lips as she walked past the knowing eyes of her fellow workers. Senor Terrazas never spoke to anyone, except Cecilia, about hours.

Santos waited until a smiling Cecilia left Ramon's office a little while later. He shook his head and grinned slightly. Ramon certainly knew how to find the perks in an assignment. Then, Santos knocked quietly on the door, and paused for a reply.

"Come in," said a relaxed Ramon.

"Senor Terrazas, I believe we may have a small problem."

By the tone in Santo's voice, Ramon knew exactly what he was referring to. "Who is it?"

"Roberto Talamantes did not come to work this morning. He is at our clinic now."

The free clinic they had established at the plant for factory workers and their families was one of the most ingenious ideas Sadeq had come up with in his plans. Whenever a worker got sick, he or she was provided free medical care on the premises of the plant. This way Ramon controlled any accidental infections that occurred and kept them silent.

Ramon muttered Iranian curse words under his breath and exited his office on his way to the clinic.

"Not yet. Not yet."

The single room held an examination table behind a white room divider on one side and three simple chairs along the other side. It smelled strongly of rubbing alcohol. Glass jars containing tongue depressors and swabs lined the counter.

As he entered the room, he saw the back of the medical officer's white coat. This man had also come to Mexico with Ramon. He heard Roberto's voice weakly explaining how he felt. Ramon knew, even before he saw the look on his medical officer's face. As soon as he got the nod, he walked grimly back to his office to use the phone.

Sadeq had provided this backup. The secrecy was the most critical part of his job. They could not vaccinate their workers without raising major questions from the local health authorities. So they let the workers take their chances. Any of them who were accidentally infected simply disappeared, along with their entire families. It could not be avoided.

This directly affected their selection of workers. They hired only the very poor people from the Colonias. Most of the other factories favored workers from a more stable background. The local community looked at Ramon's hiring of the Colonias inhabitants as a form of charity.

But there was no charity to it at all. These were the people who would not be missed. Nobody cared about them except their neighbors. And they did not matter. It was also not unusual for these people to suddenly disappear because they heard of work in another place or they took off across the river to the U.S.

Ramon knew this part of the plan would soon be completed. Still, it required control for another few weeks. He picked up the phone and dialed the number.

"We have another one. His name is Roberto Talamantes. He is here at the clinic. Follow the same procedure. And be careful. Don't be seen this time."

Ramon hung up the phone and walked back out of his office. He passed Juan as he continued towards the outside plant door. Juan turned as he passed, then threw a worried glance at the worn stool normally occupied by

Roberto. He had not seen this before. He needed to talk to Jaime. Or was it too late?

CARGO

The oil transfer pipe began to discharge into the vast holding bay of the Iraqi tanker. The pipe was almost two feet in diameter. The flow of the crude was slow at first, little more than a trickle. The trickle grew rapidly until the pipe flowed in its full capacity, virtually a solid column of black crude.

Even after several minutes, little more than a few scant inches covered the bottom of the tanker's mammoth hold. The flow of crude stopped abruptly. An indiscernible object fell out of the pipe and splatted into the crude below. Another gush of crude rolled the object around, revealing its nature. It had eyes that were open, filled with oil like dark tears. Crude gurgled out of its nose and mouth. Shiny, white nerves and stringy veins flowed with the current. The pipe belched and liberated a large object...the head now had its mangled body for company.

The flow of crude began to trickle and increase in volume until, after a short interval, the solid column of crude was again flowing. It stopped again and a crude-covered torso tumbled out. Ropes of small intestine tangled themselves around it. An entire, intact body followed it...then more body parts...heads, legs, arms and sometimes unidentifiable masses. A small burp of crude occasionally interrupted the flow of bodies. It became a slurry of oil, bodies and body parts. The slurry filled every corner of the holding tanks and every holding tank was filled to capacity. When the tanker was filled, it was replaced by another tanker, and the flow of bodies continued...

• • •

General Herndon sat on the side of his bed. He bolted toward the bathroom toilet, but only made it as far the sink. He heaved repeatedly, but only phlegm and mucous came up.

"What the shit was that...?" He heaved more and gasped for breath. "God, I hate that...I hate throwing up...I guess all that bullshit was supposed to mean something to me. And I guess asking you to just tell me what it

85

means is wasting my breath. What is this...some kind of game you play with me? Show me just a little bit and see if I can figure out the rest? 'Oh, General...great calamity is about to hit mankind...you get three guesses as to how it's going to happen.' Am I so thick that this is the only way you can reach me? Why do you torture me with this crap? All day long...with each breath I draw...burnt flesh...that's all I smell, burnt flesh. I fear going to sleep at night...I dread it. I fear for my mind. I don't know what I'm supposed to do."

TRAINING

Farid did not like his new assignment and he took it almost like a demotion. He had headed "Project Trojan Horse" as it had become known among his peers. His project's real name remained held secret...a name that only a few on the highest level of the Coalition were privileged to know.

The success of the project brought great pride to Farid. However, until the past two years, he had not received any indication that anything would actually become of his work. He had begun to believe that the skill and knowledge he had gained over the years was going to be wasted and never put to use in the manner that the Ayatollah had envisioned, or used to strike the Great Satan.

Now, he could see things falling into place. Farid's network had managed to place incredible numbers of highly trained commandos at key points across America. He had also perfected their disguises. They blended in flawlessly throughout the United States as restaurant bus boys, construction laborers, agriculture workers, menial toilers or any type of worker an illegal alien could be. The camouflage was ideal.

He knew that this would be his last direct dealing in the field of crossing of human cargo across the American border. Actually, it had been more than a year since he himself had actually done the crossing. Others he had trained handled the day to day smuggling of men into the U.S. now.

His new assignment put him under the tutelage of two men previously unknown to him. He had been instructed to cross these two and obtain a number of residences in the shabbier part of San Antonio, Texas for them. Now he returned to those houses.

"Come in, come in...did you find everything?" Kaveh greeted Farid at the door.

"Yes, let us see." Mehran pounced on Farid, barely letting him in the house before snatching the plastic bags out of his hands.

Farid thought that the Americans had a word that perfectly described both Mehran and Kaveh...*Nerds.* About all that Farid knew about the two Iraqi's was that they had attended MIT before the Gulf War and were considered to be electrical and mechanical wizards. Farid did not care much for Iraqi's, but he had been forced to learn tolerance for them since the emergence of the Iraqi/Iranian Coalition. After all, the Ayatollah had predicted that they would unite to fight their common enemy.

The two men continued to dig through the bags almost giggling with delight. They had given Farid a whole laundry list of gizmos to purchase at electronics supply houses. They had spent several days sending Farid out for various mechanical parts. He did not have a clue about the functions the parts would perform. He had also been instructed to purchase two, used utility vans.

Kaveh looked up at Farid with bright-eyed enthusiasm. "Today, we will teach you to build a...ahh...what should we call it...a...ahh, I believe the Americans would call it a 'poor man's cruise missile'."

True enough, depending on the price of the used van, the total cost ran usually under ten thousand dollars. Still, the van was hardly a cruise missile. But, when loaded with explosive, it would yield a destructive force that would dwarf the power of any conventionally armed cruise missile.

Farid did not understand the mechanical and electrical wizardry, but he immediately comprehended its application. They planned to rig a van with remote viewing optics mounted to look out the windshield and with further gizmos to make the van operable by remote control. The ready availability of the materials made it easy.

Kaveh and Mehran wasted no time and had the first van functioning in a couple of hours. "Farid, our job is to teach you and others to assemble these. It is easy for us. We have done it many times. With practice, it will be easy for you."

87

DISCOVERY

IRAN—LATE SUMMER

"Where is Sadeq?"

The President of Iran scanned the ornate room as he walked into it dressed in his formal attire. The white turban on his head covered his slight balding, but still showed the tight wave of his short, gray-streaked, black hair. He had just returned from a mid-morning meeting with the Lebanese. The tea he had drunk only served to make him more troubled by what they had discussed. The Iranians and the Lebanese Muslims had long been allies and now, the Iranians were being asked to help them.

"Sadeq was not requested to appear, Mr. President." Nasser Ghane would have to do some fast-talking to keep the man from becoming suspicious.

"Why not? I thought that he was in charge of this project."

"He is...but he does not have our advantage of seeing the whole picture." Sometimes Nasser grew tired of having to constantly explain everything to his *ally*. He knew, however, that his control over the Coalition necessitated the use of naive leaders such as this. The poor man did not even have a hint that Nasser manipulated him the way he did.

"What do you mean?"

"He is so insistent about the timing of the event. He forgets that the rest of the world is not just sitting out there waiting for him to prepare."

"The plans are progressing as scheduled, aren't they?"

"Yes, but the plans were made before this problem with Israel arose. We did not expect them to attack the Lebanese so powerfully in retribution. The Americans think that they have the right to chastise us for building a force against Israel. Their evil intrusion into our affairs must not be tolerated any more. We must attack now, whether Sadeq agrees or not. He has done what we needed him to do. Now, we must use it to our best advantage."

"When will he be told?"

"Why do we need to bother him with it? This will serve to enhance the element of surprise."

The President removed his glasses and rubbed his yellowed eyes. He replaced the glasses and looked thoughtfully at Nasser. Nasser always made him nervous. Maybe it was the way he was able to manipulate everything and everyone so easily. Was he also being manipulated even now? Possibly. Nasser had certainly risen quickly and efficiently through the ranks in the last few years. His political strength concerned the President. Nasser was not to be completely trusted. Sometimes, the hunger for political power gleamed out of his eyes, unguarded. There was only one way for Nasser to move politically. The President knew of Nasser's goal to rule the entire Coalition. He would watch Nasser carefully.

"What about our vaccinations here, Nasser. I thought that we needed more time to prepare."

Nasser's expression changed. His broad jaw tightened, and he looked out the window at the masses in the streets. The people were far enough away that they did not look human. They looked like swarming, pesky ants, darting to and fro in their unimportant movements.

It had taken him a while to become so jaded in his views. His countless years of battling the problems of mass population had finally faded the living reality of the individuals he governed. There were just so many of them. Governing them was like holding gelatin in the hand. The gelatin wiggled constantly and, if the hand that was holding it tightened in response, it simply broke into unpredictable wobbles and fell apart. It was only when the amount of gelatin was lessened that it could be effectively controlled.

"We have made good progress in the vaccination of those who contribute the most to our society. We no longer have the needed resources to provide for the others...and you know it. Maybe this will rid us of the Kurd population once and for all. Or at least lessen it."

The President gave a hard look to Nasser. He could not believe what he was hearing. This monster had been bred and groomed right under his nose. At least he was consistent. Nasser never missed a chance to exhibit his cruel visions and he used whatever means to bring them about. Now, the political arena fit him perfectly. Nasser danced around in it, never missing a beat or a chance. The direction he led the others into frightened all the people he touched. That familiar fear bathed over the President now, as he beheld Nasser before him. And yet he knew that Nasser was right. Nasser continued in a calm, soothing voice.

"Can you imagine how much easier it will be to provide for our people when we are rid of the three million Afghan refugees we have supported since 1979? And what about the fifty thousand Azerbaijan refugees we acquired in 1993? Add to that the thirty thousand Zoroastrians, the three hundred forty thousand Baha'is and the fourteen thousand Jews we have been supporting."

He paused. He watched as the horrible reality washed over the President. A few seconds here allowed the ugly truth to soak into the President's thoughts.

"We could start over. We could be wealthy nations...for those who survive."

There was a long silence as the President glared at Nasser. He hated him for speaking the things that he, himself, had been trying not to think. Then, he turned away and gazed out the window.

The President leaned on his elbow and covered his mouth as he looked at Nasser. That was one reason why Nasser was so valuable to him. He could hate Nasser instead of himself.

In another building across the city, Malik searched for Sadeq one more time. He had just disappeared... again, in his usual manor.

Malik walked to Sadeq's office and found the door uncharacteristically unlocked. He let himself in and stood there absorbing the nature of the room. It was so much like Sadeq. Everything was neat and tidy...and colorless. A large Iranian flag hung on one wall, providing the only bright colors in the room. There were no family pictures, except one of this only son. A black pipe occupied an ashtray on the desk.

Next to the pipe sat a small pile of official-looking papers. Malik gave in to his curiosity and read the first paragraph of the top page.

"We have received the last shipment of the samples and are scheduled to have them ready to mail out by the deadline agreed upon. We have only one incident to report this week. The identification was positive, and the problem was dealt with, along with all contacts immediately. All is secure. When is the variolation product to arrive?"

Malik read the last question two more times. What variolation product? He knew well that variolation was a practice carried out by his ancestors against Smallpox. Variolators collected dried crusts from Smallpox lesions and grind them into a fine powder. Then, they put a pinch of this powder into the nose of a person who had not had the disease. This invoked a very mild form of the disease, resulting in far fewer dangerous and scarring effects.

But Smallpox had been eradicated. There was no need for variolation. In fact, variolation could actually cause an outbreak of the disease because the variolated person was quite contagious. The people who caught it from the variolated person would have a full-blown case, not the same minor one as the person from whom he caught it.

Besides, where would anyone get variolation materials? He knew that the only Variola virus in the world was in two high security labs in Atlanta and Moscow. He also knew that all of it was scheduled to be destroyed. The officials would certainly never allow any of it to be used for variolation.

Even if there were a variolation product, why would Omid need any in Mexico? Sadeq certainly had some interesting secrets.

The awful truth hit Malik hard. His eyes widened in disbelief, as the implications of the situation became clear. His mouth parted and he sat back hard against the chair. No, he thought. Sadeq was working with Small-pox! And there had been at least one victim. His mind refused to comprehend it all. He reached up and held his temples. Why would Sadeq do such a thing? How could he undo the work of so many dedicated public health officials? It had taken decades to eradicate the disease. Now, Sadeq planned to bring it back without much effort at all. What was he thinking? The reality of Sadeq's dangerous insanity was suddenly very clear to Malik as he contemplated all of the consequences.

He nearly jumped out of the chair when the door clicked and swung open behind him. He swung the chair around and saw Sadeq standing there, staring at him.

"I have been waiting for you, Sadeq."

"I see that." Sadeq was looking past Malik to the communication on the desk.

"I have something to talk to you about, Sadeq."

"I see that." Sadeq's eyes glared hard at Malik, not even blinking.

91

"Maybe you should close the door."

Sadeq kept his eyes on Malik as he closed the door behind him. Then, he walked up to Malik. "What do you want to know?"

Malik could scarcely believe the self-righteous look on Sadeq's face. "What variolation product, Sadeq?" The look on Sadeq's face told Malik that he had touched on a guarded subject. Sadeq looked abruptly away, and walked to the corner of the small office.

"And what positive identification, Sadeq?"

This was all quickly making some sense now, but Malik did not like what he was seeing. Some of the mystery of Sadeq's behavior melted away to expose a horrible possibility.

"Sadeq, answer me! Do you mean that you are in possession of Variola? If there is a victim, Smallpox is no longer extinct."

He stopped and allowed his mouth to hang open for a second, as the truth dawned on him. He took a short breath. "Is that why we are producing the vaccine?" He paused. "Sadeq, what are you doing?...What have you done?!"

Sadeq's face took on a furious quality that Malik had never seen before. His pupils narrowed and his lips thinned. A small blood vessel popped up on his forehead.

As Sadeq looked at Malik, he wished he had never given an effort to save him from the Fundamentalists. There, in front of him, sat a totally ungrateful man. Sadeq had painstakingly rescued him and his entire family from certain execution. It had not been easy. Malik, with his rebellious modernization streak, was difficult to defend. Now, Malik stood before him, daring to question him and his best work for Iran.

Sadeq exploded at Malik, causing him to take steps backwards in an unconscious attempt to flee the madman. "What have I done? I'll tell you what I have done! I have done what you should have helped me do all along, except that you are so weak-minded, Malik! I have single-handedly produced an economical and efficient weapon for use in the Holy War against the enemy, Malik."

Wild-eyed and maniacal, he raved now, pacing in huge strides back and forth across the office. "The Great Satan will not stand against us, Malik! If you know what is good for your family, you will not get in the way. It is

92

already done!" He triumphantly stormed out of the office, slamming the door behind him.

Malik stepped back and fell into the chair behind him, his eyes still wide in disbelief. Then, he took a deep breath, inhaling the horrible understanding with the air rushing into his lungs. How had this happened? Panic filled him as he thought of Mike and his other American friends.

How could they be warned?

Targets

Ciudad Acuna

Santos stepped out of the office of the Macquiladora, looking for Senor Terrazas. His clicking steps quickened against the concrete as he heard his superior's voice around the corner.

"Senor Terrazas, you have a message in the office."

"What is it, Santos?" The tone of Santos' voice told Ramon that the message was urgent, so he returned to the office immediately.

It was from the Coalition, but it was not from Sadeq. This was something that had never happened before. All communication from the Coalition originated out of Sadeq's office.

But this message was from someone named Nasser Ghane. Ramon knew who this was. What Iranian did not? It was not every day that such a powerful member of the Coalition contacted an ordinary citizen like Ramon.

The message simply read: "Proceed immediately with volunteer plans. Initiate the sequence within five days. Allah be praised. Nasser Ghane"

Ramon gave Santos a surprised look. What could possibly warrant such a major change in the plan? They had understood it completely as Sadeq had explained it. The design of the plan was an analogy of the attack plan of HIV. First, the internal medical defense net and the military would be taken out. Then, the remaining population could be easily destroyed. Smallpox had been chosen over Anthrax because Anthrax was not as hardy as the Smallpox virus, and the Americans vaccinated many of their troops against Anthrax.

93

While the virus weakened the infrastructure of the nation, the second part of the plan would be implemented. For more than a year now, small groups of Coalition troops had made the trip to Cuba. Then, they crossed to the Yucatan peninsula, not drawing any attention from the Mexican government because they looked like Cuban refugees. The Cuban government had been completely helpful in this matter. The variolation volunteers were clustered up at the northern border of Mexico.

Now, however, with this new instruction, the attack date was to be moved up by several months. Ramon scratched his head, then nodded. It would be all right. His supply of samples was nearly complete now. And it would not be difficult to go ahead and activate the volunteers.

Ramon told Santos to call a meeting of the waiting volunteers for the next evening. The variolation product Sadeq had prepared had arrived only two days before. This would work perfectly.

Two days later, Behzad Sabouri stood in line with many other members of the Coalition Army. His black hair was neatly cut and groomed. He had shaved his mustache and beard. His light blue, short-sleeved shirt and his khaki-colored, casual pants were still stiff from the package. His new, brown loafers still squeezed his feet because they had not been properly broken in yet. He glanced at the inexpensive watch he had also been given.

When he had begun his required two years of service in the Iranian military, he had not known that his work would be so easy. He had not worn a uniform since he had left Iran for Cuba.

In Cuba, his work was studying English and Spanish. For six months, he went through an intense course on the languages, even using them during his off-duty hours. He and his friend, Hamid discussed everything, from having to leave their new wives, to the details of the coming assignment, all in English. He had even begun to dream in English now.

Since he had arrived in Ciudad Acuna, however, the level of difficulty had risen for a while. Officially, they were attending an on-site Spanish course. They now spoke three languages fluently. They could converse comfortably in either the language of their home, or English or Spanish. They were officially ordered to restrain from speaking in their native tongue until the second phase of the plan.

So Behzad and Hamid stood in line, talking quietly to each other in English. "What is this place?" Hamid asked.

They stood in the large back storeroom of the Macquiladora. The tall, corrugated-tin building creaked slightly with the wind blowing outside. Four loading doors spanned the other side of the room. They were rolled closed now, and it was dark outside. The meeting had been called at night to avoid questions from the Macquiladora workers. The round lights, suspended low from the high ceiling, barely provided enough light.

"It is the Macquiladora where we are preparing the infective materials."

They had not been allowed to come here previously. To do so could result in an accidental infection. They had not been vaccinated like Ramon, Santos and the doctor. The variolation would not work for the volunteers if they were vaccinated.

"Do you think it will be as easy as they say?"

"I do not know. They said we would have the disease, but it would be very mild."

"Can it be fatal?"

Until now, this mission had not appeared to have any danger involved in it. But, as Hamid watched the men in line in front of him go behind the white medical partition, he began to wonder. Behzad turned and looked into the suddenly fearful eyes of his friend.

"Yes, I suppose it can be." Behzad's grandfather had told him of the days of Smallpox, before Behzad's birth. Sometimes, the act of variolation had brought on an unexpectedly severe disease, resulting in death. He tried to ignore his own rising concern and turned back to face the front of the shrinking line. He saw some of the same concern on the faces of the other men.

Finally, it was Behzad's turn to go behind the mysterious partition. He walked around the screen to see the clinic doctor in his white coat and latex gloves. Even though the doctor had been vaccinated, he wore a mask tied onto his face for further protection. This caused Behzad's heart to skip a beat. But it was too late now...he must carry through his assignment for the Coalition.

The doctor spoke to him in Spanish. "Tilt your head back, please."

The doctor placed one hand on his head and pushed back gently. Then, with the other hand, he reached his forefinger and thumb into a small glass petri dish on the table. The dish contained an off-white powder made from the ground crusts of Smallpox sores, removed from the bodies of the Baha'is victims.

As the doctor deposited a pinch of the material into Behzad's nostrils, he ordered, "Now, take some deep breaths through your nose."

The powder stung slightly and had a sick smell that added to Behzad's nausea. The deep breaths made him woozy. The doctor kept his steady gaze on him until he felt better.

"That is all for today. You will not feel bad for several days. You may feel a little achy. Then, between ten and fourteen days from now, you will get a headache, chills, nausea, pain in your back and arms and legs and you will have a fever. You will be highly contagious at this stage. It will be carried in droplets through the air to whomever you are near. You should have four days of this before the telltale red spots begin. Try to infect your targets and as much of the general public as you can before the rash begins. Then, hide in the motel room we will provide for you. You will probably not have many spots, but they will start on your face and arms. They will spread to your trunk and legs. The red spots will become raised, and fill with liquid and pus. Do not scratch them. As soon as the blisters dry, your fever will go down and you will begin to feel better. Do you have any questions?"

A dazed Behzad looked up into the doctor's face. He had heard all of this before at meetings concerning their mission. Still, it only now dawned on him that he was going to feel very ill in a foreign country, surrounded by total strangers, who did not care. He would not be able to seek medical help. After the rash began, he was on his own.

"No...No questions."

"Pick up your assignment instructions and travel kit at the next table."

Behzad walked over to the next table where Ramon sat in front of a cardboard box containing gallon-sized sealed plastic bags. Each bag was different from all the others. Ramon looked at him, reached down and picked up the next bag and handed it to Behzad. Behzad took the bag and looked at it.

"Open it now," It was Ramon's job to see that each volunteer understood his instructions thoroughly.

Behzad unzipped the top of the sealed bag and began to look through its contents. The first item he came to was a long envelope, which he opened. A picture of a man in his fifties fell out of the package. Behzad picked it up and looked at it. Then, he turned it over. It read:

Dr. Benjamin Dawes
Home: 269 North Terrace Ave, Atlanta, Georgia
Work: Centers for Disease Control

Another picture showed the front of the building where Dr. Dawes worked. So now, he knew what his target looked like and where he lived and worked.

Behzad pulled a folded map out of the bag. It was a United States map. Within the State of Georgia, Atlanta was circled in yellow highlighter.

Ramon watched as Behzad investigated the contents of his bag, then he began to explain. He took the counterfeit working Visa and passports out of the bag and handed them to the volunteer.

"These will get you across the border without any trouble. Once you get into Del Rio, take the bus to San Antonio. Ride the city bus to the airport. Buy a ticket to Atlanta, Georgia. When you arrive there, take a taxi to this motel." He gave Behzad a pamphlet with a picture of the motel on the cover.

"Check into the motel. It is less than half a mile from the CDC. Go and purchase snack food and supplies to last you through the pox stage of your illness. Wait there until you are at your most contagious stage. Then, go early in the morning to this building. Go to your target's office and tell the secretary, in Spanish, that you must see Dr. Dawes concerning some advice on the design of a new plant in Mexico."

"What will I tell him when I get in to see him?"

"He will get up out of his chair and come over to shake your hand. Make sure you clear your throat and exhale deeply, or even cough, when you get close to him. Just talk to him about a suggested factory design to assure proper ventilation for the health of the workers. Here is a blueprint of the proposed factory. This is another chance for you to breathe on him. When he is looking at it, lean closer and breathe hard. He will suspect nothing. We have already sent him a letter informing him of your visit. Believe me, he will be so impressed that a factory will be built with human rights issues addressed that he will be happy to work with you."

"And then?"

"Go out and get as close to as many people in the area as you can, as long as the rash has not started. The more people you can infect, the more chaos you will produce for our cause. This is all the money you will need. Now pick up your travel kit and begin your trip. Allah be with you."

Behzad packed all of his materials back into his plastic bag. Then, he went to the next table and picked up his travel kit. He opened the small, gray case and found a simple blue toothbrush, some toothpaste, a small black comb, some hair cream, shaving cream, a razor, a bar of soap and a small towel. It also contained a change of clothes. The kit included aspirin for pain and Band-Aids to cover blisters, if needed.

He put his plastic bag into the case and zipped it closed. Then, he walked to a place out of the way to wait for Hamid. A pale Hamid emerged from the process, looking through his new belongings.

"Hamid!" Behzad called.

Hamid came over to Behzad.

"Where are you going?" asked Behzad.

"My assignment is in Washington, D. C. at the CIA building. Where do you go?"

"Atlanta, Georgia."

"I may not see you again, Behzad, but Allah be with you, my friend."

Hamid turned and walked with his case out the door. Behzad just watched, then turned and looked at all of the other volunteers. He wondered where they were going. One thing was sure. They were carrying death wherever they went.

SILENCED

IRAN

Malik looked over his shoulders to make sure he was not being followed as he hurried to his office. In the few minutes that had passed since Sadeq's self-righteous outburst, Malik had begun to realize the dangers that he and his family were facing. It was suddenly clear that Sadeq was the whole reason why he and his family had not been executed. And now, Sadeq's anger burned against him. He had to move fast.

He nonchalantly stopped at his lab and picked up two vials of the vaccine he had been producing for so many months. He had been vaccinated within the last four months, but his family had never been vaccinated. He had a very bad feeling about it. He would solve that problem as soon as he got home.

He knew that Sadeq had not had time to order any house arrest or restricted phone use yet, so he went into his office and called Mike's phone number in San Antonio. The phone rang three times. Then, Malik could hear Mike's voice say, "Hello..."

"Mike! I am so glad I caught you..."

"We are not able to answer the phone right now. Please leave a message after the sound of the tone."

No! Malik hated answering machines. Still, maybe he could leave the warning on the machine. The tone sounded and Malik began his warning quickly.

"Mike, this is Malik. I called to warn-"

The phone went dead.

Malik raced down the hall to his neighbor's office. Obviously, his phone was being monitored, but he could call from someone else's phone. He knocked quietly on the door. When nobody answered, he quietly let himself in and headed to the phone. He had just picked it up when the door behind him flew open. Sadeq and five soldiers wasted no time. They ran in and grabbed his arms.

"I am sorry, Malik." Sadeq's voice was too cool now. "You know I cannot let you do that."

Inevitability

Ciudad Acuna

Jaime sat next to a towering stack of boxes of postcards. The print on the postcards said, "Free Sample!" but Jaime could not read it. Even if it were written in Spanish, Jaime would not be able to read it. But after looking at all the thousands of cards with these words on them, the pattern of the letters was permanently blazed in his brain.

He peeled an address sticker off the roll and pressed it squarely in the middle of the cellophane... again. The monotony of the work wore on his nerves but at least it was easy. Jaime could not believe that Senor Terrazas paid him so much for such easy work.

Luis and Jaime had been working with Juan at the Macquiladora for two weeks now. Juan had been correct when he told them that the work and pay were good—the best they had ever seen. Senor Terrazas had hired them immediately when they showed up with Juan and asked for work. Jaime and Luis still could not believe their good fortune.

But Juan suddenly began to behave in a paranoid way a week later. He walked home with them one day, ranting the whole way about someone named Roberto Talamantes. Jaime and Luis did not know Roberto, but Juan had worked with him for a while.

"Miguel was right!" Juan muttered. "Something is wrong there. Roberto got sick and suddenly disappeared. Now, his whole family is gone."

"He just went across the river, Juan," offered Jaime, still not wanting to believe that anything could be wrong with his new job.

"No. Roberto liked his work here. And he was scared of the thieving Coyotes."

"Then he is staying with someone else while he is sick."

"No. I have asked everyone. He has not been seen...and neither has his family."

"Maybe they went to live somewhere else because they have more money now."

"No. I went to their home. Everything is still there. And there are dirty dishes left in the pan. They left in a hurry. The clothes have been hanging on the cord for four days now."

Jaime and Luis looked at each other while Juan continued. He looked down at the path and waved his arms as he spoke. "Miguel tried to tell us. I wonder what else he knows?"

"Has this happened before?"

"Roberto is the only one I know of, but I have heard of others. I just did not want to believe it."

Jaime finally conceded. "It is strange, Juan, but there is a reason. You will see."

They walked the rest of the way home wondering about Roberto, but Jaime did not want to know that anything was dangerous about his job. It had been too much of a blessing. He had earned two paychecks already.

As he reached his home, his grandmother met him at the door. "Jaime, you must take Theresa to your clinic tomorrow for more medicine."

The clinic doctor at the Macquiladora had been treating Theresa for her dysentery. He had apparently found the right medicine. Theresa was looking better now. The dark circles under her eyes were slowly fading away, and it had cost Jaime nothing at all. As one of the advantages of working at his job, Jaime and his entire family could receive free medical care. In fact, they were encouraged to seek help for every sniffle. Jaime had never known of such a caring boss as Senor Terrazas.

Luis was assigned to clean-up chores the next day. Jaime watched him out of the corner of his eye. Luis stacked up the empty boxes and put them by the big door leading to the loading bay. He carefully wiped the dust from every surface and began to sweep. The wide push broom slid along the concrete, making a hissing noise. As soon as the sweeping was done, Luis emptied the trashcans into a big plastic bag and set it by the big door.

Santos signaled the beginning of the fifteen-minute break at mid-morning. Jaime slowly stood up from his stool and stretched. It felt good to stand up again. The stool was very hard on his thin seat. He looked over at Luis who was leaning on the broom by the door. As Jaime crossed the room towards Luis, his eyes were drawn to the big door and he wondered just what was behind it.

"What's in there, Luis?" He motioned his head toward the door.

"The storeroom. That is where all the boxes of cards are stored after you put the stickers on them."

At the end of the break, Santos saw the two boys standing by the door, and ordered them to clean the storeroom. Jaime smiled, looking forward to a change from his stickers, but Luis knew how much work was involved in cleaning the place. He had cleaned it only two days before, and he could not imagine that it had gotten dirty so fast.

They opened the door and stepped in. The sounds of their footsteps echoed loudly because of the high ceiling. The dim lights allowed the sun edging the loading doors on the outside wall of the room to beam into the darkness. To the right, they made out the stacks of boxes that reached the top of the ceiling. Now, Jaime knew what had happened to all of the boxes he and the others had filled.

"What did they do in here?" Luis could not believe the mess.

On the left side of the room, the white curtain partially concealed the tables. The trash can by the first table brimmed with strange items. Jaime saw a pair of inverted, latex gloves sitting on top of the rest of the trash. He also saw why it smelled so bad. Splashes of vomit clung onto all the insides of the trash can. Another trash can over flowed with bits of plastic bags. Dust covered the floor and a small pile of white powder partially wrapped the leg of another table.

Each boy grabbed a trashcan and emptied it into a bag. They folded the legs under the tables and leaned them up against the wall. Then, they closed the white screen and put it by the tables. Grabbing the broom, Luis began to sweep the floor. Jaime picked up the dustpan and held it while Luis swept the dirt into it. The white powder was very light so it flew into the air with some dust. It found its way into Jaime's nose.

Jaime wrinkled his nose and closed his eyes when it began to burn. Then, he sneezed violently. The dust pan flew out of his hand, hitting Luis and sending dust and white powder all over him. Then, Luis sneezed too.

The boys sniffed and laughed at each other.

"Salud," said Luis.

"Salud!" repeated Jaime.

102

MESSAGE

SAN ANTONIO, TEXAS

The blinking of the red light caught Jacob Thompson's eye as he stepped into the kitchen. His original goal was to grab a bite of whatever he could find sitting unguarded in the refrigerator. But, now, the curiosity nagged him more than the empty spot in his endlessly hungry stomach.

He pushed the replay button on the answering machine. Maybe, all the recent attention he had paid to that cute little brunette had been worth it after all. He had left a message on her machine asking her to call back.

His mother had left the first message on the machine. She had gone to the grocery store, and called wanting to know what flavor of ice cream to get. Jacob knew she would guess the right type. He pushed the button again.

A woman's voice began apologizing. "This is Debbie Howard. I'm sorry to bother you at home, Dr. Thompson, but Angie is running a very high fever. Could you call me at 653-3479 as soon as possible, please? Thanks."

Messages like that always dominated the answering machine. Jacob's father, Dr. Mike Thompson was one of those rare doctors who could actually be reached at home. Jacob pushed the button again.

"Mike, this is Malik. I called to warn—," was all it said. Jacob thought it was strange. He had heard of Malik and seen his pictures. But, Jacob had never heard his voice before. Obviously, something had gone wrong with the message. It meant nothing at all.

Jacob pressed the button on the machine that erased all the messages, and continued his search in the kitchen, totally forgetting about all of them.

DESPERATION

TEHRAN

Malik had to do something. The very fact that Allah had seen fit to allow him to live despite the predicament he found himself in proved to Malik that his cause was sanctioned. Sadeq still needed him for something.

Sadeq had ordered him to be on house arrest. Two soldiers stood stationed inside his office as he worked. His phone was closely monitored, and every time he went anywhere, the two soldiers followed him like nosy little puppies. They watched and listened to every thing he did and said. They only let him have privacy as he relieved himself. And this, they did begrudgingly.

Another duo of soldiers followed him when he left work. It made him look like some kind of dignitary with an armed escort. People along the crowded streets stopped what they were doing and watched as he and his detail walked by.

Fortunately, the two guards posted at his house only stood outside the door as long as Malik was not home. Sadeq figured that Yahya, Malik's wife, was not a threat to the cause. She was, after all, only a woman. What could she do?

Malik depended on that error in Sadeq's wisdom. Yahya was free to do whatever she wanted in her house, though the phone there was also closely monitored. The two house guards stood in absolute boredom, shifting their weight to keep their legs from falling to sleep, all day long. In the meantime, Yahya very busily fulfilled the wishes of her husband.

The guards only entered the house when Malik came home. They followed Malik to every room and listened to every conversation. They had no idea that Yahya and Malik communicated so well in code.

"Yahya, it is time to send holiday gifts to our friends. If we send them now, they may get them in time." Malik had continued the holiday gift tradition he had learned in the U.S.

"Yes, Malik, what would you like me to send this year?" She knew that the gifts would arrive at their destination within two weeks, which would be a month earlier than they needed to be sent. She gave no hint of the discrepancy.

"Go to the caviar factory and buy some of their finest product. It is one of our most famous exports. I am sure that they will enjoy it." Malik thought that bragging on Iran's produce could not hurt his precarious situation.

The meaning of the whole conversation slipped by the attention of Malik's constant companions. And, the guards never had a hint that Yahya was even aware of all the details of the attack. Besides, what could a woman do? They did not know that Malik had shared his fears with her before the heat had been turned up. The children had been given their instructions.

The next morning, Yahya went to buy the gift. Looking cautiously around, she slipped a waterproof bag containing Malik's warning into the can. Then she shipped it to Mike.

Yahya did not see him. The man had turned away quickly to hide his face. As he turned, his lips tightened and his eyes shifted from right to left. He waited until Yahya left, then hurried out the back door.

PHASE ONE

CIUDAD ACUNA

Omid Farrahi, AKA Senor Ramon Terrazas, took pride in the work he had accomplished for his country. The samples were all ready to be mailed now, and the volunteers had been sent to their target destinations. The trucks backed up to the loading doors and the workers loaded the samples, so they would be mailed within a day.

"Be careful with those!" he barked. Nothing could happen to spoil the plan now. The volunteers were beginning their infection, even now.

"**D**r. Vickers, you have a call on line two."

"Thanks, Jill." Terry Vickers lifted the receiver to take the call. "Hello." He stroked his trim, white beard with his free hand.

"Terry, this is John. Are we still on for tonight?"

John Fortenberry worked in the administration office. John and his wife, Johanna, had made plans with Terry to go out that night, since it was a Friday. And Terry was looking forward to it.

"Sure, let's go! Give me twenty minutes to close it down up here. I just have to throw some cultures into the incubator. You want to meet at the entrance?"

"Sounds good to me. Are we still going to Jack's?"

"Yeah. Why not?"

"OK. I'll meet you in a few minutes."

Jack's was a combination restaurant and dance club that was only two blocks away from the main gate to Fort Detrick. It was also a very popular place, so a fifteen-minute wait greeted Terry and his friends before they could be seated.

They sat in the waiting area talking. A T-shirted waitress pushed the swinging doors to the kitchen open and took their drink orders. Terry and John ordered beer, but Johanna wanted a wine cooler. As they sat and waited, Jill and some of her friends came in. Terry knew most of them. They worked in his building and he had seen them on the elevator or in the hall-way. They sat and waited for a table. A Friday night mood permeated the atmosphere.

After devouring steak and shrimp dinners, the trio and the other diners were drawn to the club portion of the building. The drumbeat of the music called to them, and they moved their drinks to a small table at the side of the dance floor. Flashing colored lights pulsing out of the light machine cut into the darkness of the room. The lights danced with the beat of the music.

People continued to crowd into the large room until there were no more seats at the tables. The dance floor throbbed with the movement of bodies in the smoky air.

Off in one corner, a dark-skinned man occupied a small table. He looked Hispanic, but he was not. He was there to do a job. He was not feeling well, but he had taken some aspirin, so he was able to smile and be friendly. And that was his job.

People walked by, looking for a table. He nicely invited them to sit down at his table. They took him up on his offer, glad to find a seat. Then, he leaned forward to talk to them in the loud music. He made sure he got his infective mouth as close to their defenseless nostrils as he could. Eventually, he began to cough. His new friends quickly excused themselves to go to the dance floor. After all, it was flu season, and they wanted no part of it. But flu was not the problem here. And it was too late to get away.

New York City

D r. Joel Rudman raised his glasses off his good-sized nose and rubbed his aching eyes. He knew he was not supposed to do that, but he had been up for thirty-one hours now and he did not care anymore.

His double shift in the ER was a payback. Bonnie had taken his shift last week so he could go to his cousin's wedding in Boston. The wedding was fun, but this payback thing was to be avoided from now on.

He sat back against the chair support in the middle of his back and stretched. The chair squeaked out its protest at being stretched that far.

He was supposed to be treating patients right now. The waiting room was completely full, and the other doctors were pulling their fair share. But, they were not as tired as he was.

Out in the waiting room, an odd collection of patients waited. None of them were bleeding to death or having heart attacks, so Joel figured they could wait. In his exhausted state, that seemed to be hilariously funny. They could wait— in the *waiting* room! He had to get some sleep soon.

The large waiting area held a maze of couches and chairs in a soft shade of blue to match the shades on the large windows at the front of the building. In the corners and at strategic locations by the couches, lamps shed extra light into the room. It was 11:30 at night so darkness had taken over the outside world and the shades had been closed.

The room was filled with waiting people, casting glances to the double doors that led to the emergency rooms. A nurse pushed through the doors regularly and called the name of the lucky patient who would be next. All eyes in the room looked up hopefully each time the doors opened. Then, all the patients forced to remain secretly resented the one that managed to get in, finally.

Roger Ellings sat in one of the hard-backed chairs along the wall of the room. His pale skin hung loosely off his bones. His sad eyes carried dark, baggy circles under them. He stared blankly at the tiled floor pattern. At least, he figured, he was not sitting in his usual spot in the alley behind 38th Street. The weather had turned cold recently. It had been hard, even before he got AIDS from a needle he shared with his friends. But now, the cold seemed to bite into his very bones. Maybe, it would shorten his suffering. He did not care how long it took them to call his name. He was more comfortable here, anyway.

In the other corner, Roger saw Celeste camping out the same way he was. She sat there with her gray, knit cap tossed carelessly on her graying brown hair. She tugged at the greasy little fuzz-balls on the left sleeve of the faded black coat she had gotten at the Salvation Army. She was lucky to have a coat at all, so she tried to take care of it. Her usual spot was a block away from Roger's. Roger had seen her daily for three years now as she pushed her cart from place to place. She always scowled at him when he looked at her, although he had never done anything to her. He knew, by the word on the street, that she had AIDS too. This fact alone made him feel some camaraderie with her, even though she did not have the skin spots, like he did. But there were others there in the room that he felt were total strangers to him. He could never comprehend their way of life.

A ragged family with a sick seven-year-old daughter sat in the middle of the room. Yolanda lay in her father's arms with her head on his strong shoulder. Her long, black hair draped down his arm. She looked like she was sleeping, but she kept coughing. Each time she coughed, her mother would look at her with a worried glance, then look up at the father. He gently patted the child's back until she fell asleep again. Her mother kept feeling her forehead and frowning as she looked towards the magical double doors.

Roger understood why the mother and father were there with their sick child. But why did they bring their six other children along? They ranged from ages two to twelve and they were tired and bored. The grandmother had also come along. She sat there and just watched with her tired eyes as the children played rough and fought with each other.

The two smaller children played a game of chase over the backs of the couches. One fell off with a thud and started screaming at the top of his lungs. Nobody in the family even looked at him, but his loud howls did cause the nurse's aide at the window to look out into the crowded room. Roger was impressed. Nothing ever made the nurse's aide look out before.

Two other siblings chased each other around the room, tripping over peoples' feet and yelling, "You're it!" The two remaining children, who were older than the rest, got into some sort of argument. Their bickering voices grew louder and the older of the two finally reached over to slug the other one.

Roger did not know how the parents were able to ignore all this. It certainly made his headache worse. The other people in the room looked like they wanted to kill a few of them.

The fat, black woman in the corner probably would have if she had thought she could get up without the pain getting worse. She was in her late forties and her gall bladder had finally had enough. She sat, leaning forward and rocking as she held her abdomen. With each stab of pain, she glared at the loud children.

A mother in a nice pant set rocked her toddler in a squeaky chair. Each time a loud noise rose from the rambunctious crew, the toddler began to cry. He had an ear infection, and he kept rubbing his right ear and wiping his runny nose on his mother's shoulder. She had not had any idea that he had an ear infection until she tried to put him into bed that night. Of course, there were no doctor's offices open, so here she sat. She had already been there for two hours and she was also glaring. But she was not glaring at the kids. Her scowl was aimed at the parents. Why didn't they do something about the behavior of their children? Irresponsible people like that should not be allowed to be parents, she thought.

The skinny teenager with the swollen wrist sat by his father. The father kept looking at his son and frowning. "I told you to wear those wrist guards when you rollerbladed. Son, when are you ever going to listen to me?"

"But, Dad, they make me look like a Geek!"

"Well, now you're gonna look like an injured kid with a cast!"

The teenager continued to try to defend his honor. Then, he forgot and moved his arm, wincing painfully.

In the middle of the room, a dark-skinned man in nice clothes sat and waited. He was much too patient and much too content to be there waiting. He looked flushed in his face and his eyes looked like they burned. He looked like he had the flu. But he eagerly visited with everyone around him. Every few minutes, he coughed. He went from place to place in the room, as if he could not find the best seat. Within two hours everyone in the room was acquainted with him...and with what he carried.

Finally, the nurse called his name at the double doors. He walked up to her and shook her hand.

"Thank-you," he breathed into her face.

"Please come with me this way, Mr. Shirazi."

She tried not to show it, but she was always a little repulsed by people who forced her to shake hands. Still, she did not want to hurt his feelings, so she remained silent. She would wash her hands later.

She got him settled into an examination room. Mr. Shirazi looked around. These Americans sure had a wealthy lifestyle. Even their hospitals were excessive. Hospitals in his homeland would be happy to have even one of these well-stocked rooms. This hospital had eight of them.

As he waited, he was sure to handle as many items as he could in the room. He coughed, as instructed, into his hand. Then he touched the door-knobs and the handles of all of the cabinets and drawers. He touched the rails on the sides of the bed, and put his hands all over the metal trays and handlebars used to raise and lower them

Sadeq's instructions had been quite complete. He made sure to wipe his hands on the edge of the paper towel container. Every paper towel that came out of it would now be contaminated. Of course, he touched the faucet handles. He coughed onto the pillow on the bed. He rubbed his hands all along the rim of the metal stool where the doctor would sit. He contacted the entire rim of the doorway on both sides. He took the device used to examine ears and handled it thoroughly. He wiped his hands on the edges of the curtain pulled around the bed.

After a long while, Dr. Rudman came in. He reached his hand forward to Mr. Shirazi to shake hands. The patient eagerly grabbed it.

"I'm Dr. Rudman. How are you, Mr. Shirazi?" Joel could tell by the hot skin on his hand that his patient was running fever.

"I am being sick some."

Dr. Rudman looked at the chart in front of him. There was very little to go on. "Tell me how you feel."

"I am hot and then I am cold. My head is hurting and my throat is hurting too." Mr. Shirazi looked right at Dr. Rudman and coughed forcefully toward him.

"I see you have a cough too." Dr. Rudman just loved it when patients coughed and sneezed on him without covering their mouths.

"Yes."

"How long have you been feeling like this?'

"Two days."

Even though it was obviously another clear-cut case of the flu, Joel knew he should go through the formalities of an examination. It was November and it was flu season. He had lost count of how many patients he had seen with it in just the last thirty-one hours that he had been on duty.

Dr. Rudman hated viruses. There was very little he could do about them but let them run their course. Antibiotics had absolutely no effect on them. But, he hated the disappointed look patients always gave him when he did not prescribe something for them. Especially after he knew the patients had been waiting so long in the cramped, uncomfortable waiting room.

"Let's take a look, then," Dr. Rudman reached over and picked a wooden tongue depressor out of the glass jar. "Open your mouth and stick out your tongue." Joel grabbed his penlight and looked into Mr. Shirazi's mouth. Mr. Shirazi coughed.

"Sorry."

Joel had seen all he needed to see. He was sure it was flu. He pulled his stethoscope off its resting-place around his neck and listened to his patient's lungs and heart. His heartbeat was fast but that was normal for someone with a fever.

"Mr. Shirazi, you have the flu. The best thing for it is bed rest, pain-reliever and plenty of fluids." He had heard himself repeat this a million times. He could do it in his sleep. Maybe that was what he was doing.

"Go home and go to bed. You should begin to feel better in a few days." He began to fill in his patient's chart.

"Thank-you, doctor." Mr. Shirazi held out his hand for Dr. Rudman to shake. "I will do what you say."

Dr. Rudman gave him his hand and smiled a tired smile.

"Sure," he answered. Then he turned towards the door and released the big yawn he had been trying to keep hidden for the last two minutes.

Mr. Shirazi waited until Dr. Rudman turned around and left. Then, he smiled. Mission accomplished.

He went back to the waiting room and waited until early morning to go down to the hospital cafeteria. Doctors and nurses were grabbing coffee and breakfast. Mr. Shirazi stood behind them and in front of them in line. He spoke to them as they waited. And he coughed. He bought some juice and sat down at one of the little white, round tables to drink it. He sipped it slowly for about twenty minutes. Then, he got up and joined the line of the next shift of doctors and nurses. Once again, he was friendly. Once again, he coughed.

He spent the next two hours in this process. His next stop was to go to all the nurses' stations, one at a time, and ask directions to certain rooms. He spoke quietly so the nurses came closer to hear what he was saying. Then, of course, he coughed. He went to all the rest rooms and handled every doorknob. He rode the elevator all the way up. Then he took the stairs down, coughing into his hands and sliding them on the handrails on both sides all the way down to sub-level one.

He rode the elevators as often as he could, punching all the buttons, and, of course, he coughed.

That evening, Mr. Shirazi reported to the emergency room of another large hospital in New York City. His method there was the same. He kept visiting hospitals in New York as long as the blisters did not form. By the time he finished, most of the medical professionals and many of the patients in New York had ample opportunity to pick up what he left behind.

The same scene was occurring in every major city in the United States only, instead of Mr. Shirazi, the "flu" patient was Mr. Hussein or Mr. Kamali or whatever volunteer had been assigned there.

THE PENTAGON—ARLINGTON, VIRGINIA

The tour began at 10:00 in the morning. In an effort to help public opinion of the military, guided tours had been instituted on a daily basis. The fee of $5 per person was a small contribution, but even it was counted as something positive in the wake of the budget cuts. Rick Potter waited for the last tourist to finish paying for his tour.

He had just graduated from college and was volunteering here until he could find the job he wanted. As soon as the straggler turned and began walking towards the group, Rick could see that there was something different about him. He looked Hispanic, but he also looked like he did not feel well. Strange. Why would a sick person choose to take a tour?

"O.K.! Everybody gather over here and we'll get started." Rick waved his hand calling them all over to his location. "My name is Rick and I'll be your guide on this tour. If you have any questions, just let me know. I'll do my best to answer them. To start with, this is the Pentagon, the home of the U.S. Department of Defense."

He took them down the hallways describing all the significant landmarks of the structure. They had barely gotten into the second part of the tour when the straggler, who had been coughing, called out.

"Rick, I have a question."

"O.K."

The group stopped and the straggler came up to Rick. He got close to him and indicated that he wanted to say something to him quietly in his ear. Rick leaned down.

"My name is Jesse. Is there a bano?"

"A bathroom?"

"Yes."

"Sure. It's around this corner to the right. We'll wait for you."

"Thank-you." He took off towards the Men's room, coughing.

Rick could not understand why someone with the flu would want to come and infect him.

Jesse put his hand on the doorknob and turned it. He walked in and began handling every item and door handle. He coughed up some phlegm, and reached into the hand-blower nozzle, smearing it on the inside surface. Sadeq's instructions for this device were clear. It would now blow out infection and death to everyone who turned it on. In a dry state, it could survive up to 212°F. And if the intended victim did not breathe it in, the virus would still have a chance of infecting because it would be all over the "clean" hands.

Rick resumed the tour as soon as Jesse returned. They boarded an elevator. Jesse stood by the buttons and touched each one while nobody was watching. They were all listening to Rick. At the next floor, a group of five men in uniforms stepped into the elevator. Jesse coughed. Each time they passed official-looking people in the hall, Jesse coughed.

The last part of the tour ended in the cafeteria. It was a huge room with plenty of tables occupied by officials on their lunch breaks. Uniforms decorated the entire place. Jesse walked through, coughing. He stood in line and coughed.

"You really should do something about that cough." Rick was quite serious.

"I will. Thank-you." Jesse smiled as he left the room.

THE WHITE HOUSE—
WASHINGTON, D.C.

Massoud was very proud of his assignment. The White House! How many Coalition soldiers could say they had been a part of bringing down the White House? His Hispanic appearance had landed him this prestigious honor. Nobody would suspect a thing.

He stood in the line that formed on the outside of the metal fence around the grounds. As he stood there, he could see why the structure was so inaccessible. Surveillance cameras panned everywhere. As he came closer to the entrance, he saw the metal detectors checking each tourist as they approached. But metal detectors would not be able to detect the weapon he carried into the White House. He smiled at the thought. The Great Evil United States did not even know it was under attack.

As he neared the entrance, he saw the Secret Service Agents looking him over. They watched carefully as he passed through the metal detectors without any reaction. Still, one was assigned to keep an eye on him as he toured the White House. He must have fit some kind of profile they were trained to notice. It did not matter. They would never catch on. He would deliver death to the White House and leave...and all the security in the world could not stop him.

He made sure he coughed as he neared the agents. He coughed into his hand and slid it along the cords and the metal posts holding them. He touched each door handle and coughed whenever he saw someone who worked at the White House. The cold winter assured that the building stayed closed tightly. The virus had a better chance of infecting more people if the air was being recycled. Massoud coughed several times in each room.

He knew he could never directly reach the President, but there would be a chance of him catching it from the recycled air. The thought of it made Massoud cough even more often. The lady behind him offered him a cough drop. He thanked her and tried to look like he ate it without actually putting it in his mouth.

As soon as he left the White House, he rode the underground tram to infect as many members of Congress and their workers as he could. Feeling the way he was, the numerous stairs were difficult for him to climb. He climbed a few at a time and stopped to rest. Yet, his goal beckoned to him. Once again, the winter season had forced the building to be closed efficiently.

Massoud walked the halls, impressed by the majesty of the old structure. The names of the Congressmen decorated signs hung high above the tall doorways along the hall. Massoud was amazed at the lack of security here. The trusting secretaries answered his question about the location of the men's room as he asked in each office. They each smiled and gave him instructions as he coughed on them, hopefully infecting the recycled air.

Just in case, he did not infect any Congressmen that way, he went to the gallery and went as close to the front as possible. He coughed periodically as he sat there and listened for quite a while to the Speaker of the

House. Then, as the scheduled session was about to end, he went down to the exit doors of the meeting room, and coughed on the people as they left.

It was beginning to snow, now. He rode the bus to the FBI administrative building and joined the line to go on the next scheduled tour. As the tour progressed, Massoud coughed. The tour director looked a little agitated at him. He shrugged his shoulders and tried to hold in his coughs, unsuccessfully, for a while. He always coughed when someone passed them in the hall.

Then, he rode the bus all over town. He was tired, but he figured he could infect quite a few people in the closed air of the bus. Every few miles, he got off and waited for the next bus. He did this until he was exhausted, then he went back to his motel room.

AIRPORT, LOS ANGELES, CA

Amir Makhfi's volunteer packet had contained much more money than most of his fellow volunteers. He needed it to accomplish his assignment. His job was to fly on as many flights on the major airlines as he could before it became obvious that he had blisters.

His instructions had explained carefully that the air in the cabins continually recycled. Fresh air mixed with the old air every seven minutes. It took about thirty minutes to complete a flushing of the air system. Since the mid-80's, the airlines had tried to save fuel by avoiding the heating of the icy air drawn in. This was perfect for the plan. The virus that Amir shed with every breath and cough would be sent through the cabin with increasingly concentrated numbers.

Americans, especially the wealthy and influential ones, flew everywhere. Americans take about five hundred million air trips within the U.S. every year.

First, he walked through the crowds, coughing. Then, he sat in several waiting areas, coughing. Finally, he went to the gate for boarding his flight.

The flight attendant in the navy-blue suit announced that Flight 763 to Chicago was now ready to board. Amir stood and smiled. It was all right with him if he stood in line amid the other passengers. Even though he had cleared the security check with no problem, he carried a lethal weapon onto the aircraft...and nobody would know about it for another three weeks.

He walked down the covered boarding ramp and smiled at the attendant as she welcomed him aboard and wished him a good flight. He coughed three times as he passed through the first class section. Then, pushed his travel bag in his carry-on compartment, and settled down into the right aisle seat in the middle of the coach section.

The route was a popular one, so it was crowded. A man in a business suit put his briefcase into the carry-on section, and sat down next to Amir. Next to him, a newly wed couple cozied together by the window. Across the aisle sat a mother in blue jeans and her two little girls, on their way to visit their grandparents.

As the flight began, Amir visited with the businessman. The man was friendly enough. "Where are you from?"

In broken English, Amir explained that he was from Mexico City. His Spanish was better than his English was. The businessman began to talk to him in Spanish and it became much easier to converse.

Six-year-old Sarah's light brown, shoulder-length hair bobbed up and down with each of her energetic movements. Her four-year-old little sister, Jennifer, had lighter hair and was shyer than Sarah.

As soon as Sarah heard Amir speaking in Spanish, she stopped playing with the seat belt her mother had just fastened for her, and stared across the aisle at him with her mouth hanging lightly open.

"Sarah," her mother said, "it is not polite to stare."

"I know, Mommy, but that man is talking funny. What's he saying, Mommy?"

"I don't know, but it's OK, Sarah. He's speaking Spanish."

"Oh. You don't know how to talk Spanlish, do you Mommy?"

"SPANISH. No."

"That's what I said, Spanlish. I heard Maria talk like that on the phone one time, Mommy."

"I know, Dear. Maria speaks Spanish at her home."

"Oh."

Jennifer pushed the button on her seat belt and it separated. Her mother stopped listening to Sarah and fumbled with the belt, trying to reattach it.

Sarah leaned forward and looked at Amir. "Mister! Talk some Spanlish. Please?" She smiled and tilted her head pleadingly at Amir.

"Sarah!" Her mother was horrified by the thought of her daughter knowing no strangers. "Don't bother the nice man."

She looked up at Amir, who was smiling. He coughed.

"It is O.K."

Sarah's mother saw the redness of his eyes and thought he looked sick. She hoped it was not the flu.

It was not...and it was filling the cabin and recycling in the air constantly for the entire four-hour trip.

Amir waved and smiled at little Sarah as they exited the aircraft. Then, he walked to the ticket-purchasing area of the Chicago airport. Where should he go next? How about Oregon? Then, maybe he would go to North Carolina. Why not?

Atlanta, Georgia—
The Centers For Disease Control

Behzad finished checking into the motel that his instructions had ordered. He put his travel kit on the table, next to the bed. Then, he took off his shoes and rested on the bed for a few minutes. His eyes burned and he had chills and a very sore throat. That was good. He could accomplish his task.

The meeting with his target, Dr. Dawes, had gone almost exactly as Ramon had told him it would. He was certain that he had been able to infect Dr. Dawes and his whole office staff. Further, he had walked around the hallways of the building, asking directions to Dr. Dawe's office.

Sadeq's instructions had informed him that some of the CDC employees would not become infected with the full disease because those who worked with any Orthopox virus strains were vaccinated. Still, even those would feel a little sick. All the other CDC employees were fair game. They would suffer the full course of the disease. The very people who were supposed to handle an outbreak would be too sick to be very effective. They would assume it was the flu, until it was too late.

118

Behzad had placed "free samples" on the coffee tables in the waiting areas. He had handed one to each secretary and smiled as they thanked him. When he left, each one opened the cellophane wrapper, scratched the scented square and took a good sniff of the "new scent" on the postcard. Some of the lucky recipients stuffed the sample into their purses to order some after they got home. One of the receptionists even volunteered to pass them out to others who were working the labs at the time.

Behzad was sure that he had saturated the organization with the virus. As soon as he rested, he had more work to do. He washed his feverish face and went back to work.

He waited at the bus stop for the bus to take him to the shopping mall he had seen on the city map in his room. He sat on the bus and talked to the old woman he sat next. He coughed a few times. Buses recycled the air also.

He walked into each store in the mall and visited with each employee, asking questions...and coughing. At the gift store, he coughed into his hands, then handled as many items as he could. He went to the rest rooms and fouled the hand blowers as he had been instructed by the written instructions from Sadeq. Riding the escalators, he put his hands all over the handrails. Every time a group of people walked past him, he coughed.

He went to the food court and stood in line for some pizza. He coughed while he waited. Waiting in a different line, he coughed while he waited to buy fries. He did the same thing in another line as he waited to buy a coke. Then, he waited to buy ice cream. He coughed and visited the whole way.

The ladies at the perfume counters in the department stores pressured him to buy something. After he got as close to them as he could and coughed, he got them to smell the beautifully scented sample he carried in his pocket, instead.

After a while, he grew tired and he decided to go to a movie theater. There, he sat and infected everyone with two hours of more recycled air. He went out to the lobby to wait in line for popcorn...and to cough. After another movie, Behzad decided to go to back to the motel. He sat in the lobby and read the news-paper...and coughed. He carefully left a few "free samples" on the tables next to the chair where he sat.

WALTER REED HOSPITAL

S aeed's instructions were unique. He flew to the target city, where he rented a van. He took the van to a detail shop and had a sign painted on the door. The words "Fine Scents Wholesale" declared his business. Then, he drove to a department store and bought twenty boxes of five different popular men's colognes. He loaded them into his van and headed to the entrance of the Army Post.

Saeed showed the MP the bogus card that had been included in his instruction packet. The MP had seen plenty of these cards before. This was simply another deliveryman taking goods to the Post Exchange to be sold to the members of the military at slightly reduced prices. The MP handed Saeed his card and let him pass. Saeed smiled at the MP and coughed. He drove onto the Post.

Finding his way to the Post Exchange, he parked his van at the delivery entrance. Seeing his card, the woman in charge smiled and let him bring his boxes into the store. He took them to the cosmetics counter and set up a display. His job was to offer the patrons a card sprayed with a certain cologne so the customer could take a good whiff of the scent. Only, his sample cards were cards that had been produced by Sadeq's lab. They were saturated with the virus.

A young woman in a plaid, mid-length skirt, topped by a black jacket, pushed her black hair back from her face as she accepted Saeed's gift. "I've been trying to find a new scent for my husband, Pete. He's so hard to buy for. And his birthday is in two days."

She took the card and placed it under her nose. The deep sniff she took in brought the new scent into her nose...and a good infecting dose of the virus. She took the card home to her husband for his approval. Of course, he took a good sniff before he told her he liked it.

Saeed stayed at this location in the Post Exchange for the entire afternoon. He gave away all one thousand of the infected cards to everyone that walked past him. Everyone was friendly and several people chose to buy the colognes he was representing. He made a very good salesman...for the virus.

When he finished, he drove over to the hospital on the Post. Sadeq's instructions required him to go from nurse's station to nurse's station, leaning forward and asking directions. He rode the elevators and touched as many items as he could, especially door handles, elevator buttons, and water fountain handles. He found the hand blowers in the bathrooms...and every where he went, he coughed.

Other volunteers followed the same procedure at other Army Posts and Air Force Bases all over the United States.

HOUSTON ASTRODOME, HOUSTON, TEXAS

H ossein knew he would enjoy his assignment. True, he felt ill, but he knew it would not be fatal, and his purpose drove him on, despite his aching bones and head. Besides, he had always wondered what it would be like to attend an American football game.

He held a ticket in his feverish hand. He stood in the long line of eager sports fans entering the Astrodome. As he reached the entrance, he gave the older man at the door his ticket and stuffed the stub he got back into the pocket of his pants. Then, he began his work.

He got to the Astrodome an hour early. He planned to contact thousands of people here, especially since the most influential and wealthy people would have tickets to the Oiler/Cowboy game. He did not know any of the individual names of these targets. Any and all who were at the game were his targets.

He began his work by walking up a wide ramp to the left. The ramp turned to the right halfway up. He smelled the normally enticing aroma of the different kinds of foods being made and sold all along the inside perimeter of the dome on every level. The smell turned his stomach but was apparently very attractive to everyone else. Short lines of fans formed in front of the stands selling hamburgers, pizza, or fried chicken. Other fans rushed past on their way to their seats.

Hossein stood in the middle line at the hamburger stand. And coughed. He purchased a cold drink, drank a little of it, and then threw it away. He walked slowly and coughed on his way to the next food stand where Pizza was being sold. Standing in the crowded line, he coughed.

He went from crowd to crowd and line to line, getting as close as he could to the strangers in the Dome...and he coughed.

The sounds of the beginning of the game caught his attention. He acted patriotic when they played the National Anthem, and he listened to the words of the devotional...and he coughed.

After he figured out how to get to the most expensive seats by the sidelines, he stood at the entrances to those seats...and coughed in the crowds.

He circled around to the rest rooms and fouled the hand blowers the same way all the volunteers had been taught. Finally, the game began.

He watched from the entrances to the various seating sections. He kept walking and coughing on the people coming out of the seating for food or beer. He exposed many people at the beer concessions.

He actually enjoyed the game. He had the option of watching the action on the field or on the TV in every seating section. Imagine that! So many televisions! The real action unfolded right there in front of them. These Americans!

He loved the clashing sound of the player's pads pounding against each other. The whistles of the officials blew constantly, and the roar of the excited crowd was tremendous. He had never known that Americans could be so spirited over anything.

If they had known about the war he was waging on them, even now as they enjoyed the game, they would have all fallen on him, just like the players fell on an advancing quarterback. But they did not know about the war, yet. They did not react to their danger at all. Death, walked right up to thousands of people that day, tagged them, then silently walked away. It was amazing how many people a person could contact in a sports arena.

Sadeq had sent volunteers to many of the main sports arenas in the evil U.S. Hossein personally knew of one other volunteer who had been sent to the Silver Dome.

All over the United States, inconspicuous volunteers visited malls, military posts, and Reserve Units, the restaurants and establishments around them, Federal buildings, sports arenas, hospitals, theaters, subways and airports. The cold outside air was shut out. The warm air was shut inside, continually recycling through the buildings, keeping people warm...and infecting them.

NEW ORLEANS, LOUISIANA

Vicki turned her red '98 sports car into the flower-lined driveway in front of her garage. She had been fighting the five o'clock traffic for the past forty—five minutes and she was just glad to get home in one piece. Even after working for the insurance company for seven months, she never failed to be amazed by the daily grind.

She tossed her shoulder-length, auburn hair back and grabbed her purse from its safe place below her knees. She fought with the automatic seat belt and got out of the car, almost forgetting to lock it. Her thoughts concerned what she would fix for Carl for supper that night. She and Carl had shared the cooking responsibility for the four months since they had married. Carl had cooked spaghetti last night, so Italian was out of the question for tonight.

Carl's parking place stood empty, so she knew that the mail still waited in the mailbox. The brightly painted mailbox had been a wedding gift from Aunt Martha.

She hung her purse by its strap on her shoulder and pulled the mailbox door open. It squeaked. The recent rains had rusted the hinge. It only reminded her of one more chore she had to do, sometime soon. Just like the others.

She reached into the box and pulled out the mail. Walking to the door and juggling her purse and the mail, she unlocked it and stepped inside. Why was it always so hard to get into the door after a hard day at work?

She tossed her purse onto the cluttered kitchen counter and began to go through the mail. There was a 7.9% interest credit card offer. She threw it into the trash. Yeah, sure, she thought. And then they'll make me pay fees for not using the card, or for paying my bill on time. Never Mind!

She found an invitation from her mother to go to Thanksgiving Dinner. Mom was always so good about stuff like that. When did she find the time? She put it under a goose magnet on the refrigerator door.

An advertisement from a telephone company promised BIG savings. Yeah! For at least a month! She tossed it into the trash also.

Finally, she came to an interesting parcel. It was a cellophane-covered postcard that said, "Free Sample!" on one side and "Fresh New Scent" on the other side. OK, she thought, finally something free. After opening the cellophane package, she looked at the small scratch-n-sniff square. She wondered what it smelled like, so she scratched it quickly with one of her long nails.

It was a sample of a new perfume. How interesting.

She put it up to her nose, and took a good sniff. It did smell good. It could wait on the desk for future reference. She would give it a try.

Some of the virus particles attached themselves to the mucous membrane of her nose and bronchioles. They went to work immediately. All they needed were cells. They efficiently attached themselves to the outer membranes of the cells and quickly injected their genetic contents into their host cells.

Caribou, Maine

Betty removed her embroidered apron and hung it on the hook on the back of the kitchen door. She wiped her damp hands on the towel attached to the drawer handle. The coat hanging on the coat rack had an attached hood, and it was a good thing. The wet snow falling outside could be bone chilling.

She put on the coat, opened the door against the wind and pushed out towards the mailbox. The mailbox stood at the end of the rock driveway and, right now, six inches of sloppy snow covered the driveway. She would have to remind Bud to clear it before any more accumulated.

The romantic atmosphere of the Bed and Breakfast was somewhat wasted in the winter months. Most people found it too cold, but Betty and

Bud enjoyed it even more than in the warm summer season. The weather required cuddling up in front of a fire.

Most of their friends had moved to warmer climates after retirement, but Betty and Bud had decided to open this Bed and Breakfast, instead. It kept them both active and they met some marvelous people who came to visit as customers. Betty enjoyed cooking for company and she loved the chance to show off her skills. Their grown children rarely visited. They lived across the country and that made it difficult to get there too often.

She carefully picked her way to the mailbox to get the mail. The letters and magazines in her arms made it a bit more difficult to keep her balance on the way back to the house.

After she took off the coat and hung it on the rack, she picked up the mail. The Griffins had sent a letter reserving a room for early spring. Good. She always loved it when they came for their yearly visit.

The electric bill looked ominous. The extra need for heat always sent this bill too high. She was not looking forward to opening it. She put it aside.

She picked up the women's magazine. This was much better than the electric bill. She loved the new recipes she could find in these pages. Thumbing through the rest of the mail, she found the "free sample." It said, "Fresh New Scent," so she opened it, scratched it and smelled it. It did smell good. She put it on the desk. Maybe she would buy some of the new scent for her daughter for Christmas.

SAN DIEGO, CALIFORNIA

C armen tried to ignore the sound of the four fighting children in the passenger seats of the used mini-van she was driving. She did not know what the school cafeteria had fed them, but it had surely made their behavior hairy! They had been bickering since she picked them up after school and hour ago.

She took them with her to the grocery store. That proved to be a big mistake. The oldest, in fourth grade, tried to fill the basket with snack items. His hunger did not care if it was only four o'clock, but she could not afford his appetite on her minimum wage salary from the discount store. She insisted that he put it back, and he rebelliously yelled back at her.

She still did not know exactly what to do to him to discipline him. Darn it! Why didn't that no-good ex-husband of hers send that child support check this month? How did he expect her to raise his hungry son on her measly salary?

As she drove under the carport by the mobile home they were renting, the kids threw the doors to the vehicle open before she could cut off the engine. They raced to the mailbox. Carmen did not want to see what was in the mailbox. It was always bad. It was always bills. More bills. Bills she could not pay...and bill collector's notices.

That did not stop the kids from fighting over them. Carmen unlocked the door and the family poured into the cramped living room. The two oldest still wrestled over the mail. As they grappled it, a small, white postcard enclosed in cellophane wrap dropped out of the stack and fell to the floor.

Carmen always hated those things. They grabbed attention by littering the floor, demanding that the lucky recipient bend over and pick them up. It was always something that required money...money she did not have.

Usually, though, they were not wrapped in cellophane. Her oldest daughter, who was six years old, grabbed it up and ripped the cover off of it, scratching the scratch-n-sniff with what was left of her chewed fingernails. "Mom, it smells so good!"

"Give that to me."

Her fourth-grade son intercepted the transfer. "Me first." He snatched the card from his sister's hand and stuffed it up to his nose for a whiff.

"GIVE ME THAT THING!" Carmen had had enough for the day. She seldom yelled, so when the kids heard her outburst, they gave her the card and scattered in every direction to get out of her way. She stood there in the now-deserted living room until her anger died. Then, she lifted the card to look at it. She put it up to her nose. It smelled great. But so what? She could not buy it.

Kansas City, Missouri

I t was a very busy morning at Dr. Halston's office. Sammie, his receptionist, was doing her very best to keep the patients happy and the doctor on schedule, but things were taking longer than expected. Mondays always went like this.

The office door opened and Sammie winced. Not another walk-in! It was just the mailman, making his morning delivery. Sammie thanked the man and threw the pile off to the side of the desk to be dealt with later.

By six PM, the frantic rush of patients stopped. Sammie drug her feet as she finished setting up for the next day. She saw the forgotten stack of mail. Her feet were killing her, so she sat down on one office chair and plopped her feet up on the other one. As she picked up the stack, the cellophane-covered card dropped out of it into her lap. She opened it, scratched it and smelled it. She carefully placed it back onto the pile of mail. The doctor might get an idea for her for Christmas.

At least there was something nice at the end of the day.

New York, New York

A nthony smiled for the first time as he left his shift at the factory. His job was not interesting or easy. It was just a job. It paid for his food and, more importantly; it paid for his beer.

And it paid for the rent on his apartment. He turned off the sidewalk and climbed the cement stairs up to the door of his building. His key let him in. Then, he closed the door and walked to his mailbox.

He seldom even got any mail, but he never gave up looking. Maybe, he won a sweepstakes prize, or something. To his surprise, something free waited in his box today; a scented card with a new perfume. Now, if he only had a girlfriend to wear the scent for him.

He tore open the cellophane wrapper and rubbed the surface. It smelled pretty good, so he rubbed it on his work shirt and pants. Anthony smiled. See? A person did not have to be rich to smell good.

Washington, D.C.

Mrs. Catshell thanked her housekeeper for the heap of mail she gave her. This was a daily task. Even though most of the mail went to her husband, the Senator, she received a good amount addressed especially to her.

So every morning, she went through her mail. This morning, she found the usual smattering of requests for money or invitations to private parties. She considered these to be a chore, but, for Daniel, she went and did her best on his behalf.

A brightly-colored card in the stack demanded her attention. She opened the cellophane and smelled the lovely fragrance. She would be sure to give this to her husband so he would know her new preference.

Brackettville, Texas

Angie had a huge bunch of packages to mail today. She told her children to say in the car while she went in to mail them. As in many small, rural communities, the people of Brackettville were forced to go to the Post Office every day to get their mail. There was no mail delivery to individual homes.

To take some of the hassle out of this, the Post Office provided a counter where people combed through their mail and stuffed all the unwanted mail in the trash can standing next to it. All day long, patrons threw their junk mail into this can before they even got out of the Post Office with it.

Angie's kids knew this and they loved it. While Angie stood in line to mail her packages, her two kids came into the Post Office and headed straight for the trash can. They dug for possible treasures they might find there.

Today, they found several brightly-colored cellophane-covered free samples. They opened each one, and smelled them eagerly. When Angie came out of the other room, she chided them. "Get out of there! I told you to stay in the car! What do you think you're doing?'

"Mommy, look! Free samples! Mommy, come smell! It smells GOOD!"

"Put that down and let's go!"

"But, Mommy, they're free!"

Angie walked over to them and smelled the sample. "It does smell nice. Now, let's go."

Angie and her kids did not know what kind of treasure they had brought home.

JESTER HALL, TEXAS UNIVERSITY, AUSTIN, TEXAS

Amanda Meek and her sister, Tina, pushed the glass doors open on their way into the lobby of their dorm. They had walked the long tree-lined sidewalk from the history class they shared, laughing about their professor's sudden sneezing fit. He had quickly dismissed the class, hurrying out the door of the lecture hall when he could not stop sneezing. Tina and Amanda thought that was great. Free time!

They walked up to the window of the office. "Mail please."

"Sure." The girl in the window disappeared for a few seconds and came back with a small handful of mail.

"Thanks."

"Let me have it!" demanded Amanda. They were in college, but it did not matter; they were still sisters, and sisters were supposed to fight.

"Well, wait!" Tina tightened her grip on the mail as Amanda grabbed at it. It all fell to the floor. They laughed as they picked it all up.

They stopped to look through it. There was a letter from their friend, Courtney, at Texas Tech University. Jessica had also written to them from Angelo State. Tina handed the phone bill to Amanda.

"I believe this is mostly yours."

Then, she inspected the cellophane-wrapped postcard.

"Cool." She ripped into it just as Amanda grabbed it from her and looked at it. Amanda held Tina off by keeping her back turned to her. She scraped at the square and smelled the lovely fragrance.

"Here, Tina, smell this. It's cool.":

Tina sniffed at the card. "What is it?"

"Some new perfume. Let's order some."

They took their mail up to their room to show to their suite-mates.

CIUDAD ACUNA

R amon and Santos walked down the empty walkways of the Macquiladora plant. The sounds of their heels clicking on the cement echoed through the quiet building. The workers had been released and the factory was closed.

"I leave on the plane tomorrow morning," said Santos.

"Have all the final bills been taken care of?"

"Yes, Omid. All you need to do is give the keys to the new tenant. They will arrive tomorrow. Did you find any information on the two workers that did not come to work on the last day?"

"Oh, yes, Jaime Pacheco and Luis Hidalgo missed work, but it does not matter, Santos. It is too late now. The infection has been spread and the Americans will not be able to stop it now, even if they find out about it. Still, I will check on the boys before I leave."

Ramon smiled at his accomplishment. The infected volunteers successfully sought their targets. Still, the most effective phase of the attack had been the mailing of the twenty-five million infected scratch-n-sniff cards. One-third of all of the American households received them and these would surely infect the others. The bill for the mailing cost only six million dollars. It was cheap, as far as warfare went, and it was much more effective than bombs, missiles and jets, which were much more expensive than a virus.

GLITCH

CIUDAD ACUNA, THE COLONIAS

J aime had felt the first chills shortly after reporting to work at the Macquiladora the morning of the next to the last day of his job. He had not thought anything about them at first. Then, his head had begun to hurt a little and his eyes started burning. He sat down next to Luis during the afternoon fifteen-minute break.

"My head hurts so bad!" Luis confided to Jaime.

"Mine too. Does your back hurt?"

"Yes, and I feel cold."

"What do you think it is, Luis?"

"I don't know. Maybe we should go talk to the doctor."

"No, Luis! Don't your remember what Juan told us about Roberto? He felt sick and went to the doctor. Now, he and his family have disappeared."

"Where is Juan, anyway?"

"Over there talking to Cecelia."

They waved at Juan and motioned for him to come over to them.

"What do you want?" Their bad timing put a frown on Juan's face. He always liked visiting with Cecelia. Now, Cecelia walked off to visit with Ramon.

"You two don't look good. What is wrong?" he said with a quieter voice.

"We are sick. Tell us what was wrong with Roberto before he disappeared," Jaime demanded.

"His head hurt and he was hot with fever."

Jaime and Luis looked at each other.

"Is yours the same?" continued Juan, suddenly very concerned about his friends.

"I don't know. We are just sick. Maybe it is the flu or something."

"Well, don't tell anybody." Juan was whispering emphatically now. "Especially Ramon or the doctor."

"Why?"

"Because that is what Roberto did. And do you see him or his family now? No! You have to get out of here before Ramon or the doctor find out you are sick."

Juan's brows were crossed now in something similar to anger. He had been trying to warn Jaime and Luis for weeks about the danger and they had not listened to him.

"You are right, Juan. We will stay for the rest of the day." Jaime turned to Luis. "Try to look like you feel well, Luis."

Luis nodded as they stiffly rose to get back to work. Juan hurried over to his workstation and tried to hide his anxiety.

As the day grew closer to an end, Jaime's head began to pound, and his back, arms and legs began to ache. He felt himself getting weaker.

131

Exhaustion and nausea overtook them by the time they got off duty for the day. They decided to ride the bus home for the first time ever. They were too weak to make it home without a ride. They ambled over to the place where the bus would stop where Cecelia joined them. She always rode the bus home. Her heels made it difficult to walk that far. The boys sat down on the dirt pathway to wait for the bus.

After a few minutes, the bus rounded the corner and pulled up to their stop. The overloaded, white van wore bright letters printed on the sides. The driver took their coins, but did not offer any suggestions as to where they could fit into the mass of pressed human flesh that was already squeezed into the van. Everyone was on his or her way home. Nobody got off. So Jaime, Luis and Cecelia squeezed in among the other complaining riders.

Jaime's somewhat sore throat developed a tickle. He tried to ignore the impulse, but finally gave in and started coughing. Luis sneezed twice.

"Salud!" said Cecelia. She hoped she would not catch the flu, too.

Jaime knew when they were close to the Colonias. The rancid smell of the stockyards made him want to vomit. Strange, he thought, it never bothered him before.

The three of them got out of the van and turned down the rutted road to their homes. Jaime and Luis kept shivering, even though the temperature was a mild seventy-eight degrees. They struggled to their huts and went straight to bed.

As soon as Jaime's grandmother saw him, she started fussing over him. His pale face and huddled shoulders told her that he was sick.

"Jaime! What is the matter with you? You look bad."

"Yes, Grandmother, I am sick. Just let me sleep on the bed."

The "bed" consisted of nothing more than an old pallet, spread on the swept caliche ground that made the floor of the hut. Jaime lay down and his grandmother searched for something to put over him. He huddled in a fetal position and shook uncontrollably. Grandmother put her hand on his face. He was so hot. She got an old towel and took it out to the water barrel, where she dipped it into the water and squeezed it out. She hurriedly stepped back into the hut to put the rag on Jaime's forehead. He fussed at her because the rag made him feel colder so she decided to go get Ruben.

Ruben was the pastor of the Church at the Colonias. He watched over his flock carefully, and tried to help them as much as he could. His oldest daughter had gone to school and become a nurse. She came home sometimes to help Ruben with his people. She had taught him many things, so Grandmother hoped Ruben could help Jaime.

"Ruben, Ruben!" she called as she reached his small home on the corner of the street. "Come quickly. Jaime is sick!"

"Make some of the tea from the good weed, Enedelia. Bring it to Jaime's house."

Ruben's wife, Enedelia, served as the resident pharmacist when Ruben needed some of the herbal medicine he had learned to use. She opened the small bag holding the leaves of the plant, and removed some of them. After crumbling them into the pan, she added some water and began to heat it. She let it simmer to thicken the tea.

Ruben scrambled behind Grandmother and caught up with her. "What is wrong with him?"

"He is very hot and he is sleeping."

"Enedelia's tea will bring down the fever. Don't worry."

"Luis will need some, too."

"There will be enough."

Miguel, Jaime's friend, saw Ruben and Grandmother hurrying to the hut. Following them to see what was wrong, he heard them talking about the fever. Then, he saw Juan walking down the road, returning from work.

"Juan, what is wrong with Jaime and Luis?"

"I don't know, Miguel. They got sick while we were working today."

Miguel let out a deep breath and tightened his lips. His anger grew.

"I told you that place was bad, Juan! Now, see. They are sick from it, just like Roberto."

"Don't worry, Miguel," said Juan, backing away from Miguel. "They did not tell anyone they were sick. Our boss does not know anything about it."

They stood outside the hut and watched as Enedelia took the tea into the hut.

"Yes, Juan, but what if they die? I told you that place was bad. Why did you tell them it was safe?"

"I did not know, Miguel. I did not know."

133

"You must go to work tomorrow and tell your boss that they quit. Make some story. Don't tell him they are sick."

"Yes, Miguel. I will."

Jaime's sisters came home from the market to find the crowded hut buzzing with activity. When they saw Enedelia come out with her empty pot and worried face, they knew someone was sick. They pushed the cloth door to one side and went in.

The dim light of Ruben's lantern threw shadows onto Jaime's sleeping form. The tea had worked well in bringing down the fever, but Jaime was resting fitfully. Grandmother turned when she heard the girls enter the hut.

"What's wrong with Jaime?"

"Ruben says it's the flu. The tea has cooled him some. He's resting."

The sight of their oldest brother so sick made the girls panic. "What can we do, Grandmother?"

Grandmother was glad to have someone younger available now to do the bending required reaching down and holding the wet rag on Jaime's forehead. She handed Lucinda the rag.

"Put this on his head until it warms. Then, wash it out with the cold water and put it back."

Lucinda took the rag and carefully followed Grandmother's instructions. Maria knelt by Jaime and held his hand, praying for him. She knew from experience that this could be their only hope.

The fever began to subside and Jaime, though weak, felt a little better. He opened his eyes and saw his sisters caring for him.

"I will be all right. Don't worry," he managed to say weakly. His sisters' relieved looks told him that they had been worried.

"It's just the flu." He was even convincing himself.

"Do you know what day it is, Jaime?" Lucinda was asking strange questions now.

"I have only been sick for one day."

"No. Three days, brother. We have been so worried. I have never seen you sick like this."

"Well, I am doing better now. Stop worrying."

It was true; he was doing better now. His fever was lower, and his head and back did not hurt so much.

134

"How is Luis?'

"Luis is sick, but he is not as sick as you have been. Ruben and Enedelia have been taking care of him. I think he is a little better now."

Jaime and Luis felt better for a day. Then, the sickness seemed to come back on them. The cough they developed scrubbed their sore throats unmercifully. Weeping sores showed up in their mouths and on their throats, making it painful to swallow.

Lucinda was the first to notice the small red spots that formed on Jaime's face and arms. The dim light in the hut made them very hard to see.

"Look, Grandmother. Spots!" She ran her hand over Jaime's face to feel them. Their slightly raised centers caused her to itch as she felt of them.

"Ah! It must be the Measles" Grandmother said with a smile. Now she knew it would not be fatal.

"Does Luis also have spots?" Jaime knew they probably had the same thing. Relief flowed over him. Now, he could stop thinking he got the sickness because of his job. "Let's go see."

Lucinda and Rudolpho ran out the door to check on Luis. Sure enough, the same rash covered Luis' face and arms. This simply confirmed Grandmother's diagnosis. It would be all right now.

• • •

Miguel sat brooding outside his home, looking down the road towards Jaime's house. *I told them not to work there*, he thought. *It is a bad place. They should have listened to me.*

The deep rumbling of the engine of a crew-cab pickup truck drew his attention away from his thoughts. He looked up the road towards the highway to see a silver truck as it slowly made its way down the road, weaving to avoid the biggest holes. It was impossible to avoid all of them, though, so Ramon's form bounced erratically in response to them. He was having trouble avoiding the bumps because he was not really paying attention to where he was going. He looked all around at the different huts, like he was trying to find someone.

Miguel recognized him and a fear rose up in him. He knew that Ramon was looking for Jaime and Luis, and Miguel knew what would happen if Ramon found out that they were sick. He had seen it too many times before.

So, he got up and quickly walked in the direction of Ramon's truck. He did his best to look helpful. It worked. Ramon rolled down his window.

"Please, can you help me find one of my employees?"

"Yes, I will try."

"Do you know where Jaime Pacheco and Luis Hidalgo live? I need to talk to them."

"Yes." answered Miguel. He pointed to an abandoned hut.

"They were living in that house, but they have gone away."

"Do you know where they went?"

"Yes, I should not tell you this...but they left with the Coyotes to find work across the river."

Ramon looked at the empty house. "And their families?"

"They all went together. The Coyotes promised jobs for all of them."

Ramon smiled. Now, he did not have to worry about them anymore. All of his work here was finished and he could go home now. He looked into Miguel's earnest eyes.

"Thank-you," he said. Trying not to cause suspicion, he added, "If they come back, tell them they can come to work for me again, if they wish."

With that, Ramon waved to Miguel, put his truck into gear and turned it around to drive out of the Colonias. Miguel watched as the back of the truck bounced up to the highway. He slowly turned and walked back to sit and watch Jaime's house. He would turn away anyone coming to look for them.

Ramon stopped at the highway. As he looked to the right, he saw Cecelia walking towards him from the bus stop. *Ah, Cecelia*, he thought. She was the only "Souvenir" he wanted to take home with him from Mexico. She would make an excellent concubine for him in Iran, and he would save her from almost certain death and misery that would soon begin in the area.

He rolled his window down and called, "Cecelia! It is so good to see you. Would you like to go to dinner with me?"

"Yes, Ramon," she smiled. "That would be nice."

MEASLES

SAN ANTONIO, TEXAS

M ike handed his daughter, Lissa, his credit card so she could pay for the groceries and supplies while he stepped over to the tiny deli at the front of the grocery store. He leaned over the counter and spoke to the young woman carefully placing fried chicken into the display case.

"Could you fill this with coffee please, Ma'am?" He set the thermos on the counter.

The woman shot a glance over her shoulder to the coffee machine. "Can you wait a few minutes? I can give you this fresh pot. It's almost ready."

Mike checked Lissa's place in the line and saw that there was no hurry. "Sounds good to me."

The woman smiled at him, then turned back to her duties. Mike's attention shifted to the two older men sitting at a table immediately behind him. One of them was trying to get the other to talk more quietly.

"Keep your voice down, Larry." Ray had known Crazy Larry for over twenty years. Their service together in the Army had firmly cemented their relationship. When they retired, they chose houses only blocks away from each other. Now, Ray spent many hours trying to keep Larry's feet planted on the ground. Their Military Intelligence duties had permanently warped Larry's sense of reality. And Larry seemed particularly agitated today.

"I tell you, they're coming, Ray...and soon!"

"O.K. Larry, but can you keep your voice down just a bit? You wouldn't want those V.A. doctors hearing you talk like that again, would you? They locked you up for a month last time they got wind of it."

"Oh, who cares! I'm telling you that they are on their way. I can feel it in my bones, Ray. But you don't have to worry...I'm ready for them. They mess with us and they'll know real quick that they messed with the wrong guys!" Larry's voice had only gotten louder.

"For Pity's sake, Larry, be quiet." Ray instinctively looked around the area for listeners.

"Yes, Sir!" Larry reached across the small table and lightly slapped Ray on the shoulder twice, grinning and nodding his head in confidence. "I've got a few little surprises for 'em when they get here. Yes, Sir!"

Mike smiled to himself as he loaded up his filled thermos. He wondered if he'd be insane by the time he retired. But right now, he had to get on the road.

Finally, Mike, Lissa and Allan were headed in the right direction, and he knew that the further west he went, the less traffic there would be. He was looking forward to that. He would be able to visit with Lissa and Allan better, now that his constant attention was not required by the zooming traffic around him.

Within five minutes, they passed the exit to the road that led to the Institute of Biotechnology. Lissa looked down the deceptive country road as they passed it.

"There it is...that's where I'll do my thesis work."

"It's a good place, Liss. Hey, have I told you lately how proud I am of you?"

"Yes, Dad. About twenty times today, I think."

Mike smiled. His daughter's interest in his work constituted the best compliment he could ever receive. Lissa was a junior at the University of Texas at San Antonio. Her 3.8 GPA was the result of hard work, born out of an intense interest in her studies.

Still, she found time to volunteer at the Institute. She also managed to go with Mike every year when he traveled to the Mexican border to help the poor people in the Colonias. It was his way of paying back some of the blessings he had received.

Allan Simpson had accompanied Mike on his annual trek for nine years now. As Mike's physician's assistant, Allan worked with him on a daily basis. He kept Mike out of trouble and covered for his occasional clumsiness. Allan never understood how Mike never goofed up in his medical skills but so frequently messed up other things. Mike valued his friendship and they made a good team in Mexico.

They chose the week of Thanksgiving every year for several reasons. The holiday weekend was a natural time to be absent from duty. Furthermore, the milder temperatures helped the work go easier.

Since Lissa had been in college, she had been able to go with them. She arranged to have her studies done ahead of schedule so she could leave. Mike enjoyed her company, even though she fussed at them to keep them organized. She had inherited that talent from her mother.

Before Mike knew it, the car got very quiet. He looked in the rear-view mirror and saw Allan's balding head leaned up against the headrest in the back seat. Then, he looked across at Lissa in the seat next to him. She was sleeping too. Her blond hair fell into her face and covered her eyes.

He let them rest. Lissa's attempt to get her work in early had required her to give up a good bit of sleep. Allan had been busy gathering the needed supplies for the trip. Besides, Mike enjoyed the rare quiet. It gave him time to think.

He could hear the rattling of the cases and squeaking of the ice chests in the trunk. Over the nine years of this tradition, Mike had learned how to pack for the adventure. He used to pack more clothes. After several years of carting back clothes he did not wear, he learned to pack less. There was never time to worry about changing clothes. This way, he fit better with the people he worked with. He always wore simple jeans and a comfortable shirt. He knew he would be getting down and dirty. He could not comprehend living like that all the time, as the people in the Colonias did. The first thing he did when they came out of Mexico was to rent a motel room and take a good shower. It was always such a relief.

Now, most of the space in the trunk was filled with food donations for the hungry people. They brought things like rice, beans, tomato sauce and flour to give to the most needy families. The premixed, canned infant formula was one of the most important things he could bring to help their well being.

He had treated too many cases of dysentery in the babies there to ignore the major implications of the source of the disease. The water was contaminated beyond belief. The people suffered from every imaginable water-borne disease. Amebic dysentery topped the list.

It was hard enough on the stronger young adults. It was fatal, however, many times for the young babies who were infected repeatedly from the water their young mothers used to mix their powdered formula. The powdered formula was cheaper than the premixed liquid. The uneducated mothers were taught that the formula was better for their babies than their own milk. So, for the food for their babies, they dutifully denied some of their own needs so they could buy the powder.

Many times, the milk powder that was available in Mexican stores was the product that had gone out of date in American stores. The illiterate population in Mexico did not know to check the expiration date on the formula cans. Then, they mixed the out-of-date powder with infected water. Their babies were sickly and many died.

Mike would never forget Adreana. His first trip to Mexico had been quite an education. No, not an education. Culture shock was a better term. He did not know that people lived like that.

He and Allan had driven into Mexico with some sort of picture in their minds of how it would be. They had heard of the great poverty, but, they had not been prepared to step into a scene that was, in reality, worse than the scenes shown on those paid programming segments that begged for money for hungry children. As soon as they got out of the car, dozens of dirty, scantily clad children surrounded them, looking up at them with pitiful, dark eyes. Their pathetic gazes burned right into the hearts of Mike and Allan. The visitors knew they would never be able to forget these people. They would do whatever they could to help them.

They looked around and saw the women watching them from the doorways of the cardboard huts, as the cloth door covers waved in the wind. The hopelessness in their eyes was permanently burned into Mike's soul.

They approached one middle-aged woman with her hair in a long braid down her back. Mike summoned all of his Spanish-speaking abilities and told her that he was a doctor. He asked if she knew of anyone who was sick. All of the wariness melted off her face, as she smiled at them, nodded and told them to follow her. She served as their guide for the entire day.

She brought them to the meager home of Adreana and told them to wait. After a few seconds of excited Spanish in the hut, a young girl stepped out of the doorway, holding the still form of Adreana in her arms. Mike approached her, as their guide explained that the little girl was sick. The thin, small baby looked like she was less than one month old.

Mike reached out to take the baby from her mother, expecting the child to have no reaction to being turned over to a stranger. As soon as Adreana saw Mike reach for her, however, her eyes widened and she leaned closer to her young mother, crying in protest at being handed to a stranger. This was not the reaction of a newborn.

"How old is she?" Mike was confused.

The young mother answered, "She is eight months old."

Mike and Allan looked at each other in surprise. The child could not have weighed more than eight pounds. Her fourteen-year-old mother tried to explain.

"She has been sick. I took her to the clinic five times. They always put her in the hospital."

"What does the doctor say is wrong with her?"

The young mother dropped her eyes in embarrassment and shrugged her shoulders. She did not know.

"Do you mind if we take her to the clinic and talk to her doctor?"

"I will go with you." It was clear that Adreana's mother loved her.

They all piled into the car and driven to the clinic. Mike had not ever seen any clinic like this clinic. The three-room structure was about the size of his double-car garage at home. The doctor took one look at Adreana, then dropped his shoulders and looked down, shaking his head slowly.

As Adreana cried weakly in her mother's arms, the weary doctor explained, in broken English, the medical history of little Adreana. He had hospitalized her five times for amebic dysentery. Five times, he had cured her. Five times, she had gone home. Five times, she had returned, re-infected from the family water barrel. Her young mother had not been able to comprehend the need to boil the water before mixing the formula with it. Or, maybe it was because of the lack of fuel to make the required fire.

The doctor, clearly, had given up on the case. He agreed to hospitalize the child again, but he held little hope for her future.

So, Mike and Allan agreed that, the next time they came, they would bring as many cases of pre-mixed, still-in-date formula as they could haul without drawing the attention of the officials, as they came across the border. They had been bringing it across ever since, distributing it to mothers of babies.

Of course, it was too late for Adreana. Mike and Allan went back across the border that day to buy some formula for her and leave it with her mother, complete with instructions not to dilute it. They did not know if Adreana's mother understood. But, the next year when they came back, Adreana and her mother were not there. Nobody knew what had happened to them or where they had gone.

All of these memories made the time pass quickly. Before Mike knew it, he was in Uvalde. He had hardly noticed all the small towns he had passed through already. They traveled on past the Border Patrol checkpoint. Mike decided to check up on Lissa's courses.

"So, what do you think about your philosophy class?'

"It's OK, but the professor is a little strange. He's always getting off the topic, and talking about things he's seen on TV."

"Like what?"

"Like the coming of the end of the world. He told us all about all the predictions that the world would end before the year 2000. He said that maybe they were a couple of years off."

"Well, what do you think?'

"I think it's too late."

Allan jumped into the conversation. "What? You haven't seen the meteor right above our heads? Maybe the prophets were off by a year or so."

Lissa unconsciously looked up and Mike and Allan laughed at her.

"Or what about the aliens poised for their attack as we speak?" Allan would have kept coming up with more deadly scenarios, but he noticed that Mike was looking off to the left, at Laughlin Air Force Base.

Laughlin was located ten miles east of Del Rio, just south of Highway 90. The south Texas brush had been cleared just past the railroad tracks to make room for sprawling runways. The runways could not be seen because there was a low hill blocking the view, but a tower could be seen from the highway.

"My old friend, Richard Mulligan, is stationed there. We served in the Air Force together right after medical school. He went career. I didn't. Now, I work with him in the Reserve."

"You're still in the Reserve? I didn't think you'd have time for all that. I thought you gave it up." Lissa had not been around much on the weekends recently.

"No. I must get some kind of kick out of running through the bushes."

Two jets passed just behind them, and the main entrance to the Air Base came into view. Just beyond the tall brick gateposts were the static aircraft displays. The Security Police were busy screening the vehicles at the entrance. Everything looked so tidy and orderly.

"We're only about ten miles away from the border," said Mike. "Better start getting your stuff together. We're about to cross over into a different era. I swear, every time we go over there, I feel like we've gone back in time at least fifty years."

"Does Ruben know we're coming?" Allan had always had respect for old Ruben. Ruben Calavares served as the pastor for the little Church in the Colonias. He had been there for as long as Mike remembered and he knew everyone there in the Colonias, especially those that attended his Church. His thick gray hair was in stark contrast to his lively, dark eyes, but the lines on his face told the real story. Life here was hard and ugly. And Ruben had seen it all.

Ruben always waited eagerly for Mike and Allan to show up. He knew they would be there sometime close to Thanksgiving, and he tried to be a good host to them. Mike and Allan chose to sleep in their car, however, in an effort to avoid being a burden on the dear, old man and his family, but that never stopped Ruben from inviting them to sleep at his hut each year.

The sign at the red light said, "Mexico," and it wore an arrow pointing to the left. They turned and drove over a bridge that arched over a railroad. As they approached the bridge, the buildings aged, matching the ancient trees surrounding them.

It was like a different world here. Palm readers and flea markets neighbored bank buildings and stores. Money exchangers and small stores with clay pots and figures surrounded stately, old homes. The smell of Mexican gasoline being burned in old cars became stronger. Mike flipped his air conditioner from vent to recycled air in the hope of keeping some of the smell out of the car as long as possible.

As they rounded a large curve in the road, Lissa saw the U.S. border immigration checkpoint. She picked up her bag. For this trip, she had brought a large fanny pack instead of her usual purse. It was just easier to keep up with as they did their work in Mexico. Now, as she neared the border, she instinctively held it closer. Why did crossing the border make her a little nervous?

Mike drove through the narrow driveway, and stopped at the tollbooth to pay his seventy-five cents. Then, he slowly started to cross the bridge. Tall fences on both sides of the bridge arched inward at the top. A middle-aged woman walked with her three daughters on the pedestrian crossing sidewalks, carrying packages of goods that had been bought in the U.S. On the other side of the bridge, people walked back from Mexico, carrying things they had bought there.

Allan felt himself tense as they approached the Federales' station on the Mexico side. The bright, blinking red light above the drive-through meant more to him than just the necessity to stop. It meant the possibility of ha-rassment.

In the years that he had accompanied Mike on his annual trek, he had been amazed at the corruption he had seen in the Federales. He remem-bered that, on one trip, he and Mike had been detained for an hour while the Federales tried to decide how to confiscate the box of Spanish Bibles they were taking to Ruben. The Federales were not particularly religious. Rather, they thought they could make some money selling the Bibles. Mike finally bribed the guard in charge and they let them go.

The Federales always got excited over the medical equipment the group was bringing into the country. Mike and Allan had learned to hide their equip-ment and medicines under the rice and beans in the trunk. It just went more smoothly that way. Now, the party did their best to look like touristas on the hunt for booze or curios.

Mike slowed the car as they drove up to the official standing in the door of the booth. The man looked them over.

"Where are you going?" demanded the gruff official. His belly hung over his tight belt and it shook as he spoke.

"To do some shopping and go to the clubs," lied Mike. The Mexicans wanted the tourist business. Mike had given up trying to explain that they were there to help the people.

The man waved them on. Allan sighed in relief at getting in without a hassle, but he waited until Mike had driven down the road some to reach up and pat him on the arm.

144

"You're getting better at lying."

The road narrowed and became one-way. Cars lined both sides of the street. The traffic slowed to a crawl, which gave them plenty of time to take in the scenery of the tourist section of Acuna.

"Oh, look! Look at that sign!" Lissa laughed.

A bronze plaque on the wall of a club proudly announced, "Members and Non-members Only!" They all had a good laugh over that one.

Then they saw something that sobered them. A blind woman in a faded scarf sat on the sidewalk with an old tin cup in her hand. Next to her, two children wearing rags and no shoes waited. Mike and his group remembered their purpose for this trip. The somber mood in the car continued as they waited for a red light to change. They watched children playing in a schoolyard across the street.

Finally, they turned right when the light changed, and drove out past a gas station and a hotel. Small stands stood on both sides of the highway, selling their wares.

They got behind a crowded van that was serving as a bus. It stopped for passengers every two blocks, so Mike passed it carefully just as it stopped at the first Macquiladora plant.

"What do they make here?" asked Lissa.

"From what I've heard, they do a lot of metal plating and things like that. I know one of these plants makes seat belts for car companies." Mike knew this from the people he worked with in the Colonias.

"There's a new one. It wasn't here last year. I wonder what they do there?" Allan was not very good at reading Spanish.

"It says something about the mail, I think. It's been three years since I tried to read Spanish." Lissa was not sure.

The smell of the small stockyard just west of the Colonias intensified, telling Mike that they were closer. The overwhelming odor of concentrated dung lingered in the air of the people's yards and homes, but Mike had never found one of the poor people who seemed to mind. They had more important troubles to worry about. It only bothered the Americans.

The car began to bounce as it made its way down the caliche road. The ruts looked like someone had been tossing grenades on the road for fun. Mike wove all around trying to avoid them, feeling like he was maneuvering an obstacle course.

Finally, they took the left turn that led into the Colonias and passed Ruben's Church. Handmade bricks composed the huts closer to the highway. Mike saw the progress that had been made in the buildings since last year. The people had been working hard.

Some of them recognized Mike and Allan and waved, smiling broad, toothless smiles. They appreciated the help Mike brought them. A few even followed them down the road on the way to Ruben's house.

Ruben's house was average for the area. It proudly displayed a large, wooden cross on the small outside wall. He had bricked a walk to his door this year.

As soon as Ruben's wife, Enedelia, heard the car engine, she pushed the wooden shutter open on the window to see who had stopped at her house. Her mouth flew open, as she dropped the shutter.

"Ruben! Ruben! Mike esto aqui!" she yelled as she came rounding out of the door, nearly tripping over the first brick on her way out to the car. Throwing her arms around Mike's neck, she chattered so fast that Mike could not understand her. Ruben caught up with her and pulled her to his side. Mike had never seen her so excited.

Ruben shook his visitors' hands and invited them into his home. Lissa had brought a case of canned drinks for Ruben's family. Enedelia, offered some to her guests. They popped the tops, and began enjoying their drinks.

"So, how is everybody, Ruben?" Mike asked.

Ruben looked at Mike with deep concern lining his eyes. "If I did not know you were coming this week, I would have called you. The people are sick with something very bad. I have never seen it before."

"What is it?"

"High fevers, sore throats, and a rash."

"Sounds like Measles."

"No, Mike. I have never seen Measles like this!"

146

Decoy

Colonias, Ruben's House

R uben hurried his short legs as fast as they could go as he led Mike, Allan and Lissa to the home of this sickest parishioner. The warm sun would be dropping behind the Sleeping Lady Mountain to the west soon, making it hard to see in the huts, since they had no electricity. Small lanterns provided their only light after dark.

Mike tossed the car keys to Allan. "Allan, bring the car over. We'll need the medical bag."

Allan nodded as he caught the keys and went back for the car. By the time he returned, Ruben had already led Mike and Lissa into Jaime's hut. Jaime sat on his mat. Ruben did all the interpreting for them.

"How long have you been sick, Jaime?"

"Nine days, but I am getting better now. Please help my sisters and my brother. They are getting the worst part now."

Mike looked around the sparse but well-kept hut. Two young girls and another boy tossed restlessly on their mats, obviously running high fevers. Even in the dim light, Mike saw the flush on their faces and he looked at Jaime's worried face.

"If they have what you have, I need to talk to you first. Allan, bring that lantern closer. That's better. Did you have a high fever, too?"

"Yes, but it was not as bad as theirs."

"What else?"

"I was cold and shaking, and my bones hurt."

"How long?"

"Three days, then I felt a little better, but I got the spots."

Jaime raised his arms, pointing to the spots to show them to Mike. Mike pulled the lantern closer and looked at them. He put his forefinger on Jaime's rash and pressed lightly. He had to admit that Ruben could be right, maybe it was the Measles.

"And your throat was sore? Any cough?"

"Yes."

"Where?"

"Everywhere."

Mike nodded and turned to Ruben.

"You might be right. It could be Measles."

Then, he turned his attention to the three more recent patients on their mats. Grandmother moved away from Lucinda where she had been quietly sponging her forehead. Mike put his hand on Lucinda's face, then arms. She was burning up.

"Lissa, get me the thermometer."

Lissa searched and found the thermometer, and gave it to Mike. It was an electronic thermometer that measured body temperature when placed against an ear.

Mike's eyes widened as he read the result. "One-oh-four—She's hot. What have you given her?'

Ruben tried to explain to Mike about Enedelia's tea. They had also given her some acetaminophen. Mike was glad to know that Ruben had listened to his warning about aspirin and fever in teenagers. The aspirin was cheaper, but Ruben had insisted on giving her the acetaminophen instead.

Mike knelt on the swept ground and looked into Lucinda's eyes. Then, he turned to Lissa. "Get me a tongue depressor..." he started, but Lissa already had it ready and waiting and he smiled at her as he took it. He opened his young patient's mouth and looked for the telltale Koplik's spots that appear a few days before the rash of Measles. He was a little surprised not to find any. The mucous membranes of her cheeks should have had tiny, table salt crystals on them.

"Allan, can you see any Koplik's spots?"

Allan looked and had to agree with Mike that there were no Koplik's spots in her mouth.

"How long has she been sick?" asked Mike of Jaime.

"Two days."

Mike glanced at Allan and commented, "I would have thought she'd have them by now. It's not Rubella."

"Why don't we look at the others," suggested Allan.

They moved with the lantern over to Maria and Rudolpho. None of them were showing any Koplik's spots either.

148

"That's strange." said Mike. "None of them seem to have them. Have you given them the tea and acetaminophen?'

"Yes, as soon as they got sick," answered Ruben.

Mike stood up next to Allan and raised his eyebrows as he shrugged slightly. "Maybe the tea has something to do with it, Allan. What do you think?'

"Could be. Who knows what's in that tea."

"Yeah, you're right. Let's give them some antibiotics to prevent any complications. It's a virus and they'll have to just ride it out."

Ruben asked, "Will the medicine cure them?'

"No, Ruben, this is a virus. The antibiotics will only keep them from getting something worse while they are weakened from the virus. You're doing the right thing. Just help them through it."

Ruben's hopeful face dropped somewhat in response. He had hoped that Mike could cure it completely like he had done so many times with other things on earlier trips.

"Have your people had Measles shots?"

"I do not know, Mike. The doctor at the clinic knows all of that."

"Well, keep the others away from these sick ones, just in case."

"Yes, Mike, but it will be hard to do. My people care about each other and they come and try to help."

"Tell them they might get sick too. Maybe that will keep them away."

With that, Ruben led his guests back to his house. The plan had been to get a good night's rest and start seeing the people early the next morning. The next morning, Ruben opened the front room in his two-room home to be the impromptu clinic. Word had spread through the Colonias that Mike was there, so people began arriving as soon as the sun came up. The usual mix of maladies made up most of his patients' complaints. In a living condition like that in Acuna, poor nutrition and lack of good drinking water caused most of the problems. Many of the children they saw suffered from dysentery, ring worm or something related to these problems. Malnutrition was the most obvious in the younger children, whose swollen bellies made the diagnosis easy. Untreated heart disease and arthritis plagued the older people.

Late in the afternoon, Grandmother showed up at Ruben's house. "Lucinda, Maria and Rudolpho have spots on their faces now, just like Jaime's, but Jaime is getting sicker again. Should I bring him here?"

"No," said Mike quickly, after glancing around the crowded room. "I'll go there."

The people in the room watched in disappointment as Mike left. They had been waiting for quite a while. Lissa and Allan tried to handle some of the less complicated cases while he was gone.

Mike was shocked at the deterioration in Jaime's condition. His fever raged, and he was groaning in agony from his aching back and limbs. Mike looked into his mouth and saw lesions forming there. The rash looked different so he thought it might be some sort of relapse, or maybe a reaction to the antibiotics. He had never seen Measles like this.

As he looked over to Jaime's siblings, he saw that they were feeling a little better. When he came closer, he noticed that, as Grandmother had announced, they had spots on their faces...but they also had them on their arms.

He knew that could not be right. He examined them and found no spots on their trunks yet. He had never seen Measles like this before. An uncomfortable, nagging thought began to form in his mind. Something was wrong with this picture. Very wrong.

The Measles rash was supposed to begin on the head and neck and then spread down and out. This rash had begun on the face and arms first, not the trunk. A suspicion began to nag him, no matter how hard he tried to ignore it. He had been trained in rash differentiation, but he had never seen this rash pattern before. He had only read about it in textbooks. Further, he was supposedly never going to see this rash pattern. The disease that caused it had been eradicated!

By the next day, the spots on Jaime were raised and beginning to fill with fluid and Mike called Allan over to look at them. "Look at these, Allan. I've never seen this before, have you?"

"They look a lot like Chickenpox."

"No, wrong fever pattern."

"Then, what? What could they be?"

Mike motioned for Allan to follow him out of the hut because he did not want anyone to hear his ridiculous suspicions. "What do you know about Smallpox, Allan?"

A surprised, questioning look formed on Allan's face.

"Smallpox? You think this could be *Smallpox?* Mike, that's been eradicated for twenty years now!"

"I know, but these are almost classic cases. Did you ever treat it?"

"No, I only read about it."

"Well, this rash pattern fits it exactly. And there aren't any Koplik's spots. I think it's a real possibility here."

Allan watched Mike as he uttered his last preposterous words. Maybe the strain of the trip and the hard work were beginning to get to Mike. He refused to believe the possibility of the truth in Mike's suspicions.

Mike saw the doubt in Allan's eyes "Look, we've got to get a sample to a lab. I'll show you. We could take it to the clinic lab. I saw a microscope in there before. Smallpox is a very large virus...one of the few that can be seen with an ordinary light microscope."

Mike's lower jaw dropped slightly open suddenly. "Oh, my God! Lissa! Where is she?"

"I left her at Ruben's house. Why?"

"Because you and I have been vaccinated. We work in the labs with the Orthopox viruses...but I don't know about Lissa."

Allan jolted out the door on his way to find Lissa and Mike was right behind him. They entered Ruben's house calling for Lissa.

"What?" Lissa asked. She could not understand the panic in her father's voice.

"Lissa, have you had a Smallpox vaccination?"

"Uh, yeah. The people at the research lab insisted on it when I went to work there. Why?"

"Because I think it may be a really good thing they did. Jaime's rash has changed and it sure looks like it could be Smallpox."

"No, Dad. That's been killed off. They even wiped out the stocks of it at the CDC and Moscow this summer. All my professors were really excited about it because it was the first time ever that Humans made something extinct on purpose. It's gone."

Mike ignored Lissa's arguments completely as he started shouting instructions and did not even hear her last words. "Allan, where are the car keys? The clinic should still be open. Give me a needle and a couple of slides. I'm going to collect some of it to take to the clinic."

Mike grabbed his supplies and ran out the door in the direction of Jaime's hut. Lissa's confused look did not go unnoticed by Allan.

"Come on. I'll explain in the car."

They started the car and met Mike at Jaime's house where Mike came out, holding the covered needle and jumped into the car.

"Let's go."

SUSPICION

CIUDAD ACUNA—CLINIC

A fter struggling to find a place to park the car on the narrow, one-way street, Mike jumped out of the car and quickly walked down the cracked sidewalk to the clinic. Because the weather was warm, the door was left open. He walked straight through the room; past the staring patients, into the hallway that led to the back of the small clinic.

The receptionist, initially surprised by the brazen man's actions, leapt to her feet in an attempt to intercept him before he got to the back. But Mike was moving too fast for her. He had already found the doctor sitting at his desk, filling out forms. Forgetting that the clinic doctor barely knew any English, Mike ranted on to him about what he had found, until the doctor stood up, half-smiling, and shook his head slowly with a very confused look on his face. About that time, Allan rounded the corner, closely followed by the agitated receptionist.

"Oh, Allan. Good. You're better at Spanish than I am. Ask him if we can use his lab. Tell him what we've found."

"I'll try, Mike, but he looks like he's a little worried about you right now. Calm down, you're scaring the man."

Mike took a deep breath, trying to relax. He knew he had some hard work ahead of him now. Allan explained all he could to the clinic doctor, who slowly walked toward Mike and looked at his face with deep concern. He was not sure what to believe about Mike. Here stood a man he had only spoken to twice before. By the word of some of his patients, he knew that Mike came every year. He admired him for that. But what did Mike know about the people of Acuna? Mike never saw the daily struggle these patients faced just for survival. Surely, Mike was naive about the whole picture. And now, this man wanted to use his lab to confirm a diagnosis that the clinic doctor knew was ludicrous. But, he could see the panic in Mike's eyes.

"What kind of equipment do you need? All I have is a simple microscope."

"That is exactly what I need, along with some acetic acid, formalin, carboxylic acid, tannin and ammonium hydroxide. Oh, and some sliver nitrate."

The clinic doctor looked lost again.

"May I see what chemicals you have to work with here?"

"Si. Yes. You may use whatever is there."

"Gracias," Mike said, as he began digging through the cabinets in the tiny room that served as the clinic lab. It was amazing, thought Mike, that anyone could effectively practice medicine with such sparse equipment. The microscope was the same kind of instrument he had used in high school, and that was the most sophisticated article in the room.

He found some small amounts of the chemicals he needed, but he had no idea how old they were. At least the silver nitrate was stored in a dark bottle. The clinic doctor was doing all that he could with what he had.

"Allan, take Lissa and go buy fertile eggs. I'll mix the solutions for the stains."

Allan looked at Lissa. "Well, let's go. I don't know what he wants with them, but he seems desperate enough."

Mike stretched his memory, as he mixed the fixative solution for Gispen's method, then the mordant solution. Then, he mixed the ammonia and silver nitrate, until the silver precipitate dissolved and the solution took on a faint, bluish opalescence. The whole room began to smell of ammonia.

He pulled the cap off of the needle on the syringe that he had used to scrape the blister on Jaime. He had been very careful to pick at a maculo-papular lesion until it became moist, avoiding drawing blood. He smeared the material from the needle onto four slides and set them aside to air dry.

He dipped the air-dried slides in the fixative for a minute, then rinsed them with water and put them aside to air dry again. He heated the slides in the mordant mixture until the steam rose for a minute. Then, he rinsed the slides with water and heated them with the opalescent silver solution for two minutes.

He turned on the microscope and stared into the eyepiece until his eye focused on the field.

There it was, staring up at him, bold and unafraid. It's brown-black form stood out against the yellow background. A chill ran down his spine.

"Damn!" he said aloud. O.K. So far, he was right. But it was only a presumptive test. He knew time was critical now, but if he called the authorities, they would never believe him. He was having a hard enough time believing it himself— and he had seen it first-hand. He wished he could run a gel precipitation method on it, but this lab was just not equipped. He would only be able to run one more test here that might be definitive.

Once again, Allan's timing was perfect. He and Lissa showed up at the lab door just as Mike finished wrapping the slides that he had prepared. He stuffed them into his pocket.

"Here, Mike. These are as fresh as they come. I bought them off an old woman sitting in front of her house. She had to chase the chicken off to get them. They're still warm."

"Perfect. Hand 'em over."

He took the eggs and inoculated the chorioallantois with the infected needle. Looking around the meager lab, he spotted the antique incubator. It would have to do. After setting the eggs into the incubator, he stepped out of the lab, looking for the receptionist.

"Where is the phone?" blurted Mike, forgetting the language barrier.

"Como?"

Oh, crap.—Mike scratched his head.

"Uh, uhm— Tango un telephono?"

"Bueno." She gave him a quizzical look.

154

Try again. "Uhm—tiene usted un telephono?"

"Si."

"Adonde esta la telephono?"

She handed it to him. "Aqui esta."

He pulled the wallet from his pocket and searched for the number he needed. He had his code number memorized, but he did not call Tom very often so he did not know his number. It was not on the slip of paper he carried in his wallet so he would have to call his wife and ask her to look it up. He dialed the numbers and waited for her to answer the phone.

"Hello."

"Hi, Emily, could you look up a number for me?"

He said it as fast as possible—he was in a hurry. There was a long pause on the other end of the line. No doubt, Emily was trying to figure out what the problem was.

"Em, you there?"

"Well, yes, Dear—I love you and miss you, too!" Her hurt feelings translated themselves perfectly over the phone lines.

"Oh, I'm sorry Em. How are you?" He could see that he would not be able to escape an explanation to Emily.

"Well, fine. How are you? Are you O. K? What's wrong? Is Lissa O.K.?"

"Yes. We're all fine. I just need you to look up Tom Harris's number in my Rolodex there, on my desk."

After a few minutes, Emily came back and gave him the number. Then, she began asking pointed questions. "Why do you want to call Tom? Are you sure everything's O.K.?"

"Yes, Emily. Stop worrying. I just have a few questions here that I think he can help me with."

He paused, trying to think of something to say to her that would stop her worry. "How are Chris and Jacob?"

"They're fine—you know, the usual. They've been practicing for Thanksgiving dinner. I can hardly keep anything in this kitchen."

"That's good. Well, I've got to get off this phone. Tell them all 'Hi' for us." Emily held the phone out at arm's length and looked at it with a perplexed look on her face. What was he up to?

155

With Emily's paranoia smoothed out, he pushed the button down, then lifted it again to dial Tom's number. It rang repeatedly, then activated Tom's voice mail. Damned! He forgot it was a holiday for them. Maybe he could find him at home. That number also activated an answering machine. He hated those things. Tom must be traveling.

He did not have any better luck contacting Eric or Susan. He would have to handle it the best he could without their help.

"Come on!" he said to Allan and Lissa as he came around the corner. "Let's get back to our patients."

When Ruben came out to meet them, his face told them that things had gotten worse at the Colonias. Jaime was doing all right and Lucinda was apparently following the same course as Jaime. But Jaime's eight-year-old brother, Rudolpho, was much worse.

His fever was showing no sign of coming down. His flesh had taken on a dusky color and his gums had started bleeding. When Mike examined him, he found subconjuntival bleeding and the small, blood spots called petechiae on his abdomen. He was beginning to wonder if Rudolpho was suffering from something different from Jaime's disease.

Mike had read about viral diseases like this. There were a few hemorrhagic viruses around, some of which had made news lately. Ebola made all the headlines, but it was supposedly limited to the African continent. Or sometimes, it was spread by contact with African monkeys or fruit bats.

"Ruben, ask Jaime if he has been around any monkeys."

Jaime assured them that he had not. Now, Mike was confused. He had three patients with the same symptoms and one secondary with very different symptoms. He had never seen anything like this. He did not think Ebola would cause symptoms like this, and Jaime never developed the hemorrhagic symptoms.

Jaime saw the confused look on Mike's face. The doctor was having a hard time helping his brother. He looked off to a corner of his hut and a feeling of fear for Rudolpho came over him. Wondering if he had brought the disease home from his job troubled him and made him feel guilty. He quietly asked Ruben to interpret for him.

"Doctor, what do you think it is?"

Mike crossed his brows and slowly shook his head. "I'm not sure."

Jaime's guilt would not allow him to wonder any longer. "Do you think I could have brought it home from my job at the Macquiladora? My friends think that is where I caught it from."

Mike did not think it had anything to do with Jaime's job. The living conditions here were so bad that Jaime's job was at the bottom of Mike's list of possible sources of the disease. Still, he saw the concern in Jaime's face.

"Where do you work?"

"At the Macquiladora on the highway."

"What do you do there?"

"Luis and I were putting small papers on postcards. Then, we put them in a box."

"How could you get sick from doing that?"

"I do not know, but Miguel tried to tell us that it was a bad place. He said it was a factory of death."

This peaked Mike's curiosity. "What did he mean?"

Jaime told the whole tale of the others getting sick and disappearing, along with their families. Mike listened, trying to figure out what had happened. He looked at Ruben for confirmation.

"It is true, Mike. Some of the people have disappeared. And they did work at the same plant."

None of this made any sense. How could working at a plant have anything to do with getting sick and then disappearing?

"Tell me about the cards."

Jaime used his hands to show Mike the size of the cards.

"They were this big, and they were white, with big red letters on one side and blue letters on the other side. They were wrapped in clear plastic."

"What did the words say?"

"I do not know. I cannot read. Somebody said they said something about a new smell."

Allan had come into the hut a little earlier and had heard the whole story. "I bet it was that plant we saw when came in. The one that said something about the mail. You think there's something there infecting the people?"

"Could be. I've read accounts of factories, in Africa, and other places, that infected their workers with diseases carried by bats and other vectors.

That part about the families disappearing is just strange. Probably just a coincidence."

Grandmother sat next to Lucinda, stroking her hair. She did not know English, so she was not following the conversation. Struggling to rise to her wide feet, she walked over to Ruben.

"Ruben, I remember this sickness in Mexico City when I was young. Some of my cousins died from it. One cousin is blind now. It is so bad. Does the doctor know what to do?"

"Not yet. Did you say you know this disease?"

"Yes."

Ruben stepped closer to Mike and grabbed his elbow. "Grandmother *knows* this sickness."

"What? What did you say?"

"Grandmother *remembers* this sickness."

Mike looked over at Grandmother. Her eyes held the wisdom bought by a hard life, and she was trying to tell Mike something.

"What is it, Grandmother?"

Grandmother spoke to Ruben for a few minutes, pointing to her upper arm and waving with other gestures. After she quit talking to Ruben, Ruben turned to Mike.

"She says she does not know the name of the sickness, but she remembers what her parents did when everyone was getting sick."

"What?"

"One person had a shot that made a sore. They put a needle into a flame and let it cool. Then, they picked at the sore with it. They picked at another person's arm with the same needle. That person was also safe from the sickness."

Mike turned to Allan. "God! You know what she's describing, don't you? A vaccination. A Smallpox vaccination. She's seen Smallpox and she says *this* is Smallpox."

Mike paced to the other end of the hut, rubbing his chin. "But how could Jaime and Luis get this from working at the plant?"

He had the feeling that he was putting together some sort of message with a whole bunch of words missing. He still was not convinced that he was dealing with Smallpox, though it was getting easier to believe. He had to confirm his suspicion in the lab or he would never be able to convince any-one, including himself.

The next morning, Mike and Allan did their best to save Rudolpho, but he never regained consciousness. The blood found every orifice of his young body to ooze out of and left the boy still and lifeless before the sun even came up on the Colonias. Jaime bowed his head and wept while Lucinda and Grandmother openly wailed at their loss. There was no consoling them. Rudolpho had been the baby of the family. Jaime blamed himself completely.

To make matters worse, Mike saw that Grandmother was beginning to get sick, herself. He knew that she would not get a severe case, but he also knew that she was old, and would not be as able to take it as a younger person would. Her fever was mild and she was up and around.

It was Lucinda who had taken a turn for the worse. Blisters in different stages covered her face and arms. Some were filled with clear liquid; others were filled with pus. A few had broken and scabbed over. Her face grew so many of them that it looked like someone had spilled soap bubbles all over it. When she grimaced, some of them split, oozing their contents.

Mike could see her developing the signs of encephalitis. He did not think she would make it. Yet, as with Rudolpho, the very mention of taking her in to the hospital utterly panicked Jaime, causing him to shake his head frantically in refusal. He feared that Ramon would hear that they were sick.

At one point, Mike and Allan tried to take her in, despite Jaime's objections. Mike looked over and saw Jaime resting, apparently in a deep slumber. Mike motioned Allan out of the hut. "Let's take her while he's not looking. I'm beginning to think that the paranoia may be a part of the disease."

They quietly came into the hut and began preparing to transport her to the hospital. Jaime suddenly awoke and saw what they were doing.

"No. NO!" His voice was loud enough to wake Maria and Grandmother.

Mike and Allan ignored him and continued their plan. But Jaime jumped up, holding his head for a few seconds as the blood came back to his head, and he went out of the hut. Mike and Allan could hear voices calling in Spanish outside. Suddenly, the cloth door flew open and Miguel stood there with Luis and Jaime. Miguel stormed into the hut with his fists clinched and began yelling at Mike. Mike could not understand him, but he could see that he meant business. When Mike did not respond to whatever Miguel was yelling, Miguel suddenly slid his hand around his back, pulling the seven-inch blade of his knife out of its sheath tucked into the back seam of his pants.

Mike looked at the angry young Mexican in front of him. Miguel had hunched down slightly, and was shifting his weight from foot to foot, as he held the blade firmly pointed at Mike. Mike threw his hands up in apparent surrender.

"O.K., O.K.! Never mind!"

Ruben ran into the hut. "Miguel! No!"

Mike shifted his gaze to Ruben for an instant. "Tell him we're not going to take her."

Ruben quickly translated the message to Miguel, who relaxed some, but did not immediately put down the knife. He kept his glare on Mike, watching him to make sure that he kept his word. Then, Jaime came forward to talk to Ruben. He gestured towards Mike as he rattled his Spanish to Ruben.

"He says that Miguel will make sure you do not take any of them to the hospital. He says not to even try."

"Tell him O.K., fine."

Ruben spoke to Jaime, who nodded to Miguel. Miguel looked intently at Mike, then stepped outside of the hut. But, Mike could hear him as he stood guard duty at the entrance.

So much for getting his patient to a hospital. It probably was not a good idea anyway. If it was anything like Smallpox, Mike did not know if the medical personnel would be able to keep them isolated well. It might serve to spread the disease more.

Then Lucinda developed encephalitis. The intense pain and mental confusion drove her family out of their meager hut, sobbing inconsolably for her. Still, her death seemed easier than Rudolpho's bleeding death.

Mike, Allan and Lissa all loaded into the car to go back to the clinic. It was time to check the eggs for final proof. As they drove up to the clinic and walked in, they did not see the man sitting in the waiting room with his wife. Any group of Anglos caught the attention of the people here. Anglos did not normally use the clinics in Acuna, and this group of Anglos just walked into the back rooms of the clinic without waiting. The receptionist did not even react to their inappropriate behavior. She just let them go to the back and simply smiled at them as they went past her. So the man in the waiting room decided that these Anglos must be important somehow. He moved to the chair nearest the door so he could hear as much as he could.

Mike led the way to the incubator. "If it really is Smallpox, these eggs should show it by now. Of course, it's not the best way to prove it, but it is one more piece of evidence to take to the authorities."

"Who are you going to tell, Dad?" Lissa had never seen her Dad in such a worried state.

"I'm not sure, yet. I tried to call Tom the last time we were here, but I got no answer. Every authority I'd want to talk to is on Thanksgiving Break now. I'll try Tom's home, or maybe Susan's."

Mike carefully lifted the eggs from the incubator. He peeled the shell from one of the eggs gingerly. Immediately, his worst fears were confirmed.

"Damn! There it is. Big as you please. Look at those lesions. Classic Smallpox." He paused, rubbing his forehead on his forearm. "I had hoped that I'd be feeling a little silly at this point. You know...like I'd gone over-board."

It was Allan who broke the silence. "Now what?"

Outside the door of the lab the man in the waiting room had heard all that he needed to know. How fortunate that his wife had been sick that day. He knew that he could find a buyer for this information out there some-where, and this time he knew where to go to sell it.

He pulled up into the abandoned parking lot of the Macquiladora. There was only one truck parked there. He smiled as he recognized that it was Ramon's truck. His buyer was inside.

Ramon came to the door. He was miffed. He had told this man never to come to the plant, but it did not matter now. He relaxed a little.

"What do you want?"

"Senor Terrazas, I have information that I know you will find interest-ing."

Ramon was tired of this man. He thought he would never have to deal with him again. The plant was closed now, and he was trying to get ready to leave. What could this man possibly have to tell him?...And how much would it cost?

"How interesting?"

"The same as before."

Ramon was amazed. He had already paid this man too much.

"Impossible. What do you think is so interesting?"

The informant could see the hesitation on Ramon's face. He'd have to give him a taste. "An American doctor knows."

"What?!" Ramon had thought that he was home free. In just a few hours he was taking off to Cuba with Cecelia to board another plane back to Iran.

"Well, is it interesting, or not?"

"Yes. It is interesting. What? What do you know?"

"An American doctor is at the clinic on Juarez Street. He has done some tests and says it is Smallpox. The receptionist said they were working in the Colonias."

No! Ramon could not believe it. He had checked on those two workers himself. They could not have hidden it from him. And why an *American* doctor? Where did *he* come from? He paid the man and got a description of the American's car. He quickly went in to use the phone. He dialed the number.

"Yes, it's me again. We have a situation. You must take care of an American doctor in the clinic on Juarez Street. Make sure he does not get out alive. There's a big bonus in this one."

After pushing the receiver button down, he picked it up once again and dialed a different number. "This is Senor Ramon Terrazas. We have had a burglary at the plant. The thief could be trying to get out of Mexico. There will be a large reward for the Federales who catch him."

After giving the Federales the description of the car, Ramon hung up the phone. This was not part of the plan.

• • •

The red, older model Chevy Blazer cruised slowly down Juarez Street, its muffler purring roughly. The four men inside it searched carefully along the sides of the street for a certain vehicle. When they found it, they parked several cars behind it, and began their preparations. The automatic pistols had been carefully kept low in the Blazer until now. The puffy-faced man in the front passenger seat turned around to face the others.

"They are still there. All we have to do is wait. They'll come out soon enough. Be sure this time. Ramon wants these bad enough to pay big money."

Inside the clinic, Mike was trying to convince the clinic doctor of the danger of the virus. Allan translated as Mike explained what he had found on the slides and in the eggs.

"Allan, tell him that we disinfected the lab with the formalin, so he does not have to worry about spreading it from there. Tell him to watch for other patients with the same symptoms."

As Allan talked to the clinic doctor, Mike searched for the phone again. He had to get in touch with Tom, or even Susan. He had the proof he needed now so he searched in his pocket for the paper with Tom's number. Then, he went through the other pockets. It wasn't there. Oh, yes. He had left it in the car. He stepped around the corner to the lab.

"Liss, I'm going out to the car for a second. I left Tom's number in there. Be right back."

He paced out of the lab, through the crowded waiting room, and squinted slightly as he stepped out of the clinic door and faced the sinking sun to the west. Holding his hand over his brow to block the blinding light, he made his way to his car.

The puffy-faced man waiting in the car jumped to life. "That's him!"

All four doors of the Blazer flew open at the same time, spilling their intent passengers out suddenly. The automatic pistols were in plain sight now; the men were not even trying to hide them as they ran towards Mike.

Mike heard the commotion, but could not see what was going on because of the sun in his eyes. His first hint of danger was the whizzing sound of a bullet as it passed just in front of his nose. His Reserve training took over and everything seemed to go into slow motion. He dropped down and rolled behind the front wheels of a truck parked in front of the clinic.

From this location, he could see his advancing attackers because the hood of the vehicle blocked the sun from his eyes. Who was shooting at him? He had never seen them before. This had to be some kind of mistake.

But the men kept firing at him. So he dove and rolled into the protective doorway of the clinic. The waiting patients had vaulted from their chairs and screamed in terror as they ran to the back rooms of the clinic. Shards of glass from the shattered windows followed them, hitting them like thousands of tiny glass daggers. Mike could see Lissa and Allan looking out at him, their mouths hanging open in panic. The clinic doctor was shouting something in Spanish, shoving the patients into his office. Allan searched for a back exit.

Mike could barely hear him as he shouted. "There's no way out!"

Mike turned around and saw the men closing in on him as they were almost at the clinic. Suddenly, a white flash streaked past them towards the door of the clinic. It was the doctor, racing out to try to stop the men from killing his patients. His white coat seemed to stop the men momentarily. They were not expecting their doctor to run out towards them. They paused.

Mike jumped on the opportunity to grab Lissa and Allan and race out the door to his car. He could hear the doctor pleading for the men to stop shooting. The puffy-faced leader began to yell at him, then at the other men. Then, the leader simply pointed his pistol at the doctor's face and pulled the trigger.

The bullet hit its target, sending blood and fragments of the doctor's shocked face flying in every direction. The red spray came down on the white coat, leaving huge splotches scattered on the arms and shoulders.

As Mike saw the redness of the blood, his panic heightened. These men were out to murder them. He was already in the driver's seat, and Lissa and Allan scrambled into the car as fast as they could. He saw the men aiming as he gunned the motor.

Allan hastily opened the car door for Lissa, a gentleman even in the end. Just as he ducked his head to get in after her, the first bullet shattered his shoulder blade and continued on through to his right lung. The shocked look in his eyes turned to panic, then brief surprise, as the second bullet entered on his left side on its burning way to his pounding heart. The fear in his eyes slowly faded as he slumped over and Lissa, screaming and crying at the same time, pulled his limp body into the accelerating car.

A pool of Allan's blood collected on the floor of the car. They did not know who was trying to kill them, or why. It did not matter at the time. They just had to get out of Mexico. And fast.

Then, as Mike sped up to the tollbooth, the once-lazy Federales came to life. Just as Mike reached for his toll dollar, the two men in the booth began excitedly chattering in Spanish and radioing for backup. Mike glanced at Lissa's contorted face. The gravity of their situation dawned on her at the same time. As Mexican Federales in khaki uniforms vaulted towards the car, Mike and Lissa flung the doors open hard, scrambling out to the relative safety of the nearby small, painted adobe buildings.

Mike did not know who had bribed the persistent Federales to stop them at the border. It did not matter. They ran in and out of darkening alleys, dropped into peeling doorways and tripped over huge snaking cracks in the sidewalks as they scurried away. The zinging of bullets whizzing past them spurred them on.

Suddenly, all those hours of exercise and running paid off. Mike and Lissa were in better shape than the Federales. The loping soldiers soon dropped behind the refugees and lost them in the milling crowds gathering close to the silty river to take an evening bath. Mike and Lissa slowed down to avoid notice and tried to look natural. Dressed the way they were, in their dirty jeans, shirts and caps, they looked like they belonged there.

They briskly walked along the muddy river, passing scattered groups of sad-eyed people cooking on campfires fueled by dung. As long as they kept their eyes looking down, nobody noticed their blue eyes. Further down the old river, groups of men in faded plaid shirts held their plastic water jugs and bundles of meager belongings above their heads as they slowly waded across the thigh-high brown water of the Rio Grande River.

Mike and Lissa waited, then they crossed too. Periodically, Mike nervously glanced over his shoulder, searching for persistent Federales. It grew dark and the clouds in the sky effectively blocked out any light the moon may have graced them with. The icy wind began to blow from the north, signaling the arrival of the predicted northern.

The thin path they had taken was not a path made by people. Wandering goats must have carved it out of the West Texas wilderness. The bare caliche was randomly dotted with low, green prickly pear cacti that grabbed at their jeans at every opportunity. One of the hateful thorns penetrated right though the front of Mike's shoe, permanently embedded so that the small tip stabbed at his big toe every time he took a step. In the race away from danger, he did not have time to stop and perform the surgery required to remove it.

The clumps of rocks scattered everywhere were the same beige color as the caliche, so it was hard to avoid tripping over them. Once tripped over, they still did not get out of the way. They rolled in the same direction as the foot and managed to get under it a second time. Then, they slid and gave way under the weight of the foot. Lissa lost her balance once, painfully catching herself with her right hand in a waiting clump of spiky catclaw.

A foraging skunk meandered out from under a mesquite bush and crossed their path. They stopped short and allowed the respected critter plenty of space.

They heard a light scratching sound to their right, and stopped to look at it in case it was another skunk, but it was only a hungry armadillo, frantically digging in the soft dirt under a bush in the hopes of snagging some fleeing insects. It did not even look up as they went by.

The screech of an owl in a scrub-oak tree startled them and the plaintive howl of a coyote warned them of its presence in the vicinity. They heard other strange sounds that they were not able to identify.

What was he doing here? He was a physician, not a super-spy. Even in his Air Force Reserve training, he had not been trained for this. Now, with all the unpleasant events of the last few days, he was beginning to become a little paranoid. None of this made any sense. But slowly, an ugly picture of the realities of the situation began to take form in his exhausted mind. Surely not. It couldn't be.

Mike noticed that Lissa was walking slower and rubbing her temples. He knew how she felt. They had not slept the night before in the intense effort to complete the necessary lab tests. They were past tired.

As Mike lost the fight he waged with his eyelids, the slow realization diffused into his dreams. Now that the clinic doctor was dead, he and his daughter were the only professionals who knew about the virus.

Now, if he could only manage to stay alive long enough to get the information to the authorities.

Escape

A demanding itch pulled Mike from his fitful sleep. He rubbed his burning eyes and looked around, trying to figure out where he was. He had no light to turn on, not even a flashlight. The overwhelming darkness confused him even more, and made the chill of the November night sink deeper into his aching bones.

Lissa! He frantically felt around in the enveloping darkness and found the soft, muscular curve of her arm. His reluctant eyes were beginning to work now. He could barely see the silhouetted outline of his daughter's athletic form sleeping close to him to stay warm.

The Purple Sage bush and its rooted mound of caliche dirt supplied the only shelter from the nippy wind that could be found. Lissa and Mike, knowing they could not take another step, had ducked under its cover, hoping to be able to hide and sleep there for a while.

Mike kicked the stalking scorpion off his soggy shoe. Two days ago, if he had done the same thing, it would have at least given him a rush of adrenaline, but all of his adrenaline had been consumed in their frantic escape. He calmly picked up a rock and crushed the toxic vermin.

He sank back against the reassuring mound, and his eyes fell on the beige cap on Lissa's head. A sprig of her blond hair peaked out along the grimy bottom edge of the cap.

Suddenly, he remembered what he had been dreaming about. LICE! Blood-sucking, pestilence-carrying lice! Tingles began to crawl with imaginary creepies all over his chilled skin. A repulsive shiver followed down his spine.

It had seemed like a good idea at the time. Actually, it was a move made on pure panic impulse. In the hurried chase, Lissa's golden-blond hair attracted too much attention as she ran down the squalid streets of the filthy, crowded border town, trying to escape with her father. Mike grabbed the cap off the greasy head of an older boy sitting on some stairs that led up to an unseen room. They hurried off and ducked into another doorway. Lissa quickly tucked her blond hair up into the covering cap. Along with her dusty bluejeans, tennis shoes and stained long-sleeved shirt, the cap helped Lissa blend perfectly with the other street urchins.

Now, in the relative safety of the Sagebrush mound, Mike had time to worry about the unpleasant possibility of lice. Oh, well. If that were the worst that came out of this little adventure, they would be very lucky. The choice between the blood-sucking lice and the murderous bullets was an easy one.

He knew that the dull ache that had settled over his body was not solely caused by the lack of sleep. How long had it been since they had seen the first case? About six days now. Perfect timing.

The sun began to come up in the distant east. An eerie glow covered the horizon. Mike knew what direction they needed to go now. Lissa stirred as the whine of two jets zooming overhead disturbed her restless sleep. She awoke with a start and sat up, looking at Mike with a sleepy, confused look on her face. Then she quickly surveyed the area in every direction.

"Did they find us?"

"No, I think we lost them. At least, I haven't seen them. Lissa, take that cap off your head!" Mike would not be able to rid himself of that creepy-crawly feeling until Lissa took the filthy headgear off her head.

"Sure, Dad," answered Lissa. She looked almost hurt by his curt command. Apparently, she had not had the same disgusting dream that he had.

"Sorry, Liss." He did not mean to come across so harshly. Lissa began to cry.

"Oh, God! Poor Allan. I can't believe what happened!"

"I know," he paused. "How do you feel?" Mike saw that she looked pale. All her crying had swollen her eyelids. He felt a little unsteady himself.

"A little weak, I guess. And I keep getting a chill."

"Yeah. Me, too. It doesn't surprise me."

"What do you mean?"

"The fact that we had vaccinations doesn't mean that we won't have any effects."

"But we won't get it, will we?"

"No, baby." Mike hoped he was not lying to his daughter. The way he felt now, he was not so sure. He also knew that they might be contagious. The more he thought about it, the less he knew.

The deaths they had witnessed had been horrifying.

What was it? The evidence could not be right. He felt for the wrapped slide he had managed to rescue from the lab. Still there.

The flight of the jets overhead reminded Mike of their position. As they had driven towards Del Rio on Hwy. 90 on their way to Mexico, they had passed the sprawling Laughlin Air Force Base on the south side of the road. Now, he knew where they must go. The sun slowly warmed the chilly air. A merry-go-round of vultures circled overhead just to the south of them.

"Come on. We've got to go now." Mike knew they were only getting weaker, and they had not had any water since yesterday afternoon. He was running out of spit to swallow. As they trudged on, Mike could not think clearly. What did all this mean? His suspicions about the disease sounded paranoid, even to himself. What could he say to the authorities to make them believe him? He knew that the minute he explained the events of the past few days, they would all consider him to be certifiable. Could all of this be some sort of hallucination?

He knew the answer as he heard Lissa's sobs start again. They got up and let the sun lead them in a northeast direction.

LAUGHLIN AFB

Tony Espinoza sat on the stool in the tiny guard shack. He looked handsome in his blue Air Force uniform, according to his new wife. He had gotten to the Security Police building by 6:45 to relieve the SP on the night shift. The tired SP gladly turned the duty over to Tony, reporting that the night had been more than boring. Well, at least there would be some traffic in the day shift to keep him awake. He looked forward to the next rotation.

A few cars entered and left through his lonely gate. Even though this was the back gate to the air base, it served as the closest exit to use if a driver wanted to go to Eagle Pass. He checked each entering car for its required sticker and saluted as it drove by. At this gate, he did not even have the opportunity to answer questions from the occasional visitor that would come to the base. All visitors used the main gate.

Two hours later, the sun had climbed higher in the sky and, even though it was late November, the heat slowly intensified. Tony always marveled at the two-month winter of Southwest Texas. A person only needed a coat for December and January here, and there were several days in even those two months that were too warm for winter clothing. At least, it was not the summer season that often graced local residents with weeklong spells of 100-110 degree temperatures.

As Tony mused on all this, he looked up through the glass of the shack and saw something moving far away, across the highway. He rubbed his eyes in an attempt to make sense of what he was seeing. It did not work. So he stepped out of the shack and squinted toward the approaching apparition through his sunglasses.

The outline of two people formed as they came closer. They were walking toward him. Illegal immigrants always crossed in this area, but none of them were so stupid as to walk up to the Air Base gate. What could they be thinking? Maybe, they had some sort of emergency. It looked like the boredom of the morning was about to be broken.

As he stepped closer to the highway, he saw why the two images kept blending into one. One of the wanderers leaned on the other for support. Their faltering steps were dragging, kicking up the caliche at each move.

They could not be illegals. As they moved closer, he saw that the shorter one had blond hair. She was a young woman. The other one looked like a man. He could not see the man's hair because he wore a sweat-stained cap. Tony saw the misery on their faces as they approached the highway, so he began to walk towards them.

"Stop," stammered Mike. "Don't come any closer—for your own sake!"

170

The Plan

Laughlin Air Base, Thanksgiving Day

Mike was barely able to stand there, supporting Lissa's weight on his own shoulder, as the young Security Police guard stared back at him. Confusion was replaced with suspicion in the inexperienced guard's eyes. Mike did not blame him.

Their narrow escape from Mexico had been harrowing, and Allan was dead now. That thought, alone, kept the reality of the situation alive in Mike's head. Still, the temptation was to hope that all of this was a simple case of paranoia. He did not want to believe what he knew to be true. The determination quickly returned as the picture of Rudolpho's gruesome death replayed itself in his mind. Many more people were in grave danger of suffering the same way Rudolpho had. He had to warn somebody.

Tony Espinoza carefully watched Mike as he tried to decide what to do next. "What do you mean? Why shouldn't I come any closer to you?"

"Look, we could be carrying a lethal virus. If you come any closer, you might get it. Stay away."

The young guard was still having trouble comprehending the problem. Mike suddenly remembered his Reserve training. "O.K.—I'm officially declaring myself to be a possible biological agent. Please call your Medical Group Commander, Col. Richard Mulligan, and notify him of the situation."

Tony did not like people in civilian clothes giving him orders. He knew what he was supposed to do so he left Mike and Lissa standing outside and went into the shack to call the Command Post.

Mike could see Tony in the shack. The guard was on the phone, talking excitedly into the receiver and gesturing to them. Mike could make out what he was saying.

"He's insisting on seeing the Medical Group Commander, Sir...Just two, Sir...one male and one female, Sir...Yes, Sir."

Tony stepped out of the shack and quickly returned to his original position in front of his visitors. "I've notified the Command Post. They're on their way."

Lissa's weight was becoming too much. Mike lifted her arm off his shoulders and gingerly lowered her to the gravel. She smiled up weakly at him to let him know that she was all right, then he turned back to face the road and wait for the authorities. The guard kept his distance, but looked over at them periodically with a curious look on his face. Nothing in his training covered these events.

Finally, a convoy of navy blue vehicles made its way hastily down the road to the shack. Mike was apprehensive and his stomach was churning slowly. What could he say to them that would convince them of the gravity of the situation?

The convoy came to a stop, raising a cloud of caliche dust that drifted over the vehicles with the slight breeze. Men in blue uniforms spilled out of the doors and paced towards Tony. So far, Mike did not see his friend in the group. Then, another van rounded the bend in the road and joined the line of parked vehicles. Dr. Richard Mulligan stepped out of the passenger's side, squinting towards Mike and Lissa. He scrutinized the pair of visitors who had caused all the commotion. Then, a familiar smile came over his face.

"God! It's you, Mike! What the hell do you think you're doing?" He glanced down at Lissa. "Is she all right?"

Mike shrugged. "I don't know, Richard. We've been through a lot."

"What's all this stuff about being a biological agent?" Richard began to walk towards them.

"No. Don't come over here without proper gear. We've been up to our elbows in something—something fatal and contagious. I know you're probably going to think I'm crazy, but I think it may be Smallpox."

At this announcement, Richard stopped walking and gave Mike a strange look. He could see that Mike had been through some sort of trauma...maybe too much trauma to make sense. Lissa's hunched form on the ground told him that Mike might be holding up well to a very bad set of circumstances.

"What happened, Mike?"

Mike gave him a condensed version of the events of the last few days, explaining the symptoms of the disease carefully. "And I don't know if we're contagious. She and I both have had vaccinations within the last year because of our work with related viruses. But our clothes may be saturated with it. We were in the trenches with it...up close and personal."

Richard turned to one of his men and told him something that Mike could not make out. The man headed off to the van at a trot. It was apparent that Mike had been out in the South Texas sun for too long. Richard certainly did not believe that Mike had been working with Smallpox. It had been eradicated thirty years ago and he had just read a report that it was now extinct. The authorities had announced that the last cultures at the CDC and in Moscow had been killed in a much-publicized event. Mike's allegations were impossible.

Further, he had not heard anything about a shoot-out across the border. If the Mexican authorities had wanted to catch him, they would have alerted all of the law enforcement people on both sides of the border. He had not heard a whisper. Still, he could see that Mike had been through something. He was obviously too stressed to be rational. Richard decided to humor him.

"O.K., Mike. We're taking you in. If you're carrying anything, it's only on your clothes and possibly your skin. If we can avoid direct contact with you, it shouldn't get to us. We'll put you in isolation to make sure. Don't worry."

"What about notifying the CDC? Somebody's got to get on top of that situation. It's bound to spread."

"O.K., Mike. Don't worry now."

With that, Richard turned and called out orders to his men. Mike was not sure of what he had expected to come out of his announcement, but this was not it. Richard did not even seem to react. He certainly showed no understanding of the danger. Mike could not help feeling a little let down and confused. Didn't anybody else see the problem? He turned to Lissa and went to help her get ready to move. The men transported them in isolation to the base hospital in Dr. Mulligan's van.

As they entered the hospital, Mike noticed that the place was very busy. The nurses were rushing around with frenzied looks on their faces, trying to tend to the many patients. Richard saw the look on Mike's face.

"We've got a flu outbreak, I'm afraid. Must've been a strain that wasn't in the flu shot. Most of these people have had their shots."

Mike's eyes widened. "Are you sure it's flu?"

Richard saw where he was going with that question. "Well, doesn't it look like flu to you?"

Mike had to admit that these patients had the appearance of people suffering with flu. Many of them wore pained expressions as they rubbed their temples or shivered uncontrollably. But he'd been fooled once already this week.

Then, as they turned the corner, Mike noticed it. It sat innocently on the desk at the nurse's station, totally ignored by everyone passing by it.

A postcard.

A simple postcard.

A simple postcard with a scratch-n-sniff section. It had been scratched off already. It was exactly as Jaime had described it.

"Wait!" called Mike as he came to a halt in the hallway. "That's it. That's one of the postcards my patient was telling me about."

Richard stopped and looked back at Mike. The poor man was worse off than he had thought. Now, he was getting paranoid over a postcard.

"O.K., Mike. We'll check it out."

Richard led the way into the isolation room Mike was to be staying in for the day. He hated to see his friend in this state. Richard knew that Mike would be embarrassed over it all later on.

"Look, Mike, we're going to let you rest in here for a while. Just take it easy. Get some sleep. I'll be back to check on you later."

With that, Richard turned and exited the room, leaving a frustrated Mike to wonder what to do. Lissa drug herself over to one of the beds covered in stiff, white sheets and plopped down on it with a sigh of relief. Mike watched as she fell to sleep within two minutes. Then, he admitted to himself that the other bed looked much more inviting than the red, vinyl-covered chair in the corner of the room. He sat down; planting his weary body on the lower portion of the bed as it creaked in protest. His eyes grew heavy. He was exhausted. He decided to close his eyes for just a few minutes to rest them.

• • •

The clear, blue sky was quickly replaced with dark, ominous clouds. Lightening danced erratically in the clouds. Then, he saw it. The tornado was the biggest he had ever seen. The thick, black core reached all the way down to the earth, shifting its destructive path unpredictably. It was moving too fast. Mike could feel the debris hitting his face with increasing force, until every particle stung, forcing him to raise his arm to cover his face. Still, all he could do was stand there. He saw people being swept up into the voracious beast.

"IT'S COMING! COME ON...LET'S GO!"

But nobody could hear him. Or maybe they were all ignoring him. He grabbed a few of them, and tried to get their attention by shaking them. But, they just kept gazing off into the view, as if they could not even see the killer.

"It's just a rainstorm," one person said.

As they refused to listen to his warnings, the tornado grew larger and more fierce by the second, engulfing everyone in sight. Then, it seemed to notice *him*. It leaned its huge, spinning top towards him, and its tail soon followed. As it got nearer to him, he could see and smell that its core was made of rotting death. He screamed, but no sound came out of his mouth. When he finally got his voice back, the roaring of the tornado drowned out any sound he could make. He tried to run, but his feet locked themselves to the ground. He struggled and pulled his legs as hard as he could. No good. All he could do was wait to be eaten alive by the great beast, which abruptly grew huge fangs. Suddenly, his wife and family stood next to him. They seemed to be pulled towards the swirling mass. Lissa was the only one able to resist the power. He reached out and grabbed onto the others, but he could not hold them. The force of the monster sucked them into the blur. Then, all he could see was blur. Once, he thought he could make out an arm—Chris' arm—but it was covered with awful sores and bruises. Finally, the Blur began to rend his skin from his body.

• • •

Then he awoke.

The light in the room had changed. He snapped his arm up so he could read his watch. He had been sleeping for an hour. Lissa snored quietly on the other bed. Then, he remembered where he was. He sat up quickly and rubbed his eyes.

Nobody had even been in to check on them. He could hear the nurses as they walked down the hall. "You got 26B?"

"Yeah, what about 23A?"

"No time. They're sleeping anyway. The other shift is waiting for report."

"God! Have you ever seen anything like this before?"

"No. And I hope I never do again. We're out of beds. The next one that comes in will just have to ride it out in the hall."

"Must be some other strain than what they predicted. These people are pissed. They say they got the shots, but they're catching it anyway. All I can say is that I'm glad my shift is over. I've got a killer headache and my back's in total rebellion. I can't wait to get home and off my feet."

"Me, too."

Mike quietly got up and walked over to the door. He pulled the door open and looked down the hall. The place was chaos. The personnel scurried around trying to take care of all their patients, but it was not working. Mike could see that the food tray bus was still sitting in the hallway. Normally, it would have been removed many hours ago, after lunch. Partly filled out charts sat, unattended, on a cart nearby. Heads would roll over that if things were normal.

He closed the door. It was obvious what was happening. This was not a flu outbreak. It had spread out of Mexico, and he could not convince anyone of the problem. He had to get a message to Tom or Susan before it spread any further.

He buzzed the nurse's station. The flashing red light blinked repeatedly, but he got no answer. He knew he probably would never get one. He noticed the phone on the nightstand next to the bed. When he picked up the receiver, the dial tone sounded a little strange. He started to dial, but the phone started ringing on the other end after the fourth number had been pushed. Apparently, he was on some sort of hospital line. He'd forgotten to dial 9 to get an outside line. He hung up the receiver and picked it up again. When he dialed 9, a recorded voice began to speak.

"I'm sorry. All outside lines are in use at this time. Please hang up and try again later."

Damn! He had to get in touch with Tom. Hearing a nurse come down the hall, Mike hurried to the door and stuck his head out to speak to her.

"Nurse! I need to use the phone to call a colleague of mine. The one in here isn't working. Is there something wrong with the lines?"

The nurse slowed momentarily. A confused look came over her face. "Dr. Mulligan didn't leave any instructions about you using the phone. I don't think he meant for you to be talking on the phone. You are supposed to be resting right now."

"You mean I'm not allowed to make any calls?"

"I don't think so. If you'd like, I'll ask Dr. Mulligan the next time I see him."

Now, it was Mike's turn to wear the confused look on his face. "Yeah. If you would, please," he said, knowing that he would not be able to do any better.

He stepped back into his room and closed the door. Apparently, he wasn't in isolation at all...more like house arrest than anything else. Now he knew that Richard thought he was crazy. So much for trusting him! He would have to do something else. The alarm had to be sounded somehow, only now he would have to get past Richard to do it.

Lissa's rhythmic snoring changed its pace as she began to wake. She turned over and peered out of one eye at her father. Mike knew what he had to do. He began to search around the room. He opened the door to the restroom and walked in. Lissa could hear him rattling something. When he returned, he had several empty toilet paper rolls in his hand and in the other hand, he gripped their brown paper covers. His determined eyes searched the room for something else.

He stepped over to the portable IV console and began to attack it. He pulled at the back of it frantically until the cover came off. Then, he reached inside and quickly removed the batteries and put them in the pile with the other things he had collected. He was not finished yet.

Tape...He needed tape. He peeked outside of the room. All clear. He quietly walked down to the deserted nurse's station and opened the desk drawer. He ripped off three long strips of the tape he found, closed the drawer and returned to the room. He hung them on the edge of the bed stand.

After he stuck two of the rolls together, he stuffed tissues into the middle until they were full except for the outer two inches on both sides. He put one large battery into each end and stuffed more paper in after them. Then, he taped each end to keep it all from falling out. He made another one just like the first one. He unfolded one of the paper covers and turned it so that the labeled side was facing up as it rested on the table. Carefully placing the two rolls he had just constructed on the label of the paper, he wrapped them in the paper and taped the ends tightly. Then, he began to pull on the IV console again.

This time, he dislodged a rectangular piece from the console. It had plenty of knobs and buttons and he taped this to the outside of the brown paper covered bundle. He was not finished yet.

He picked up the TV remote control and began to remove it from the chain that secured it to the bed. He looked at it with satisfaction and stuffed it into his pocket.

Mike could feel Lissa watching his efforts. Her confused look told him that she did not understand.

"Lissa, we have to talk."

Lissa answered him. "Why, Dad? What's wrong? What are you doing?"

"Listen very carefully to what I have to say. I may have to do something in a little while that you never thought I'd do. I just want you to understand it. You're going to think that I'm crazy...everybody else does. And when I do it, maybe I will be."

Plan B

Laughlin Air Force Base, Thanksgiving Afternoon

Mike spent the next few minutes outlining his plan to Lissa. Lissa listened with her mouth slightly open in disbelief. Every few words, she tried to interrupt with a small "but" to try to understand what her father was telling her.

"Look, it's obvious that they're not going to let me get a call through to Tom or Susan. Take a look out in the hall and you'll see that it's already spread to this Air Base. I've got to alert the authorities before it gets any further."

"But, Dad, do you really have to do all that? Can't you just sneak out and use a phone somewhere else?"

"I thought about that, Lissa, but it's the holiday and I just can't get through to anyone by phone. This is my only option."

"But what if something happens to you?" Her exhaustion led to tears streaming down her cheeks over the thought.

"It's going to be O.K. I have to do it for people like your mother who haven't been vaccinated. I just have to."

With that, he pulled Lissa to him and held her tight. He was not so sure as he had just let on. In fact, he was scared to death. This type of desperation went beyond his basic nature. He let go of her and held her back at arm's length to look into her eyes.

"Just do what I told you to do...and remember that I love you."

"O.K., Dad. I love you too," she answered renewing the stream of tears.

Mike turned and walked slowly to the door. He opened it carefully and peered out. This time he did not want to be seen. The halls were still busy, but all of the people in the halls were patients or their families. The staff was, as Mike had hoped, gathered in a small room with charts. They were discussing the patients and filling the next shift of nurses in on things they needed to know.

He stepped out of the room and strolled down the hall like he was supposed to be there, smiling amiably at the people he passed. Everyone ignored him. As he reached the nurse's station, he noticed the postcard still sitting on the desk in the corner. He nonchalantly turned into the station and walked over to the desk to retrieve the card. He wanted this for evidence. He stuffed it into his pants pocket with the slides he'd made in Mexico.

So far, everything was going as planned. His heart stopped momentarily as he suddenly saw two Security Police standing at the entrance of the small hospital. They looked tired and bored. That would work great for Mike. He strolled right past them, smiling and tipping his head slightly. They hardly even saw him. The chaos of the place made him nearly invisible.

As he rounded the corner on the sidewalk outside, he came to an abrupt stop. He saw Richard across the parking lot by the van. Fortunately, Richard was facing the other way, talking to another man in uniform. Mike turned around and quickly walked out of sight in the other direction. When he got to the other side of the building, he stopped and looked around. He knew what he was looking for. It just took a few minutes for a landing T-38 to show him the way he needed to go. It was not very far from the hospital to the landing strip.

He walked on the sidewalks along the manicured lawns, avoiding attracting any interest from anyone. His pace was steady and confident, even though his mind was far from sure about he was about to do. Maybe he was crazy. But he did not know any other way.

As he neared the hangars, their large size began to intimidate him. Who did he think he was? This was the United States Air Force for pity's sake. How did he think he could do this? These were not stupid, untrained people here. No. On the contrary, he knew that these people knew their stuff. And they had been trained to prevent the very kind of event he was about to cause. He kept his mind on Emily and how he had to protect her. He was the only one who could protect her now. That thought kept him from simply turning around and going back to the hospital. It had to be done.

The personnel at the hangars were also in the process of changing shifts. Mike stepped into one of the hangars that was the closest to the T-38s parked on the runway. There would only be a skeleton crew on duty anyway because of the holiday, not to mention the sickness. As he surveyed the inside of the building, the slight whistling of the wind outside made the hangar seem even emptier. Now, he needed to make himself a little more inconspicuous.

His searching eyes fell on a pair of light blue overalls that were hanging on a hook at the opening of a short hallway. He looked all around the room one more time to be sure nobody was there. Then, he walked quietly over to the hallway and slid the overalls off of the hook. He scanned the small area for a utility closet and stepped into it to put the overalls over his own clothes. Just as he was putting his last shoe back on, he froze. The sound of the two male voices approaching his location caused his heart to race and reminded him to be careful.

"Man, it's slow today. At this rate, the day is going to last forever."

"Well, at least we'll get off for the Christmas Holidays."

"Yeah, but I still wish the day would go faster."

"Cheer up. Luke is due in any minute now. That'll give us something to do."

The voices faded down the hall and out into the hangar. Mike waited for a few minutes, then he cautiously opened the door to peer out. All clear. The sound of huge engines approaching the hangar drew him out to take a look.

He grabbed a clipboard from a nearby desk and casually carried it over to a door facing the runway. He saw two men standing just outside the door, facing the nearing T38. He assumed that these were the men he had just heard in the hallway. A dark blue jeep drove up to them and a young member of the Security Police jumped out, grinning broadly as he came closer to the two men.

"O.K. What are you grinning about, now? Don't you have anything else to do but come over here and bug us?"

"Sure I do. Like finding my way to the mess hall. Now, all I have to do is find a place to take a big nap. You have a TV anywhere?"

"What?" The noise of the T38 grew louder now.

"That was the best pumpkin pie I ever ate. Even better than my mother's. Course, my mother never cooked any. But you gotta find your way over there today. There's mountains of food and not many people to eat it. They'll give you all you want."

"That explains why we can't see your belt buckle!"

By this time, the T38 had taxied up to the front of the hangar and the pilot slipped out of the cockpit. He had to unfold to get out of it because he was so tall. Luke Shipman stretched for a second. When he pulled off his helmet, his close-cut black hair stood out in contrast to his pale blue uniform. He pulled off his gloves as he came near the other three men.

"So why is everybody in such a hurry to refuel me? You'd think it was a holiday or something."

"Yeah, yeah. We're coming. Don't remind us." The taller man motioned to the other man and they went out to the T38 to refuel it.

Luke continued over towards the Security Policeman, smiling. "What's eating them?"

Mike stood quietly behind them as they watched the men in their refueling task.

Luke looked around. "Sure is quiet...that must be some kind of damned flu."

"They're all out with it. Wouldn't surprise me if they closed the flight line."

Luke and the Security Policeman stood facing the T38 with their arms folded. Mike saw the pistol in the SP's holster. It had probably never been used except for target practice. That was about to change.

When the two men who were refueling the T38 turned and walked towards Luke, they were shaking their heads. Mike had to duck back behind the door to avoid being seen.

"O.K., it's ready Hot Shot. What's your big hurry anyway?"

"Just keeping busy, I guess. I just can't stand the boredom today."

It's now, or not at all, thought Mike.

He sprung out from the door and grabbed the pistol from its resting-place at the side of the startled SP. Everything began to go in slow motion as the SP reacted and turned, using his leg in a full-swing kick aimed at Mike. Mike jumped to the side, avoiding the kick, and grabbed the pilot's left arm, causing him to turn with his back facing Mike. With the pistol pointing to the pilot's head, Mike began to back up slowly, pulling the pilot by the arm that was now forced high in his kidnap victim's back.

The SP, who was now recovering his balance, looked up and realized the situation. The other two men stood there with their mouths hanging open. The SP began to come towards Mike, his pupils narrowing.

"Stand back, or I'll shoot him!" Mike yelled in his most authoritative voice. He had to convince the SP of his sincerity. The pilot began to struggle, but Mike pulled up harder on his arm. "Be still!"

"What do you want?" yelled the pilot.

"We're taking a little ride. Get into the T38. Don't try anything stupid or I'll shoot."

The SP stood by, his hand still absently grabbing what should have been the pistol in its holster. There was nothing he could do to stop Mike without endangering Luke.

"Hey, man! Don't be stupid! You're just gonna get yourself killed pulling a jackass stunt like this. Let go!" he said, trying to persuade Mike.

"Don't try to stop me!" Mike shouted as he climbed up into the back seat of the cockpit.

Luke put his headgear on his head and began to set the controls. The madman behind him was probably capable of anything right now. He had to think fast. He knew that once he got up into the air, it would be a question of who was the hostage of whom. Of course, he would never do something suicidal, like purposely crashing the T38. Still, he began to formulate a plan that would keep the thief from having control over the powerful hardware. God knew what the lunatic was planning to do with it.

The control tower passed them as they taxied down the runway.

"Where to?" Luke asked.

"The public airport at Atlanta, Georgia."

Mike could see the other pilots scrambling for their aircraft in response to the attack. His only guarantee that they would not blow him out of the sky was the pilot. Mike began to worry about the pilot. He was being way too quiet.

Like he was calculating something.

OLD FRIENDS

SAN ANTONIO, TEXAS—
THANKSGIVING AFTERNOON

Emily caught the phone on the fourth ring, just before the answering machine took over. The Caller ID announced that the call was from Laughlin Air Base. She did not know anyone there, but she knew that Mike did. It was probably something about the Reserves.

"Mom."

The familiar voice of her daughter caught her by surprise. What was Lissa doing at Laughlin Air Base?

"Lissa? Why are you calling from Laughlin Air Base? Is everything all right?"

The sobs that began pouring out of the phone answered that question. "No, Mom. Everything is terrible." She paused to blow her nose. "I can't...I don't...I don't even know...how to tell you what...what has happened. And now Dad..." The sobs began again.

"Dad, what? What has happened? Is your Dad all right? Lissa! Talk to me!"

"Oh, Mom. There is this outbreak...of Smallpox. Then, some men...tried to shoot us. Allan is dead. We got away across the river but now...Dad is...Dad is...CRAZY!"

"What do you mean? Did he get shot?"

"No, Mom...At least, not yet."

"What do you mean, 'not yet'? Slow down. Tell me everything. Please!"

Lissa filled her mother in on all the events of the last few days. When she recounted what Mike had told her in the hospital room, Emily nearly dropped the phone.

"He said he was going to do *what*? God, he *is* crazy! Well, where is he now?"

"He told me to wait for an hour after he left before I called you. He's been gone for an hour and fifteen minutes, now. He said he wanted you to get hold of Tom or Susan somehow. He didn't have Susan's or Eric's home phone numbers. He said to tell them everything and to tell them that he would be flying into the public airport at Atlanta...on the T38 he hijacked! Mom, he's crazy! What are you going to do?"

Emily thought about it for a second. "I suppose I'll do just what he asked me to do. What else *can* I do? Now how can I find Susan?"

Mike had done plenty of other crazy stunts before...just for entertainment. But this...this was past crazy. She went to work on the problem, trying not to imagine her Mike as a hijacker. Oh, yes. Susan had a cell phone number that she gave her on the card she sent them announcing her change of address in Atlanta. Emily just had not put the number in the address book yet. Now, where was that card? After she found it, she rang the number.

ATLANTA, GEORGIA

S usan would never have dreamed that she'd be sharing Thanksgiving with Tom. She had been working with him on her job at the CDC. After all this time, who would have guessed it? But there she was, not only enjoying her time with Tom, but also wearing his ring. They had decided on a Christmas wedding with all the trimmings that she could throw together in such short notice. She had so much to do.

First, she had to send the invitations to a whole bunch of people who were not going to believe what they were reading. She and Tom had been such good friends for so long. Suddenly, they were getting married? It did seem strange, even to her. The minute the invitations were sent the phone would ring off the wall.

RING!

Wait a minute, she had not sent any invitations yet. And that was her cell phone ringing. She had turned the ringer off on her other phone. Who could be calling?

"Hello?"

"Susan? This is Emily Thompson. I'm sorry to call you on your cell phone, but I couldn't get hold of you on the other one."

"That's O.K., Emily. I had the other phone turned off. Is everything all right?"

"Well, no. To be honest, you are probably not even going to believe what I'm about to tell you. You have to, because we need your help."

"Well, what's wrong, Emily?" Susan had all sorts of awful scenarios rushing through her mind. Emily told her the whole story. Nothing she had imagined was as bad as what she had just heard.

"God! When did he leave?"

"I'm not sure. Maybe about thirty minutes ago."

"O.K., I'll see what I can do from here. We don't have much time. Stay by the phone."

She pushed the end button on the cell phone and jammed it into her purse. Tom was sleeping on the couch in front of the football game.

"Tom, wake up! Major emergency! Wake up and listen. Mike's in trouble and he's on his way *here*!...in a T38 he *hijacked* to get here. We've got to do something."

LUKE

ABOARD THE T38

M ike looked out of the cockpit and saw the two fighter jets that had been tailing them since their take-off from Laughlin. His stomach was queasy, but he couldn't let it interfere with his plans now. So far, the pilot was simply doing as told, but he was not sure how long that would last.

"I know you think I'm crazy, but there are some things you don't know about. I don't want to hurt you. I just have to get to Atlanta...now."

Mike began to tell Luke about everything that had happened. Luke was not really listening. He was thinking.

"I know what you're thinking," continued Mike.

Luke answered him in his mind. *Oh, no you don't, Buddy or you'd be plenty worried right now. I'm not your hostage anymore. You're my hostage,*

186

and right now, we're headed straight to the Gulf of Mexico where I have a little surprise for you.

Mike kept talking. "And they have distributed all these postcards laced with the virus. They're everywhere. I got this one off the desk at the nurse's station at Laughlin. You want to see it?"

Mike pulled the card out of his pocket and waved it in front of Luke's face. Something uncomfortable began to nag at the back of Luke's mind. He had seen that postcard before, or one just like it. Could it really be covered in a deadly virus like the madman was saying? Maybe he wasn't a madman at all. What if he was right? Many of his friends had been out with a strain of flu, even though they had all gotten the flu shot together. What if it *wasn't* the flu? He began to listen to Mike's ranting. The only crazy thing the man had done was to hijack his T38. That was pretty crazy. But wouldn't that be what he would have done if it had come to it and he felt that national security was at stake? Something about Mike told him that this was not really a madman.

Suddenly, Mike reached up and over his seat and unzipped the first six inches of Luke's flight suit. Before Luke could even react, Mike slipped the "Bomb" into the suit and zipped it back up.

"What?...What was that?" Luke sputtered.

"Insurance."

"What do you mean *insurance*?"

"Just in case you're planning to do something stupid like ejecting. I've got my finger on the detonator and you do not want me to let go!"

Luke could see the "detonator" with Mike's finger lightly pushing on one of the buttons.

O.K. Maybe he was a madman after all. Luke carefully turned the T38 to a different course and dropped all thoughts of ejection. O.K. He wouldn't do it. Besides, if he ejected and let Mike ride it out alone into the Gulf of Mexico, he'd lose his favorite T38.

SUSAN

ATLANTA, GEORGIA—THANKSGIVING DAY

They did not have much time. Susan did not know how long it would take a T38 to fly to Atlanta, but she knew she had to beat it to the airport. She had made a few quick phone calls and found that nobody wanted to be bothered on Thanksgiving afternoon. The director had given her complete control of the situation.

Tom pulled up to the door of the building where they worked and let Susan out, before he parked his car and followed her. The lot was nearly empty because of the holiday. Susan talked into the phone with one hand as she ran around her office grabbing things with the other. Tom stuck his head into the office.

"Come on. We'll need the suits."

"Right."

"Hurry. You know the Air Force is already moving into position."

"Yeah. The Guard is already on the way. They'll meet us there."

They ran down the empty halls to the lab that held the Racal suits that would be used to protect them from any contagious disease they might encounter. Carefully checking to see that the batteries and air tanks were fully ready, they grabbed two of them and raced out the door. The security guard peeked into the room to see what all the rush was about.

"Sorry, Ben. I'll explain later. Major rush."

With that, they bound out the door.

When they got to the airport, the National Guard unit that Susan had called in was already there, waiting for them to arrive. They were checking their weapons and gathering on the sidewalk. Tom had pulled the CDC van right up to the sidewalk, totally disregarding the sign prohibiting parking in that spot. This was official business, after all. A curious crowd had collected around the Guard unit.

Susan jumped out of the van with her helmet tucked under her arm. The rest of her suit already covered all of her body except her head. When

Tom joined her, he was just beginning to struggle into his suit. Susan took the opportunity to address the Guard.

"Gentlemen, this is a tense situation. We may be forced to take action against both the Airport Security and the United States Air Force if they do not comply with the orders of the Secretary of Defense. We have orders to take two men into custody. These men may be carrying a lethal virus. It is imperative that Dr. Harris and I are the only ones that come in direct contact with these men."

She looked down the sidewalk and saw the vehicles that told her that the Air Force version of a SWAT team waited already inside, probably getting ready to blow Mike away.

"Let's go."

Susan and Tom took the lead as they pushed their way through the holiday rush of travelers. The hurrying patrons turned and watched them as they noticed them heading towards the boarding gates. Suddenly, the crowds disappeared, leaving a clearing. At the end of the clearing, the Air Force team, readied themselves to receive Mike. The sharpshooters had already begun to set up. A quick glance out at the runway told her that they had arrived at the airport before Mike. There were no Air Force aircraft out there.

One of the Air Force men looked up as Susan boldly marched into the cleared space towards the group. He straightened. "Colonel Packer, look over there." He pointed to Susan as she neared them.

The Colonel's eyes narrowed as he turned to face her. Who did she think she was? Nobody was allowed to be in this space at this time.

"This area is off-limits right now. Turn around and leave immediately."

His barked order did not even slow Susan down. She kept coming towards him at a steady pace. "What is your name?"

"My name is Colonel Packer. I have the authority to have you arrested immediately if you do not leave."

"I have been given authority by the Department of Defense to apprehend the two men on the T38. They may be highly contagious with a lethal virus. Your men are not trained in such apprehension techniques. My orders supersede any you've been given."

"Like Hell! We've got a kidnapped pilot and a hijacked T38 and we'll handle it the way we see fit!"

189

"I don't think you understand the situation. Anyone coming close to either of these men is in grave danger of contamination. Our orders from the Secretary of Defense take precedence over your orders right now. Stand down!"

By this time, Susan was standing face-to-face with Colonel Packer. The Colonel glared at Susan. The veins on his neck stood out and his face was so red that Susan could almost feel the heat coming from it. Still, she did not back down. She could feel her own face growing red.

The men who were with the Colonel stood holding their weapons, ready for anything to happen at this point. The Guard unit behind Susan waited tensely to see if the Colonel would give in to Susan.

The silence was broken by the squawking of a radio in the hand of one of the men in the Colonel's group.

"Sir, the T38 is on radar now."

Rescue

Aboard the T38

"We're approaching the Atlanta Airport now." The pilot had been silent until this announcement.

"Good. That did not take long. Looks like we kept our tails the whole way."

"Yeah. And they'll land right along side of us."

The pilot fell silent again for a few seconds. "Are you sure you want to do this? You know, of course, that the sharpshooters will be training their weapons on you the minute you get off the aircraft."

"I know. I guess I just have to take that chance."

This time, it was Mike who grew silent. Luke glanced back...and saw that Mike's finger was no longer pushing the button. Wait a minute...he should have blown up when Mike's finger came off that button.

"What's wrong with your detonator?"

Mike looked down and saw that Luke had seen his finger off the button. He looked up at Luke's questioning face. Then, he picked up the remote, pointed it at Luke and pushed a button, smiling.

"I just changed your channel."

"What?!!"

"It's just a TV remote."

"Well, why the hell did you tell me it was a detonator?"

"Just like I said...Insurance."

"Damn!!! And the Bomb in my suit?"

"Batteries and toilet paper rolls...Sorry."

"Well, I'll be damned!"

Luke surely did not want anyone to know about that. But, Mike was not gloating in his trickery right now. He was worried about his exit from the T38.

"Look...if...if they...kill me...show them what I'm carrying in my pockets...try to tell them what I told you. I'd hate to get this far...and still not get the message sent."

The pilot disengaged his radio. "What is your name?"

"Mike Thompson."

"O.K. Mike. I think you may be onto something. I disagree with your methods, but I can almost see your line of reasoning. If you're right, my family has also been exposed...and that thought scares me. Maybe, I can help you out...some. I'll be your hostage...I won't struggle or anything. Keep me right by you...and move around a bunch...the shooters won't be able to take you down...I think."

Mike could not believe what he was hearing. For the first time, somebody partly believed him. He could sure use any help he could get right now.

As the T38 rolled to a stop, Mike's stomach began to tighten in anticipation of the next few minutes. He was fully aware that they might be his last. "Let's go. I'm sure they'll be here any time now."

The pilot released the latch that held the cockpit closed, and they both got out, stretching from the long time of being cramped up in the T38. From the distance, they could see the flashing lights of the emergency vehicles heading their way in fast-moving lines. Many of them were blue, telling Mike that the Air Force was arriving in force. The cold wind made their eyes sting as they watched the arrival.

191

"Well. Take your hostage...now."

Mike pulled the pistol out of his pocket and held it up to his hostage's head. He kept the safety on, though, so that nothing would happen to his new partner. Luke brandished a pained expression for the benefit of his expected audience.

The vans and cars screeched to a halt a little way away from them. The doors flew open and uniformed men yelled and jumped out in all directions, hiding behind the vehicles. Mike kept his grip on Luke and moved around as much as possible to avoid the aims of the weapons trained on him. He began to wonder if this would really keep him safe.

Suddenly, a white van pulled forward. Mike could not see what the words on the side read. The side doors slid open and two figures appeared in the doorway as they stepped out of the van. They were wearing bright orange RACAL suits, complete with helmets, and they were walking directly for Mike and Luke.

"Stop, or I'll shoot! Don't come any closer!"

The two figures stopped immediately in response. A very red-faced Colonel picked up a bullhorn and addressed Mike. "These people have come to take you into custody. Go with them peacefully, or *we'll* shoot." The man seemed to be angry. It was almost like he wanted to shoot him.

Mike saw no need for the stolen pistol in his hand now. He carefully lowered it to his side and bent down to place it on the runway.

The figures began their approach again. Mike could not see their faces because the facemasks were so fogged up on the inside. They gestured to Mike and Luke to wait there, then they came on up to them. From a bag that one of them was holding, they pulled out a folded material and shook it to separate the sides. It was some sort of headgear with a filter and an oxygen mask attached. The taller figure gestured for the two men to put it on their heads. Mike and Luke looked at each other in wonder and shrugged. Then they did as they were told. It was better than being shot on sight.

The orange figures each took one man by the arm and began to escort them through the group of soldiers that had now moved closer to them. Mike did not understand why he felt so comfortable with this unexpected change in his plans. They walked through the mixture of Air Force and National

Guard soldiers, suddenly grateful for a peaceful exit. Mike did not know where they were taking them, but he did not care at this point.

They reached the white van. Mike could now make out the words on the side. The emblem of the CDC was plainly displayed. The orange figures allowed them to get into it first, before they followed and pulled the door closed behind them. The taller of the two climbed into the driver's seat and started the ignition. With a hard turn, the van retraced its entry path onto the runway and exited the gate.

So far, the people in the suits had not spoken to Mike or Luke. The two prisoners looked at each other across the van, not having a clue about their destination. Mike could not stand it any longer. "Where are you taking us?"

The suited figure in the back of the van with them reached up to loosen the helmet of the suit. Mike could have swallowed his tongue when he saw the familiar red hair that had been hidden in the fog in the helmet.

"God! Susan! What...How...How did you know?"

"It's O.K., Mike. Emily called me and told me what you were up to...or at least she tried to explain. Do you know how close you came to being killed right there? What the hell did you think you were doing?"

"How did she get you? I tried several times and there was never an answer."

"On my cell phone. You still haven't told me what you're doing?"

By this time, Tom had struggled out of his helmet. He turned for a short glance at Mike.

"Tom! What are you doing here? I've been trying to call you at Ft. Detrick. Why are you here?"

"I'll explain later. What the hell is wrong with you? How are we going to explain this? Start talking!"

"Well, what did Emily tell you? Lissa was supposed to call her. I don't know if she got it straight. What did she say?"

It was Susan's turn to demand answers now. "It doesn't matter now. Start from the beginning."

JUSTIFICATION

CDC—ATLANTA, GEORGIA— THANKSGIVING DAY

It took the whole trip from the airport to the CDC complex for Mike to try to explain the events of the last few days. Susan rubbed her hands through her hair nervously as she listened intently to what Mike was telling her. She never took her eyes off him. Mike felt like she was trying to decide whether or not to believe him. When he finished his explanation, she continued to stare at him with the same questioning doubt on her face.

Finally, they drove up into the driveway at the back of the building that housed Susan's office. She had stopped any pretense of believing that Mike and Luke actually carried any infectious disease.

"Come on."

Mike had a sinking feeling in his gut. What if his own friends did not believe him now? He remembered the slides and the postcard in his pocket. His hand reached down to make sure they were still there.

"Let me show you these slides. Oh, and I have one of the postcards."

They were walking quickly down the hall to the elevator now, as Mike fished in his pocket for his evidence and tried to keep up at the same time. Susan led the way into a reception area that separated her office from the hallway. Mike stopped in his tracks.

There, in the trash can, a little postcard exactly like the one he had in his pocket lay proudly across the top of the other refuse in the can. It had already done its job. The scratch-n-sniff section was mostly scratched off.

"Oh, My God!" He stared at it in disbelief. Up until now, he'd been convinced that it was a local infection. Suddenly, it was clear to him that this was more than just a coincidence. Those cards were apparently everywhere. This was done on purpose. But what purpose? It made no sense. Who would want Smallpox to come back?

"What?" It was Susan.

"That card. It's exactly like the others."

194

This time it was Tom who spoke to Mike. "Look, Mike. I don't know what your problem is, but it's got to stop...now. I don't know what you've been treating, but it could not be Smallpox. It's been eradicated, and now it's extinct. You know...there are plenty of other viral diseases with similar symptoms. Monkeypox produces exactly the same symptoms, at first. Did your patients have any contact with squirrels? You said they did not have much to eat. Maybe they hunted squirrels. If they ate any unprocessed organs from them they could catch the disease. They don't have fuel to cook with, do they? That is just one possibility. And as for your slides, that test is only presumptive anyway. Now you've gone and gotten us all involved...and it's probably only some new sort of Chickenpox or something. What if you're wrong, Mike?"

Mike felt his face grow hot in anger. His fists clenched subconsciously. He knew what he'd seen—hell, he'd nearly been killed finding out about it—and these people had the nerve to doubt his integrity. In the mean time, a fatal epidemic was spreading unchecked through the country. Friends or no friends... they were wrong!

"But what if I'm right? What is *wrong* with you people?! Why can't you see what's going on here? What do I have to do make you understand the situation? Millions of people are going to die as it is—we have to stop it *now* before it gets any further."

Susan could see the determination on Mike's face. "O.K., it sounds pretty gruesome...and it's a good thing you've alerted us to it. But stop ranting about it being Smallpox. That's impossible...and it makes you sound insane or something. Let us check it out. It'll only take..."

The sound of her cell phone ringing interrupted her. She reached for her bag and fished out the phone to answer it. "Hello?...Oh, Hi, Emily. Yes. He's right here and he's still in one piece...though I still don't know how. Here he is."

Susan handed Mike the phone. "Em! Are you O.K.?...Well, read it to me then...Oh, My God! Listen to me. DON'T open that cellophane wrap. Burn that card...now!"

Susan and Tom couldn't stand it any more. "What?"

"So you think I sound insane, do you? Well, Emily just opened a package from Malik in Iran. It appears that he may be insane also! Read it again to me slowly, Em."

Mike recited the words of the note to Susan and Tom.

"Mike, I am so sorry to have to tell you this news. But I hope it is not too late to help you some. It appears that our friend, Sadeq, has been very busy preparing a biowarfare attack on the U.S. His plans are to use Smallpox since we can vaccinate our own people against it. Please advise your government to prepare enough vaccine and begin to distribute it immediately. I do not know the timing of the attack, but I know it will be soon. I have tried to tell you this sooner, but Sadeq has managed to keep me quiet. Your friend always, Malik."

They stood in the office just looking at each other. Finally, Susan blinked hard and broke the spell. "O.K. Damn it! You were right. Now, we have to act and we have to act fast! It may be too late already."

"What do you mean?"

The quiet in the building began to swallow them. It was more than just a holiday emptiness. Suddenly, Susan remembered. "We, the CDC, are in the middle of a *flu* epidemic right here at our building. Gentlemen, I think they may have thrown one of the first bombs right here in our midst...and we didn't even notice it."

Tom grabbed the phone and punched in numbers furiously.

"Who are you calling?" Susan was asking as she turned to work on the computer keyboard.

"Detrick. I've got to know if they're also having a *flu* outbreak."

"Have you two been vaccinated lately? I have because of my lab work. It's the same with you, right?" Mike asked.

Susan and Tom looked at each other for a second in thought. "Yeah. A year ago," was Susan's answer.

"Same here," added Tom. Then, he scowled. "The last time Smallpox was used in biowarfare was by the Colonists against the Indians...right before they massed an attack against the natives."

Mike caught his drift. "You don't suppose..."

Susan pushed her chair rolling back from her computer so hard that she nearly fell back. She caught herself. "Shit!!! I can't believe it."

196

"What?"

"We were actually in the process of eliminating our stocks of vaccine! There are only two thousand doses left. God!! What are we going to do now? It'll take at least three weeks to make more of it." She looked around. "And that's when we have a full house. Only the people that work with the Orthopox viruses are vaccinated. That's only a fraction of us. How are we going to make enough that fast?"

"Well, don't count on your two thousand doses, either," said Tom.

"What do you mean?"

"I work with the military, Susan. I can tell you that the second they get wind of this epidemic, they'll be knocking on your door to confiscate it."

"What for?"

"For the generals and the politicians, the *important* people in the world!"

"But what about the rest of the us?"

Tom just shrugged.

FIRST WAVE

NEW YORK CITY—THANKSGIVING DAY

D r. Joel Rudman massaged his temples in an attempt to ease the pain behind his eyes. It just was not fair. He was not supposed to get sick. He was supposed to be the doctor. How was he supposed to help the patients when he was sick? And he had taken the damn flu shot. But, apparently that did not matter. His patients had been telling him the same story all week. Why couldn't the people in charge of predicting the flu strains get it right?

The acetaminophen he had taken had not even come close to lessening his agony. Even his hands hurt as he grabbed the bottle of ibuprofen, wincing as he struggled with the childproof cap. He was beginning to feel weak. But, he had to keep going. Much of the staff had called in that morning to say that they could not make it to work that day. Every one of them had the flu.

Outside, in the waiting room, the growing masses of sick people would soon be pressing down the door, especially if he did not step up the pace. He could not call up to the floors for reinforcements. Most of their staff members had also not shown up that day. Some had not even called in. They just did not get there. Nobody had time to check on them.

The patient rooms brimmed over with moaning patients. Many of them were unceremoniously dumped in the halls. The few nurses that had reported to work moved in slow motion like Dr. Rudman. They refused to give in to the pain. They just kept working, as if working would protect them somehow. But even those began dropping into chairs in exhaustion as the day progressed.

The ringing in his ears increased until it finally began to drown out the constant sound of his name being called. He looked through his headache as he moved in his surreal surroundings, barely responding to the people around him as they spoke to him. The automation that his body had learned through years of ER service kept him moving in some sort of order, though he did not fully comprehend all the stimuli around him. Something kept him going...he did not know what.

He had a very hard time getting anything done because the patients kept wandering into the ER, since there was nobody directing them out in the waiting room. It took precious time and energy to convince a worried relative to go back out and wait with the others, especially since he had not dared to show his face out there in the last hour. Every time he did, the crowd ran toward him and he had to use more energy and lots of headache to yell at them to get back. He could have really used some security.

Once again the doors opened and Joel braced himself to yell at whoever was coming in without being called. He took a deep breath and turned around to attack the intruder, but he stopped as soon as he saw a policeman at the door.

"Finally! What the shit took you so long?! Get out there and keep them off my back! I can't work like this. Just keep them out of..." Joel's words choked back into his mouth as he watched the expression on the policeman's face turn into a grimace. The huge man tensed as he drew his revolver and pointed it at Joel.

Joel's mind saw all of this in slow motion. He saw before him something that did not make any sense...but why change things now? Abnormal was now the normal. This whole scene fit neatly into the day's activities. Suddenly, Joel was too tired...it was too much. He dropped his hands to his side, looked deep into the man's eyes and shook his head. "So shoot me, Man...Please."

The big man struggled and nearly shuddered as he looked around him slowly. The hardness in his eyes melted and moisture gathered into tears. His hands shook as his holstered his revolver. He dropped his head and blubbered, "I...I'm sorry. I just...I don't know what got into me. It's just that my...daughter...Jennif..." Great sobs escaped from the man as he buried his face into his hands.

Fueled by the adrenaline jolt, Joel moved over to the man and grabbed his arms. "Where is she?"

"In the car...the traffic jam...too far to carry..." The man looked up at Joel. "Can you come take a look at her?" Joel could only pity the poor man. He looked him in the eyes.

"I'm so sorry. There's just nothing I can do for her now. I'm out of medicine...Just go back to her and be with her...I'm sorry." The hopelessness of his situation sank in to his weary mind. There was no hope. He could not help Jennifer...he could not help any of them...he was too tired now...he had to rest. He sat down, put his head on the desk and closed his eyes. He could hear his patients calling to him from their beds in the ER. They had been waiting there for about an hour. But Joel could not bring himself to let go of his temples and go tend to them. He slowly drifted into a fitful sleep.

It was an unfamiliar sound. The knocking. The pounding. It seemed to beat in the same rhythm as the throbbing in his head. Then, it stopped. Dr. Joel Rudman looked up just in time to see the panicked crowd rushing towards him. He closed his eyes and felt every finger as they gripped him, shaking him out of pure frustration. But the pain faded away slowly, as Dr. Joel Rudman slipped into unconsciousness.... Just in time to escape the worst.

Roger Ellings backed away slowly from the mob squeezing into the door of the hospital. His back hurt so badly that he sat down on the curb slowly. He could see Celeste at the end of the mob. She was pushing with all her might. Roger had seen her curled up in a ball, rocking and holding her head earlier. Life on the street was never private. He had risked walking up to her to see if he could help. This time, she did not run away from him...she stopped her rocking for a few seconds and peered out at Roger with one squinting eye. They had leaned on each other all the way to the hospital, a few blocks away. They knew they needed some help.

But Roger could see that they were not alone. Something was very wrong at the hospital. People of every description had waited patiently in the biting wind until a sudden panic had taken over. Now, the crowd shoved into the hospital until no more bodies could fit in the lobby.

Roger remembered seeing some of the people before when he had been there two weeks ago. The ragged family with the sick little girl was back...only now there were three sick children. The father held one on each shoulder and the mother balanced another on hers. The parents looked sick. They were flushed and they squinted their eyes against the light. One of the children in the father's arms looked as if someone had beaten her. Dark bruises covered her arms and legs. She lay so still that Roger thought she might be dead.

The piercing scream of police sirens silenced the angry mob, as the people looked up towards the approaching sound. The solid mass began to melt away as the people scattered in response. Roger slowly rose to his aching feet, turned and ambled back to his place on the street. There would be no help.

ASTRODOME—HOUSTON, TEXAS

S tan Lewis checked his watch for the date as he turned into the massive parking lot of the Astrodome. It was the right day, right? Yep. This was the right day. He had impatiently waited for today for two weeks. These tickets in his pocket were gifts that Russ had given him when he was resting at home after a mild heart attack. Russ had shown up after going to another game, baiting the old man with promises of the chance to go to the big game on the day after Thanksgiving. Russ had known that if anything would get Stan going again, it would be the hope of going to a game. So, Russ had promised to take him. Stan had done his part. He had recovered well from the attack. He had done everything he was supposed to do, including not smoking, so that he would be ready.

But when Stan had called Russ to see what time to be ready, Russ' wife had told Stan that Russ was sick that day. He had the flu. Russ had been too sick to talk on the phone, so his wife had told Stan to go on to the game and have a good time. That was just what Stan was going to do.

He had tried to call Jim and Larry, but they had the same flu. Then, he decided that he would go by himself. Surely, he could find someone to visit with there. He had read that the game was sold out. Maybe, he could scalp the extra ticket and give the money back to Russ. But, there were no people waiting to buy tickets.

In fact, Stan parked his car in the first row. This was a first. He always had to park a country mile away when he came to a game. As he neared the entrance to the dome, he caught a glimpse of a sign on the door. No, it couldn't be! Now, he knew why the few people who had shown up were turning and walking towards their cars.

The game had been canceled due to illness of a majority of the players.

HOUSTON, TEXAS

William Stephenson waited for the taxi he had called over an hour ago. It was a good thing he had given himself plenty of time to get to the airport. What was taking so long? He did not live that far away from the airport. He got out of his plush living room chair and went to the phone to call the company again. Just as he finished dialing the number, he heard a loud honk from the street. Pushing the curtains aside, he saw that his taxi was finally there. He hung up the receiver, grabbed his leather bag and his briefcase. He draped his coat over his arm, locked the door and set the alarm. The taxi driver honked again in irritation.

William took a good look at the driver. He was obviously of foreign descent. The man looked like he was from the Middle East. He wondered if all taxi drivers were that impatient. After all the time he had just waited, William did not appreciate having to hurry now.

He got into the taxi. "Airport, please."

"Sure. I am sorry to make you wait so long. There are only three of us working today. All the drivers are having the flu."

"Really?" William was not really interested in the taxi company's problems with personnel.

"But it will not be a problem getting there. Look. There is no traffic today."

William glanced out the window. Sure enough, the traffic was very light today. It looked like it did on a Sunday morning. William crossed his brow over that one. This was the day after Thanksgiving. The traffic was supposed to be hell with all the after-Thanksgiving shopping. This concerned William because his store was supposed to be having a big sales day today. Where were all the people?

The taxi screeched to halt in front of the unloading area of the airport sidewalk. No porters came out to help him. The parking lot was only partly filled and the airport was not crowded with holiday travelers as he had expected it to be. Another taxi pulled up behind his and a group of business travelers spilled out on all sides. Two of them were obviously sick.

"Come on. You'll be fine by tomorrow. It's probably just a twenty-four hour bug." The boss was trying to get them to hurry along so they would not miss their flight.

William took his carry-on and began his trek to the ticket counter. Only one person worked at the counter where there were usually at least three.

"Where is everybody?" William asked, smiling.

"They all called in sick. Oh, and I hate to tell you this but your flight has been canceled."

The attendant said this just as the small group of business travelers William had seen unloading caught up with him at the counter. The boss went ballistic. "What do you mean! It can't be canceled! We have to be in Miami for a meeting at one o'clock!"

"I'm sorry, Sir, the whole airline is down, except for emergency flights. Most of the personnel have that flu. You wouldn't want a sick person to fly your aircraft, would you?"

"Well, no, but..."

"I tell you, if I were you, I'd go home and hide out until this thing passes. It's everywhere. I'm probably going to catch it from some sick passenger." He suspiciously eyed the flushed young man standing behind the boss. "Are you sure the meeting is still on? I hear that many places are at a stand still. I'd check it out if I were you."

"Thanks."

William turned around to go back to the taxi stand. The boss cursed all the way behind him. William was going to have call his publisher and let him know that he would not be making it to the meeting. William did not cherish the thought of sending his book to him by e-mail. His publisher had promised him that they would try a new restaurant. Oh, well, maybe he could collect his meal the next time they met.

The small group stood at the taxi stand in front of the airport. There were no taxis to be seen anywhere. There were not even any buses. Come to think of it, William had not seen any buses running today. How the hell was he going to get home?

BOOMERANG

IRAN

"What have you done?! Are you crazy? Why didn't you talk to me first? Do you have any idea what you have done?" Sadeq pounded on the desk in front of him, then turned and continued his rapid pacing in front of it.

"Sadeq, it was time. We needed to begin the Holy War now, not later. It does not matter when we start it, only that we did. The evil U.S. should be feeling it by now. They are completely defenseless. The surprise worked, just as you said it would."

The council member was trying to keep up with Sadeq, but he only succeeded in intercepting him on his turns.

"But don't you see? *We* are not ready yet either! Our own people are not vaccinated yet. We have only vaccinated about thirty percent of the men...and none of the women!" Sadeq surprised himself with these words. He usually did not worry about the women. But one particular woman was on his mind now. His daughter was four months pregnant with his first grandson. The ultrasound had confirmed it just last week. A Grandson!

The Council member spoke calmly and soothingly to Sadeq, trying to slow his rage. "Sadeq, please try to understand. We have very carefully vaccinated the most productive members of our population. It will not hurt us to thin the society of some of the others. And we can start to vaccinate our most prized women now."

"You fool! It will take at least three weeks for the vaccinations to be effective! We may not have that long! It may already be here."

CDC

S usan pounded desperately at the keyboard as Mike and Tom frowned over her shoulder. At the final screen, they looked at each other in panic. The CDC was the main source of the vaccine in the world. There were only five hundred doses in Switzerland and the doses in India had been destroyed long ago because of storage problems. Israel did have about one thousand doses to spare. But even they had started ridding themselves of the useless stuff since the virus had been exterminated. That meant that there were only three thousand five hundred doses available worldwide.

"What can we..."

The door to the outside office slammed and they all snapped their heads in that direction to see why. The red-faced form of Director Charles Abbott exploded through the office door and went straight for Susan.

"What the Hell do you think you're doing?!!! I just got a call from the Air Force. Please tell me you have a reasonable explanation for your actions!...Well?"

Mike had never seen Susan stammer before. "Mr. Abbott, I called you ahead of time and you told me to handle it. I did just that."

"Yes, but did I tell you to barge in on a military operation and seize control? I don't remember that at all. But you stood there and told the Colonel to cease and desist his operation under *my* authority! Now, I have the whole Department of Defense breathing fire down my collar."

He stopped yelling long enough to look around the room at Mike, Luke and Tom who had backed out of the way and were standing there trying to look inconspicuous.

"And who are these people?...Oh, My God. These can't be the 'carriers' can they? What the shit are they doing in *here*? Why aren't they in the slammer?"

"The slammer is for people who are possibly infected with something that we do not want to spread. First, the main 'carrier' was recently vaccinated because of his lab work. Besides that, the virus has probably been spread all over the nation by now anyway!"

"What do you mean? I have not been alerted about any cases of Smallpox...anywhere."

"That's because it's in the early stages. Everybody thinks it's the flu. Wait a few days...then you'll know for sure."

"Damn it, Susan! That's impossible! What makes you so sure it's Smallpox, anyway?"

Susan gestured with her eyes towards Mike. "Maybe, you should talk to him."

Mike took his cue and explained the whole story to the Director. Charles Abbott just stood there listening in amazement with his brow crossed. When Mike got to the part about Malik's message, his doubting expression suddenly changed.

"And this man actually said that this attack was to occur? How did he say they would do it?"

"He didn't. The message was smuggled out of his nation in a can of caviar. There was not a whole lot of room for details."

Susan jumped back into the discussion. "We're confirming the virus identity now. It shouldn't take long to confirm the nucleotide sequence. But Mike, here, says he thinks he knows how they did it."

"How?"

"It has something to do with these scratch-n-sniff postcards. We're testing the scratch-off section for virus. If there is virus in it, anybody who scratched it would be effectively infected. Think about it. If they do not breathe it in sniffing it, they'll have it under their fingernails for later infection when the person rubs his eyes or nose. Sneaky. Really sneaky. And we don't have any idea how many of these cards were sent."

"Yes, we do" interrupted Mike. "A whole warehouse full, all the way to the ceiling."

Understanding began to cross the Director's face like a shadow. "Oh, God."

"And that's only half of the story. Only about three thousand doses of vaccine exist in the world." Susan wanted him to have the whole picture.

The silence in the room grew intense as everyone waited for the Director's response. But, he had no response. He was deep in thought and it was going deeper into a form of depression. How could this happen on *his* watch? He stood up straight and walked back out the door.

Susan waved him off as the door closed behind him.

"That man...I'd feel so much better if...*anybody* else was in charge right now. He's such a...hard ass! I don't like the way he got so quiet.... It means his little pencil-pushin brain is squeaking." She threw herself into a chair.

Mike's mind began to meander through the events of the last few days. A picture formed. He was standing in Jaime's hut one more time. Grandmother was saying something. What was it? Suddenly, he reached forward and grabbed Susan's shoulders.

"I know how to multiply the vaccine! The poor countries used this method when they could not afford to buy many doses of the vaccine. It's not like having enough for everyone, but it'll sure put a dent in the task." Mike saw the confused looks on the faces of the people in the room with him. He was moving fast in his excitement.

"What are you talking about, Mike?"

"One person gets a vaccination. When the blister forms, a needle can be used to prick at the blister and then on the arm of someone else. This can be done as long as the blister is still shedding virus. There's no telling how many vaccinations can be made this way from each one we have here. It just multiplies it. Jaime's grandmother in Acuna told me that that's how her people did it."

206

Susan added, "You'd have to be careful not to break through the inner layer of skin, or your donor could get pretty sick."

"That's right. But given this crisis, I think it might just be worth the risk."

"You're right, of course."

They spent the rest of the evening constructing a plan to best use the available vaccine. By the next morning, when the nucleotide sequence of the virus had confirmed its identity, the plan was complete. They triumphantly marched to the Director's office to fill him in on the plan.

Rubbing his sleepy eyes, Charles Abbott opened the door when they knocked on it. It had been a long night for them all.

"The sequence is positive for Variola," Susan announced. "But we have a plan."

The Director raised his eyebrows in hopeful surprise. "Let's hear it then."

They explained it to him and watched as the pleasant expression on his face slowly slid off and was replaced by scowl instead.

"Well, I'll consider it, but I have to contact the Pentagon first. I'm also calling in the rest of the troops." He had been hoping that his personnel would be returning in better numbers now that Thanksgiving was over. He began dialing numbers. The first two numbers he dialed only gave him continued ringing. But, the third number he called actually got answered.

"Hello? Is Len there? This Charles Abbott at the CDC...Oh? I'm sorry to hear that. What have you given him for it? Tell him to stay in bed and drink lots of fluids. This year's flu is sure a bad one...Keep in touch."

Susan's face mirrored all the other faces in the room staring at the Director. "Flu? You know damn well that he doesn't have the flu! Why didn't you tell him?

"It wouldn't help him any. There's nothing that can be done. He'll just have to ride it out."

"Don't you think that they have a right to know what they're dealing with?"

"Susan, please remember our policy in cases like this. If there is nothing we can do about it, there is no need to panic the public. Panic will only make the situation worse."

Silence followed. At least for a few seconds, until Susan could catch her breath after the Director's revelation. "And the public? Aren't you going to let them know?"

"Why? What good would it do? What can we do for them?"

"We've got to give them some sort of warning! That's our job, remember? I can't believe you intend to keep silent!"

"That's exactly what I intend to do. And I expect you to do the same. Now, excuse me. I've got to call the Pentagon."

Susan and her friends stormed out of the Director's office in disgust. The Director dialed the numbers to the Pentagon. The phone rang repeatedly. Finally, someone answered it.

"Who is this? Where is General Simmons? He's the one who's supposed to answer this phone."

"Uh, sorry, Sir. The General's not in today. In fact, there're only a handful of us here today, Sir. Some sort of Flu. May I take a message?"

"Have you been there long? Is this your usual assignment?"

"Uh, no Sir. I just came in from an assignment in Israel. It's chaos here sir. That's funny. I just realized. The only ones that are not sick are us new people. So nobody knows what to do exactly."

"I need you to do something for me. Call the White House and tell them I need to speak to someone in charge there. I don't have a direct line."

"Uh, O.K., Sir. I'll try. It may take me some time to find that 'direct line' you're talking about. I'll tell them to call you...if I can get them."

Charles had never dreamed he would ever have had that conversation with anyone on the other end of that line. He looked quizzically at the phone as he replaced the receiver.

After about thirty minutes, his phone rang. It was not the official at the White House. It was, instead, the confused young man again at the Pentagon. "Uh, Sir?"

"Yes? Did you get them?"

"Well, sort of, Sir...I mean I did talk to someone there, but they're closed because everybody there's sick with the flu. Even the President's coming down with it. Is that why you needed to talk to them?"

"No. I need authorization to use this vaccine."

"Vaccine for what?"

"It's not the flu...It's Smallpox. We have the vaccine that you might need to distribute.'

"Smallpox? Huh...That's why I didn't get it...I was vaccinated in Israel."

"Just send someone over to pick it up. Please find someone with some rank and try to explain it to them."

"Yes, Sir."

Susan walked in on the last part of that conversation. Her jaw dropped a little in shock over what she had heard. "They're coming to take the vaccine?" Her face was reddening quickly.

"Yes. Should be any time now."

"But...what about the plan? We need the vaccine! Do you know how many lives we could save?"

Charles Abbott had suffered through enough of this impertinent woman. "Don't you get it? There's nothing we can do! It's too late! Your 'public' is on its own now."

"But, why? If you let us, we can save millions of lives. The effect of the vaccine supply we have will be multiplied exponentially. You've got to give us a stab at it."

"No, I don't. We have long established procedures. We've trained and trained...if the vaccine is limited, it goes to the military. We've gone over this scenario a thousand times...now we just do it."

"I just don't believe...!"

She slammed the door so hard that the glass rattled.

Snack Bar—CDC—Midnight

Tom, Mike and Luke followed Susan, then watched as she stamped back and forth in front of them, raving about what she had just heard. She had motioned for them to follow her as she exited the office. Now, they sat at one of the small tables in the snack bar on the ground floor of the building. The grill that was normally manned by a cook was now abandoned. So, the only food available was locked away in the brightly-lit rows lining the room.

209

"Come on, Susan. Calm down. You're gonna stroke out if you don't cut it out." Mike knew her temper, but he had never seen it at this extreme before.

"We've got to do something. That bastard's giving away the only thing we have. The Army's going to show up any second and take it all away. And what for? *For the important people.* The generals and politicians. Nobody else counts. And do you think for one moment that *they* will vaccinate anyone else from their vaccinations? Hell, No! They couldn't care less. And those important people are probably already exposed anyway. That's how I would do it if I were going to plan an attack on a nation."

Susan's words echoed off the walls of the empty room. Tom tried to interrupt her solo. "But what can we do? The man will not listen to sense right now. He's resigned to inevitable mass extermination."

"Well, who cares if the leaders live. There won't be anybody to lead. The mortality rate of the virus depends on a couple of things. Normally, it ranges between forty and sixty percent...Or it did. Who knows what our attackers have done to it.... And even if they didn't do anything to it, the population hasn't seen it for decades...that's enough to raise the mortality. The overcrowded population will nearly ensure that it will be at its highest virulence. That's how these things work. That vaccine is all we have!"

"Tom, you're the military man here. You think you could talk some sense into them?" Mike was still hoping.

"Yeah, that's just it, Mike. I am the military man here, and I'm telling you...they won't listen. If you think the Director's being hard-nosed, just wait till you try to talk to the people who came up with the very policy he's defending.... The people are on their own."

"But there's got to be something we can do. I've always hated that man...he's a true bastard...follows every rule to the letter, whether it makes sense or not." Susan stared at the walls as her jaw set and her eyes narrowed in anger. "We can't just sit by and watch this happen. Let's go *explain it to him.*"

She charged out the swinging metal doors of the snack bar and hit the stairs running. She couldn't wait for the elevator. The others were right behind her.

When they reached the office, they found that the Director was not there. The phone rang. They all looked at each other, still breathing hard from the stairs. Susan picked up the receiver.

"Yes. This is the office of the Director...No, he's stepped out of the office for a few minutes. May I help you?...I'm sorry, we have decided not to give you the vaccine. We have designed a plan of distribution of our own..." Everyone in the office could hear the yelling coming out of the phone. Susan held it away from her ear in defense. Then, she hung up the receiver.

"Well, what did they say?"

"You heard every word I did. They're on their way."

"Good." It was Charles Abbott entering the room who added this word to the conversation. "Now, go get it ready for them. That's an order!...Well, get on it!...Now!"

Susan's face went from red to crimson in an instant as she lunged toward the Director. Her right hand grabbed his collar and her left hand gripped a section of his hair.

"You listen here, you son of a bitch!" The Director tried to shield his face with his arms and squirmed in her grip. "I don't give a Damn about your blessed training and protocol...we have a chance to save huge numbers of people.... And that's just what we're going to do...whether you read that in your specs or not!" She shook his collar hard and released him so that he fell backwards onto the floor, staring up at her with his mouth hanging open.

She turned and nearly pulled the door off its hinges opening it to go out. Tom, Mike and Luke followed her in a hurry. They had a hard time keeping up with her as she led them all the way to the vaccine storage facility. Suddenly, she stopped and faced them. The cool look on her face surprised them. She smiled a sly smile.

"I have a plan."

CDC—Later that Morning

The phone kept ringing. Just as Tom was about to give up, some one answered it.

"Hello?" The voice on the other end sounded tired.

"Isaac? Is that you?"

"Yes. Tom? Where the hell are you?"

"I'm in Atlanta. Why?"

"Cause this place is deserted. Most everybody has called in with the flu. I thought maybe you had it too. Why are you in Atlanta?"

"It's a long story. I just called to see if there was a flu epidemic going on there, too. I guess you just answered my question."

"Tom, you gotta get back. The place is nearly shut down. It's weird. The only people who are not sick are the people in our office. We're trying to man the whole place."

"There's a reason for that, Isaac. Now, listen carefully. You're not dealing with the flu. It's Smallpox. That's why our people haven't come down with it. We all had the vaccinations because of the pox viruses we work with."

"That's impossible. Smallpox is..."

"I know, I know 'eradicated'. Not any more. Anyway, I'm dealing with it here with the CDC."

"We've got calls from all over at the bases and posts. They think it's a pandemic of flu."

"Well, it's not. Get on the phone and tell them what they're really dealing with."

"Are you sure? How do you know?"

"Just listen to me. We confirmed it with the nucleotide sequence. Now do what I told you to do."

"Are you coming back?"

"I don't know. I hear that it's pretty hard to get a flight. I'll be in touch."

In another room, Mike was on the phone also. He fingered the clear, plastic straw-like strand containing vaccine as he waited for someone to answer the phone on the other end. The straw was sealed off in four small bubble compartments. The vaccine itself was colorless. Finally, someone answered.

"Hello?" It was Emily.

"Emily, where are the kids?"

"Mike! God, I needed to talk to you. What's going on? It seems like the whole world is sick. I heard on the TV that it's the flu. Do you still think it's Smallpox?"

"Yes, that's what it is, Emily. Now, listen carefully. Is anybody sick?"

"No, not yet."

"I want you and the kids to stay at the house and keep away from everybody. Don't let anyone come over. Keep yourself isolated. You are completely unprotected."

"What about you and Lissa?"

"Don't worry about us. We've been vaccinated. Lissa should be getting home any time now. I told her to get out of Laughlin as quietly and as fast as she could. I'm sending you some vaccine. Now here's what you do with it. It will look like a set of connected bubbles. Take one bubble and pierce it. Squeeze some out and rub it on your upper arm. Then, take the needle and prick your skin where you rubbed it with the vaccine. Be careful not to go too deep with the needle. Don't draw blood. Do this to the boys, too. See that they stay home for the next two weeks."

"What? Two weeks! That's impossible! You know how Jacob is going to react to that? He'll go out just to show me he can."

"Tell him it'll be the last defiant thing he does. The only way to avoid dying of Smallpox, or worse, is to stay away from everyone right now. You won't be protected for at least that long. Stay in!"

"How are you going to get it to me?"

"Let's just say I have a delivery man. He'll show up at your door shortly. Let him stay with you until I can get home. He's got more vaccine to distribute around there."

"O.K. More mystery. When will you be home?"

"I don't know. I've got some important things to do right now. The vaccine has to be distributed somehow. I guess that means me. I don't know how long it will take, but don't worry. I'll come home as soon as I can. I promise."

Mike kept giving Luke his last minute instructions as he drove him to the airport. Luke was still in his flight suit, stuffing vaccine into the sports bag he carried with him and trying not to scratch his new vaccination. As they drove past the chain-link fence, they could see that the airport was deserted.

So far, so good. Luke would find a way to fly to San Antonio. He carried with him the first allotment of the only hope for survival.

CDC—Noon

"Now look, Ben. If you see anybody coming let me know immediately." Susan had enlisted the aid of the security guard to watch as she, Tom and Mike went into the vaccine storage facility.

She pulled the warm gloves over her hands and entered the huge room, with Tom and Mike close behind her. They wore the gloves also. The vaccines had to be kept at −20°C to ensure their potency. The room they were stored in was not that cold, but it was cold enough that mist puffed out of her mouth every time she breathed out. She rubbed the frost off of one of the glass doors in front of the vaccines. The label on the door announced that these vaccines were Smallpox vaccines. Each batch of ten straws had a white label around it holding them together and identifying them. There were twenty batches in each box. Susan began lifting the boxes out of the freezer and stacking them on the floor. Mike and Tom followed her example.

When she had pulled them all out, she went to another part of the room and rubbed the frost off another label. This was the polio vaccine. It, too, was colorless, but it was in small vials, also packed in boxes. She pulled out one of the boxes and opened it, removing a vial for further inspection.

They worked diligently for two hours. They had just finished the last batch. Suddenly, the door to the room opened and Ben stuck his head in.

"We've got some company. Military types. What do you want me to do?"

"Meet 'em in the outer office. Deny them access. Tell them we have decided not to hand over the vaccine."

"What if they insist?"

"Send them in, I'll talk to them."

Ben closed the door and went to the outer office to meet the men.

"Everybody ready?" asked Susan.

Mike and Tom nodded.

214

Out in the outer office, Ben waited for the arrival of his guests. The clicking sound of their boots and the straps of their weapons alerted him to their close position. The door burst open.

"Where's the vaccine?"

"Stop where you are. You are not permitted entry into this facility."

"We're here to pick up the vaccine. Now, where is it?"

"The CDC personnel have decided that the vaccine is not to be surrendered."

The Captain looked at his men and they pointed their weapons at Ben. "I said that I came to pick up the vaccine, and that's just what I'm going to do."

"I'm sorry, you are denied entry to this facility."

In the storage room, Mike, Susan and Tom jumped at the sound of the gunshots just outside their door. Mike ran to the door and opened it. There, on the floor, was the squirming figure of Ben who had been shot in the legs and abdomen. Mike raced to his side and looked up at the Captain. Ben's convulsing form slowed its motion and became still.

"He's dead! What the shit do you think you're doing?"

"They told us you would offer resistance. These were our orders if you did."

Susan stepped out of the storage room. "What do you want?"

"For the fortieth time, we came for the vaccine."

"Well, you can't have it. It belongs to the people."

Tom grabbed her. "Just give it to them. Can't you see they'll kill for it? It's not worth it!"

Susan glared at the Captain as a confident smile came over his face. "Finally, someone speaks our language. Sergeant Wilkes, begin the loading."

Four men pushed past Tom and Susan and began loading the vaccine boxes into the ice chests they had brought. Mike, Tom and Susan watched the men haul the last of the vaccine out of the room.

The captain turned as he started out the door. "Thank-you!" he said sweetly as he smiled and walked out after his men.

Susan glared at him as he left and even after he was gone, she continued to glare at the door he had closed behind himself. Finally, after a few seconds that felt like a few hours, the hatred exuding from her eyes resolved into relief. She pulled loose from Tom's grip and looked down at the limp form on the floor, then back up at Mike. She turned her shocked expression to Tom.

"You were too right. Poor Ben."

"The first of many, I'm afraid. We must be under some kind of martial law."

"SHHH!" Mike warned. "They're not out of the hall yet!"

Finally, Susan gained control. "Tom, you deserve an Oscar! Such concern! You're really talented."

"How long do you suppose it'll take those meatheads to figure out that they've got the wrong vaccine?"

"Who knows? Maybe they won't at all! But we'd better be gone by whenever that is. Let's go."

They grabbed the ice chests out of the closet and put the real vaccine into them. The boxes of Variola vaccine were labeled "Polio."

As they gathered the vaccine, Susan smiled.

"What?" asked Tom.

"I was just thinking. Those *important* people are in for quite a disappointment. Too bad it's not a Polio outbreak!"

LAST CHANCE

IRAN

Sadeq clutched his bag, holding it close to his body. The traffic outside his car only bothered his driver. Sadeq's mind was elsewhere. He stared off into the crowds, not even seeing them.

It had taken precious time to get his hands on the contents of the bag. The ice pack that accompanied it made Sadeq's skin cool...or was it the panic he was feeling?

"Can't you go any faster?" He knew that chiding the driver could not make him get there any faster, but somehow, it made him feel better. This was the only thing he could do for his only grandson.

Sadeq did not even wait for the driver to open the door for him. He jumped out immediately and ran into the house. "Yousef! Where is Salehi?"

"One moment, Father. I will get her for you." Yousef disappeared around the corner in an effort to find his wife. A few minutes later, he returned with Salehi in tow. "Here she is, Father."

Sadeq quickly unwrapped his parcel as Salehi gave it a worried glance. "What is it?"

"Gamma globulin. Maybe it can protect her and the baby."

"But she is fine. We have been watching her for any sign of the virus."

"Yes, I know. But she was at the party with that woman that Omid brought back with him from Mexico. That woman died today. There is no time to waste. She has to take this now."

FIRST BLOW

WASHINGTON, D.C.

Senator Daniel Catshell watched as his wife writhed in the bed. He had never seen her like this before. Her labor pains twenty-nine years ago had not even caused her to toss like this. He picked up the receiver of the phone to call the doctor. Still busy. Just like it had been for the last thirty minutes. Finally, he left his wife's side and went down the spiral stairs to summon the housekeeper.

"Maria!" No answer.

"Maria!" Still no answer. Where could she be? He noticed that the breakfast dishes still sat on the table. He was going to have to light a fire under Maria, apparently. He had noticed that Maria was very quiet and a bit cross this morning as she served him his breakfast. Yes, she had even been moving slower then, come to think of it. But where could she be now? He needed her to help him with his wife.

The heels of his shoes clicked loudly on the kitchen floor. It made the house seem so empty. Oh, that's where she was. The door to the basement stood open, revealing that the light was on down there. She must be doing the laundry. He pulled the door open wide and peered down the stairs. What he saw did not make any sense. A worn, black woman's pump teetered off of the last step at the bottom of the stairs. He carefully walked down the first three steps. Then, he saw it.

Maria lay in heap at the bottom of the stairs.

"Maria! Are you OK?" No answer.

AUSTIN, TEXAS

Tina Meek managed to open one eye. The little bit of sun that beamed through the blinds stabbed her in the eye, so she closed it again. She did not know what time it was. She only knew that she felt like she was going to die. Why didn't Amanda help her? That was what sisters were supposed to do when one was sick. Where was she, anyway? Tina had not heard her even walk into the room.

She agonizingly rolled over in the bed. The sheets rubbing against her skin sent stinging needles all over her body. Finally, she was able to focus across the dorm room at her sister's bed. She wanted to scream, but she did not have the strength. All she could muster was a little whimper. It did not change the sight across the room. She *had* to get up and over to Amanda now.

She moved the bedspread off of her legs and immediately started shivering uncontrollably. Then, she painfully sat up, slid one leg off the bed and followed it with the other. She felt light-headed. Bracing herself with her arms on the side of the bed, she pushed up to attempt to stand. Blackness crowded in on her eyesight as she fell, unconscious, into the vomit that her sister had spewed across the floor, shortly before she had passed out.

Outside the room, Brandy Meeks knocked on the door. No answer. How did those girls think they were going to pass their history course if they did not even bother to get up and take the exams? She had heard a rumor that classes could be cancelled, but it had not happened here yet.

She gave up on them and turned to walk back down the hall of the dorm towards the cafeteria. A strange sound emanated from the TV room as she passed it. She stopped and turned back to peer into the room. Everyone in the room was glued to the screen.

"Hey, what's going on?"

"SHHH!" was the response.

Now she had to see what they were watching. She settled into a nearby seat to watch the screen. What she heard sounded like some sort of science fiction film. The live broadcast from CNN was warning people to stay home and avoid public places until the flu epidemic had passed its worst. People in New York were being instructed to call the officials for pickup of any corpses. They were to be wrapped in sheets and placed on the sidewalks.

But Brandy had not seen any bodies and did not know of anyone who had died of this flu. "Oh, sure. I'll just stop my life and fail all my courses because of a little flu!" She flipped her dark hair back and made her way to the cafeteria.

New Orleans, Louisiana

Vicki's auburn hair lay in a jumble above her head in the bed as the TV blared on. Carl was by her side, but he was in a deep sleep as far as she could tell. The light in the room must be playing tricks with her stinging eyes. His skin had taken on a red hue. She closed her eyes and opened them again, but the color was still there.

Some man was rambling on about a rumor about the flu that she and Carl were suffering with together. Did she hear him say Smallpox? Couldn't be. Now she must be hearing things on top of the ringing in her ears. She knew that Smallpox no longer existed.

Still, she began to wonder. What were all the red spots she was getting on her arms?

San Diego, California

Carmen finished pulling the last of the blankets from the bedrooms to the living room floor. She had had enough of running from room to room when each kid yelled. How did they all get the flu at the same time? Why didn't they tell people who were contemplating being

219

parents about times like this? One thing for sure...she would have had a few less if she had known.

Her four little patients had no regard for the fact that she felt lousy too. That was the most unkind thing about this whole little episode of mother-hood. She was not even allowed to be sick. Every time she started to sit down, one of them called her or threw up everywhere. Her own stomach was pretty queasy too. But she could not sympathy vomit any more. There was nothing left.

She had tried to get them to a doctor, but there was no answer at any of the doctor's offices or even the hospitals. She had gone from door to door along the curved lane of trailers. Only one person had bothered to answer the door. The poor old lady had coughed so hard she started to bleed, so she slammed the door on Carmen. Everybody she knew had the flu. So she just did what she could for them at home.

One by one, she carried them all into the living room and laid them down on the pallet she had built. Only one of them moaned pitifully for a few minutes before he fell into deep sleep. The other three did not even flinch when she carried them. They were limp and two of them must have broken their fevers. They were cold.

Avoiding thinking about what that meant, Carmen finally sat down on the couch, then slid down until her head was resting on the cushions. Her aching, weary eyes fell on the form of some official talking into a micro-phone. She could not really hear what he was saying, but by his body lan-guage, he appeared to be hiding something. She pushed the remote to turn up the volume. The writing below his face announced that he was some-body named Charles Abbott and that he was a Director at the CDC, what-ever that was.

"Director, what are the estimated percentages of infection in the U.S. population?"

"Frankly, it is hard to say at this time. Communication lines are not what they should be because many of the health officials in most communi-ties are also sick. We really can't say how many people are infected now."

The woman who was interviewing him pushed her straight, black bangs from her eyes and moved closer. "Director, what about the rumors that this is not the flu? Some people say that it is Smallpox or Ebola. Could there be any truth to these rumors?"

The man violently shook his head in denial, then looked off to the left. "Absolutely not! This is simply an unusually virulent strain of flu. The same thing happened in 1918. This is just one of those cyclical things that hits the population periodically. But that's all it is. Just the flu. Nothing more."

"But there are reports of some people having large blisters all over their bodies or bleeding to death like Ebola. Have you heard these reports?"

"Of course I have heard them." The man was getting agitated with the woman. "You have to understand that, under such stressed conditions, ridiculous rumors always begin to circulate around the people. It is just fear that is not under control. The wise person should ignore these false stories and concentrate on getting over the illness."

"But, Director, I have personally seen some of these blisters. Are you telling me that I did not see what I saw?"

The Director's face grew red and he looked toward the camera for a second. Then, he pushed the microphone from his face and stormed off, muttering something to himself that sounded like he was trying to convince himself.

"Director?"

"No more questions!"

The camera came in on a close-up of the woman. "So, there you have it. Are they just rumors? The CDC is not answering any more questions. This is Laura Gilliam, reporting live from Atlanta."

Carmen closed her eyes. She did not care anymore about what it was. She only knew that she felt like she was dying. And if she did, who would take care of her children?

CARIBOU, MAINE

Betty had never seen Bud help so much around the house. But, then again, she had never been so sick in all her life. Her head and back attacked her with racking pains and she kept vomiting. Even the smell of tea brewing in the kitchen set her off. She had begged

Bud to go outside to eat. The slightest smell of food brought on the dry heaves.

The view on the TV in front of her was incredible. Some woman news anchor dominated the screen. Only, Betty could not see the bottom of her face. It was covered with a surgical mask. Her anxious eyes darted around her as she spoke. She was holding the microphone with her latex-covered hand. Betty turned up the volume with the remote.

"Not sure how long we will be able to keep broadcasting from this location. As you can see, small groups of roving gangs are looting the area." The camera panned the scene. Across the street from the camera, glass crashed as three men hit the locked door of a small drug store with large stones. The ear-piercing alarm did not even slow the thieves down, as they ran to the pharmacy at the back of the store.

"The epidemic has sparked theft of unusual items from the stores. Medicines are of premium value to these people, as are latex gloves and disinfectants of every kind. The rumors that this is Ebola or Smallpox have spurred a complete paranoia and panic, despite official denials from the CDC and other health organizations."

Betty smiled. She knew she was sick, but she was sure that it was not Smallpox. She still bore the remains of a large scar on her arm. All the people her age had been vaccinated as children. She could not get Small-pox. Or, at least, that is what she thought. Still, what were the raised red spots on her arms?

NEW YORK, NEW YORK

Anthony drifted in and out of consciousness as he lay on the torn plaid cover of his couch, one arm draped down to the floor. He had no knowledge of how long he had been sick. Time did not matter when his head hurt so much.

An old woman was talking on the TV, answering questions from the same anchorwoman who had been on the screen for days. He had tried to switch the channels to get rid of the woman, but nothing else was on. Some of the channels showed nothing but snow. So, it was this woman or nothing. He did not even care any more.

All the woman's talking about Smallpox did not worry Anthony. What he had was not like what she was talking about. He never had any red bumps that grew into blisters. He was, instead, covered with small bruises that had now begun to run into each other. He fought to raise his hand from the floor to wipe his nose. When he finally caught the irritating drip on the back of his hand, it was bright red...It was blood. But, he could not care anymore. He had to try to stay conscious, so he concentrated on the women on the screen.

The anchorwoman introduced her guest. "This is Velma Addison. She is eighty-five years old. She lived in Africa as a child, with her father who was a missionary at the time. Velma, was there Smallpox in Africa?"

"Yes. I remember it well. I had to help my father. He ran out of vaccine and there were still thousands of people who were not protected yet."

"Sounds like the situation we're in now. What did he do?"

"Some of the elders of the tribe we worked with told us about a practice they had used for generations against the disease. When a person came down with it, they would gather the crusts of the blisters and grind them into a fine powder. Then they would make a small wound on someone they wanted to protect, and rub in a little of the powder."

"Didn't that give the person a case of the Smallpox?"

"Well, yes, but it was usually a mild case, with only a few scars."

Anthony allowed himself to slip into unconsciousness. If this was what it had come down to, he did not want to be a part of it anymore.

TEXAS A&M UNIVERSITY

D ry heaves rocked Lindy every few minutes. It was the smell. She had given up eating. It was a total waste of time and she was not sure how much time she had.

It had been hard to leave her family right after Thanksgiving Dinner to get back to work on the paper that was due only two weeks later. The whole grade for the course was based on this paper. It had to be good. But the day after she finally got to her room, she discovered that nothing was open. She had checked before she left for the holiday and she knew that the library was supposed to be open. The sign on the door simply read, "Temporarily closed due to illness." Great! Now how would she finish the paper?

Looking for help, she discovered that everyone was either gone or sick. Her calls to the professor's office and her messages to his E-mail all went unanswered. She had given up her family time for this?

She decided to go back home, even for the two days left. She ran down the creepy, empty halls of the dorm. She shuddered as the emptiness began to close in on her. She looked over her shoulder instinctively, and fell on her face. Scrambling up to her hands and knees, she shook her head and looked around to see what she had tripped over. A hand!

The arm was stretched across the floor of the hallway from one of the rooms of the dorm. Deep bruises covered it and blood trickled from the nail beds. Lindy vomited immediately. She could smell the blood. Then, her curiosity got the best of her.

She stood up and peeked slowly around the door. She vomited again. She recognized the girl as a Resident Assistant she had seen before. The girl was not breathing. A trail of blood flowed from the corners of her eyes. Lindy closed her eyes and gagged. She took a deep breath. Then, she ran.

West Texas

Michelle Robbins rummaged through her kitchen, not really knowing what she was looking for. Maybe she was hungry. No, not hungry. She lost her appetite every time she thought about them.

They were all in the other room. She had put them there herself. Her meager attempt to erase the memories by covering their bodies had not worked. Every time she walked by the door to that room, it all came rushing back to her. Every single horrible death. She had witnessed every single one.

There were no other sounds of humans to be heard, besides the sounds of her own footsteps and her constant mumbling to herself. The house sat in the middle of the sprawling ranch, so there were no neighbors. The only living things Michelle knew of in the area were her dogs and the Angora goats that her mother and stepfather had raised. The goat kids romped and played with each other as if nothing were wrong. Well, if they could ignore it, so could she.

That was why she had not buried any of them yet. To do that would be a confession that they were dead, and she was not ready to confess that. Nothing was wrong.

She went to the TV and turned it on again. Snow. Nothing but snow. She fed channel numbers into the system over and over. There was nothing but snow. The system must be on the blink. That was all.

She picked up the phone, again. She dialed Bonnie's number. It rang repeatedly. The answering machine did not even work.

She felt as if she must have entered a mysterious parallel universe when she came home from her trip to Cozumel. Traveling on the ship had relaxed her completely. She was ready, now, to get back and pack to go begin the next semester of her Junior year at college.

But, everyone at her house had come down with something. She had been the only one well enough to help any of them. All her attempts at getting help had failed. Then, one by one, they all died...and now, she was beginning to feel sick, herself.

She had to get away. She could not let that happen to her. Not now. She stuffed a few things into her old gym bag and swung it over her shoulder. Being careful to latch the gate behind her, she stepped up into the old black pickup truck and made the engine roar into action. She would be at Bonnie's house within a few minutes.

An eerie feeling crept over her as she realized that she was driving the only moving vehicle on the highway.

Where was everyone?

OKLAHOMA

Janie wiped the sweat off of her brow. It was not hot. She was just sweating. Then a cold chill ran down her back. She walked into the kitchen and went straight for the sink. She stared at the word "antibacterial" on the soap dispenser as she frantically pumped it until her hand was completely filled with soap. She did not realize that this was the third time in twenty minutes that she had washed her hands. Her expression went blank as she scrubbed her hands. She had not even noticed how raw and sore her skin was becoming. She just did not feel it. She had other things to feel.

She went back to her task, tucking the meaning of it all as far back into her mind as she could manage. The only problem was that it kept escaping, rushing to the front of her thoughts, filling her ravaged eyes with more burning tears. Every time she thought she was completely dry, she found herself sobbing, out of control, one more time. She wiped her eyes furiously so she could see her work.

The needle and thread kept going in and out of the material, making a line of sewing. The only problem was that she could not make the line straight. She had sewed for her children many other times, but never while they were in the garments. And she had never sewed sheets onto them before. This would be the last time she would ever sew for them again. She had to do her very best for them. But how could she sew a straight line when her shoulders kept throwing her around with every sob?

Finally, she stuck the needle and thread into the big cloth tomato and inspected her work. Jennifer, her fifteen-year-old daughter, now wore her final gown, made of the prettiest sheets her mother could find for her. Her auburn hair was set off so well by the rose colored flowers on the sheets. Janie had always been so very proud of that hair. Now streaks of it escaped the seams at the top of her shroud. She was such a beautiful girl.

"Jim! Jim! Come help me. I can't carry her by myself...Come on, Jim!...It's the last thing you'll ever get to do for her!"

But Jim did not answer. Jim did not even hear his wife of twenty years calling him. The bottle of Vodka on the floor next to him was protecting him from hearing it. Jennifer had been the last one to leave.

Only a few hours before, he had carried his only son, Brent, out to the curb, like the trash. He had just left him there, wearing the shroud that his mother had soaked with her tears as she sewed it for him. A part of Jim had stayed there on the sidewalk as he walked back into the garage and pushed the door button to close it. He knew he could not do it again, not for his baby

226

girl. Not for Jennifer. His hand had grabbed the bottle as he walked back into the house. Now, he could bear the pain. He wanted to stay drunk. He did not want to hear his wife.

It was bad enough to have to carry his mother out and leave her there. At least, when his father had died of a heart attack five years earlier, Jim had been able to honor him properly. The funeral had been very expensive, but his Dad had gone out in style. Now, his mother was laid across the sidewalk like the dry Christmas tree, waiting to be hauled off. Only, nobody was hauling anything anywhere.

The piles of bodies leaked body fluids until they dripped off the curb and ran into the gutters. The virus was an equal opportunity killer. All the young people and children who had not been vaccinated had become sick. The weaker ones died quickly, especially as the virus exhibited its most potent hemorragic form. But the older people who had been vaccinated as children were not safe either. Their vaccinations had long since lost their potency. They only protected the victims partially.

The older population had indeed been vaccinated at an early age. But, now, they were much older and the virus, like all other diseases, was much harder on them now that they were weaker. Equal numbers of old and young died.

Jim and Janie did not know it, but they represented the group most able to resist. They were old enough to have had previous vaccinations, but they were not old enough to be weakened too much to fight it off. They would survive. But they did not care. They had lost all that mattered.

SPRING, TEXAS—THE SUBURBS

The shots rang out and echoed back to their origin. Every sound wave seemed to slap David in the face. He jerked his face back and winced, causing some of the scabs on his face to split and start bleeding again. His aching head made it hard to look into the sun. He opened one eye to inspect his target and swatted furiously at the flies that were landing on his face and arms. He could see through the sight that he had accomplished his goal.

227

The twenty-two-caliber rifle he held, still pointed towards the street, had been the prized possession of his father. Only a few months earlier, the two of them had driven out to the range and his father had performed the rite of passage. The day after David's tenth birthday, his father had ceremoniously handed him the rifle, after a long dissertation on proper care and safety. Then, David had been allowed to fire the heirloom at a target in the range until he had become very accurate. His Dad had been so very proud of his son's "good eye." Now, it seemed that David had not lost any of his talent.

The German Shepherd's body lay leaking bright, red blood in a rivulet that joined the others coming from David's other victims. The bodies of three other dogs, a vulture and two cats were strewn randomly around the body of his father, now partially wrapped in a blanket and taking its place among the others on the sidewalk. In a way, he felt sorry for the animals.

Their owners had died and quit feeding them. These were the lucky ones that had been able to escape their confines, as many are so adept at doing. Now, they roamed the streets looking for bowls of dog food...or carrion if no dog food was available.

The cats were quiet and sneaky about their feeding. David had not noticed what they were doing until they had succeeded in eating off most of one of his father's hands. Now, he sat guard over the body. An early warning system had developed in the area. Even the cats could not sneak up without sending hordes of buzzing flies rising into the air. But he was beginning to worry about a few things.

The dogs, as their ancestors had done many years ago, were forming hunting packs. As their hunger burned deeper, they became bolder in their search. One pack, consisting of a Sheltie, a Dalmatian, a Labrador, a Pekinese and a few mutts, charged at the pile of bodies from all sides suddenly while David was sleeping with his head propped on the barrel. By the time David was roused enough to get his senses together, they had managed to rip large chunks from several bodies, including his father's. Then, there was the problem of ammunition.

When he ran out of what was in the torn box at his side, he would have to venture to a store or something. He was still very weak from the virus so he was not sure he could make it to the end of the block, much less the store. Then, the vultures arrived.

228

Shadows of the circling vultures glided across the lawns and bodies. David shot a vulture attempting to feast off of his father's body. The vulture landed with a thud on the body and immediately vomited partially digested human carrion all over it. David vomited too.

David gritted his teeth down hard as he fired at the hated vultures. He watched as they neatly picked the other bodies on the neighboring sidewalks clean. Sure, he knew his neighbors and hated that the beasts were consuming their bodies, but he had so little ammunition. His father was not going to be like that. No, not his father. Not a skeleton with chunks of red meat hanging loosely off at the ligaments.

No. Not his father.

The buzzard slowly circled above David's house. He had seen what had happened to the last buzzard that had tried to feast at that house. It was not a problem. There was plenty of food to be found and nobody would be guarding it. The buzzard scanned the area for a snack.

It had not always been this way in this location for the buzzard. He had lived enough years to know what hunger felt like. For the most part, the humans in this area kept the food out of reach for the buzzards. Occasionally, he had snacked on a dog or a cat, but, usually, even these food types were whisked up off the roads as soon as the cleanup crews discovered them. Life was to be barely sustained by finding unfortunate rabbits or skunks that had been hit on the roads. But the buzzard had only tasted of human flesh once when it had been dumped out of a car that had quickly sped away. The feast had only lasted until other humans found the body and carried it away.

Now, the buzzard ate human flesh until he was full. It was a novel sensation. The buzzard circled above the carrion, waiting to have a tiny empty space to fill with it. The other buzzards joined him in his sky dance. For once, there was enough food for them all. Instead of fighting over the prey, they simply moved over to the next body. Everyone had plenty.

At first, the humans had tried to bury the carrion, as they always did. But, for some reason, they had suddenly stopped burying it and it began to pile up all over the suburb. The number of humans moving around lessened and the moving vehicles were rare. Feeding was easy.

It would be a good year for the buzzards.

LAURA

ATLANTA, GEORGIA

Mike, Tom and Susan avoided the only crowded portion of the streets around the hospitals. The rest of the city streets were wide open and mostly abandoned as people stayed home because they were sick or tending to others who were sick. They passed the looters in the downtown area, staying as far away from them as possible. Finally, their destination loomed before them.

Parking Tom's four-wheel drive right in front of the entrance to the BNN building was not even questioned. Nobody was there. The door was not locked, though the echoing of their footsteps in the halls made the building seem to be empty. As they entered the foyer of the building, they looked for the directory to the offices. Laura Gilliam's office was on the sixth floor.

The office was deserted. Susan began searching the desks for clues. "There's got to be some way we can contact her. Look for cell phone numbers."

"Here it is!" called Tom, holding a card in the air.

'When Laura answered their call, she sounded surprised. "Hello?"

"Laura Gilliam?"

"Yes. Who is this?"

"You don't know us. My name is Dr. Mike Thompson and I'm waiting with my friends Tom Harris and Susan McGill here in your office. We have seen some of your broadcasts and we have information for you."

Laura's headache was getting worse.

"Like what?" she snapped. She did not have time for this. It was bad enough that she was the only one left broadcasting. How did this happen?

She and Jason had been sent to Canada to do a special on Thanksgiving traditions in Canada. The trip had been fun with Jason taping her in various beautiful locations around Canada as she interviewed local people about their traditions.

Then, as they returned to the U.S., many of the employees of the broadcasting company had called in sick with the flu. She had not even had a chance to unpack her things before she was ordered to be back on duty again. Now, she could not get in touch with anyone from the company. They were on their own, prowling the streets, looking over their shoulders and jumping at every sound. Some of the people they had seen roaming the streets had looked at her with crazy expressions on their faces that reached out and shook some of her confidence. She had to wonder if anyone sane was left out there to hear her broadcasts.

The streets had grown strangely silent, except for the sounds of the alarms and shattering glass. Now, somebody was calling her on her cell phone. It was a sound that she had not heard for a few days now. Well, at least it meant that somebody was listening.

"I'm sorry," she continued. "Who did you say you were?"

"Dr. Mike Thompson. We have been at the CDC headquarters. We think you'll be interested in what we have to say."

"Are you a physician...or a lab jockey?"

"Both. If you'll tell us where you are, we'll meet you there."

"I'm right in the middle of downtown...at Jaspar Park. You know where that is?"

Mike checked with Susan.

"Sure. We'll be there in a few minutes."

Jason's camera spanned the area while Laura described the chaos around them. If nobody survived, at least her filming would leave some sort of documentation of what went on. A small band of looters went about their business at a drug store across the street.

"As you can see, the looting goes on, unchallenged by any police. One has to wonder if there *are* any police."

The thought gave her the creeps. Suddenly, she felt very vulnerable. The chilly wind blew around them, masking any other sounds around them. Her nervous eyes began to search the place for someplace less open.

Then, she noticed that the band of looters was not there anymore. "Jason, where did they go?"

"I don't know. I don't see..."

Jason's head lunged forward with the force of the brick that hit him from the back. His panicked eyes sent Laura flying towards him, but it was too late. He fell with a hard thud on the ground and did not make another wiggle. Laura searched in all directions for the source of the brick as she crouched down, holding one hand on Jason's limp form.

A red flash jumped into the corner of her sight. She instinctively fled in the other direction. But, a grass vine caught her high heel and sent her tumbling hard onto the ground. She looked up just in time to see the vicious countenance of her attacker.

"Now, I've got you! Not too smart, huh?"

As he bent closer to her, she felt the cold blade at her throat and smelled the liquor on the man's breath. She looked to Jason, but saw that he was not even resisting the other man, who was no more than a teenager, rifling through his pockets and taking his wallet.

Then, she saw it. Or, maybe, she was just wishing that she saw it. No. She heard it too. An approaching vehicle was careening straight for them. Her attacker looked up from his task momentarily. That was all she needed.

She grabbed his wrist with one hand and straightened his elbow with her other arm. Her knee contacted the elbow from beneath as she raised it hard and fast. The dull crack, followed by his shrieking, confirmed that the technique had worked just as it had been promised that it would. She rolled out from under him and began kicking at his face and neck with her pointed shoe. Her final shot was to his groin. He doubled up and tried, in vain, to crawl away from his attacker. She just kept kicking him everywhere, and probably would have kicked him to death, except that a strong pair of arms grabbed her shoulders and began pulling her away. She twisted suddenly, breaking her holder's grip, and swung her fist toward his Adam's apple.

But Mike raised his arm in a block. "Whoa!! Wait a minute!! I'm on you're side!!"

The hair on her neck was still standing up as she narrowed her focus to see Mike. She stood poised to continue the battle if necessary, breathing heavily in response to the adrenaline pumping through her body.

"I'm Mike Thompson. You O.K.?"

Laura shook off the grass from her sleeves. "Yes. But Jason's not." She motioned towards his still form lying on the grass.

Tom joined Mike as he went to help Jason. Susan stood next to Laura. The attacker had crawled out of sight somewhere. Laura was still shaking.

"Looks like you came just in time. They came out of nowhere. We were filming and they circled behind us. Why do people have to become animals when there's a crisis?"

Susan was still in shock over the Army's attack on them that morning. "I don't know, but it's not just individuals. The government is even out of control. The military attacked us this morning over the vaccine!"

Laura's expression changed to surprise. "You have vaccine?"

"Yes. That's why we needed to talk to you. We need a way to spread information to the public. We have a plan that will spread the vaccine exponentially through the remaining population."

"But aren't you with the CDC? I've been in constant contact with them, and all they can do is deny the possibility of Smallpox."

"Yes. We saw your last broadcast where you interviewed Dr. Abbott. The man is not to be trusted. The bastard is lying through his teeth. He wouldn't listen to reason, so we took things into our own hands." Her face was turning red as she remembered the confrontation.

"But, I didn't think there would be any vaccine. The virus is supposed to be extinct! Didn't I read about vaccine being destroyed not too long ago?"

"That's right. We don't have much. The military wanted it for their own use."

"I can just imagine that. But how can you multiply it?"

Susan explained the plan to Laura as Mike and Tom slowly got Jason up on his feet. "Is he going to be all right?" Laura asked Mike.

"I think so. You might try to keep him still for a while. He may have a concussion. But don't even think about taking him to a hospital. The ones we passed were being swarmed. I don't even know if anybody is on duty there."

"Well, that does it. I don't care about the gun laws. I'm packin from now on. There certainly weren't any police here to help us when we needed them."

Susan looked at Tom and Mike. "You know, she may be right. It looks pretty rough out here. We ought to get some protection before we go."

Laura gave a slight cough. Mike gave a knowing look to Tom and Susan. Then, he spoke to Laura.

"How are you feeling? Are you coming down with it?"

This time it was Jason who answered for her. "She's had an awful headache all day. And I'm starting to get one too. You think it's the Smallpox?"

"It could be. Why are you the only ones working from your building?"

"We have been out of the country on assignment."

"That explains it, then. When did you get back home?"

"About a week ago."

There was nothing Mike and Tom could do for them. The epidemic had not reached the point where there would be recovering patients. They had brought the necessary supplies to make serum whenever they found someone who had recently had the disease and recovered. But, so far, they had not found any of those. They knew that Laura and Jason would just have to ride it out. They only hoped that the broadcasters would be able to accomplish their task of information dissemination before they became too ill. They outlined to Laura all the information they wanted her to get out to the public. They left them with two doses of vaccine and plenty of sterile needles in case they found people who were not infected, and instructed them on how to vaccinate others and keep spreading the protection.

"Now what?" Tom questioned Mike. He seemed to be the one with all the ideas.

"We need vehicles. Ones we can trust...even on bad roads. There's no telling where we'll end up. Four wheel drives would be the best choice."

"Just looking, I'd say that we can have our choice. I bet the dealerships are abandoned too. Where could we find some, Susan? You know this place."

Susan directed them to the new car lots, concentrated in one area. "Do you think you can find something to fit the bill here?"

Mike surveyed the lots. "Perfect! Let's go."

The crashing glass led to the piercing alarm that split the eerie silence of the streets. Susan kept her hands on her ears as Mike and Tom used a crow bar to open the box where the keys were kept. They searched for the I.D. numbers they had found on the window stickers of their selections. As they exited, the deafening sound only got worse as it was piped through the loudspeaker system outside.

234

Mike opened the door of his new ride and yelled out to the others, "Now, we go shopping!"

Supplies

Sunset Mall—Atlanta, Georgia

S unset Mall had never seen a Saturday evening like this one. The three four-wheel drive vehicles pulled up into an empty parking lot. The internal security lights were the only ones being used that night, even though it was only eight o'clock. An audible alarm sounded in the building, but nobody was reacting to it. Police were noticeably missing. Mike used his headlights to sweep the outside of the mall for any signs of activity.

Susan drove up beside him and motioned for him to follow her. She took the lead and drove to a secluded alcove behind a tall wall. She rolled down her window to talk to Mike. "I think this is the outside door to the store we need."

Mike surveyed the area. "Looks like it's locked up tight. And that's a metal door. We won't be able to break through it. We'll have to go through the mall to get to the inside entrance."

"The closest one is just around that corner. But I bet it's locked, too." Susan had not thought about having to break into the mall.

"Well, at least it won't be made of metal. We can break the glass."

They drove around the corner to the mall entrance. Parked next to the door was a black Corvette. It still had its sale sticker on the window, and it looked deserted.

Tom looked in both directions quickly. "Where do you suppose the owner is?"

"No tellin. But I bet he's inside."

"Maybe. There's only one way to find out."

"Let's go."

Mike fished the flashlight out of his vehicle and scanned the mall door. Tom followed with his revolver. The door had already been forced open.

"So now we know why the alarm is sounding." Susan's heart began to pound. Her nervous eyes leapt from shadow to shadow as they opened the mangled door and stepped inside the building.

Rows of shoes and bags greeted them as they advanced into the store. The alarm almost drowned out the normal background music, still playing in complete ignorance of the situation. Mike led the way, followed by Susan and Tom, who periodically turned around to check behind them. Susan could feel the eyes of the mannequin following them. She kept glancing back behind them, half expecting them to be advancing on them somehow.

They turned in the direction of the inner mall. Another locked door stood between them and the rest of the mall. It, too, had been forced open. Mike put his forefinger up to his lips to remind the others to be quiet, as they slipped through the doors and stood there looking around.

Susan motioned for Mike to follow her. The deafening alarm increased its volume within the mall. An elephant could have charged them and they would not have heard it coming.

They passed the stores one by one until they came to the sporting goods store they were looking for. Susan waved at the others and pointed towards it. Once again the door was locked. Once again, the door had been forced.

They peered into the store and saw no movement, so they pulled the sliding doors apart and went in. The cash register had been thrown down and was lying upside down with its drawer wide open and empty. Susan moved up to Mike's ear and said, "Let's go somewhere else. They might still be here."

Mike shook his head. He was sure the looters were gone. He turned and started towards the back of the store. Susan grabbed his arm and turned him back to her, trying to get him to leave the store. Mike jerked his arm away and glared at her for a moment. Then, he turned and started walking to the back of the store. Susan turned back to face Tom as if he could control Mike. He just shrugged. Reluctantly, she set her jaw and began to follow him into the store.

They inched into the store, inspecting every hiding place as they went. Finally, they found the items they needed in the camping supplies section. Tom stood guard with his revolver, as Mike and Susan put together sleeping bags, lanterns, fuel, cook stoves, batteries, instant cold packs, flashlights, tents and warm clothes. These would be needed because the motels may not be open for business. Nothing else was. They stuffed as much as they could into ice chests to carry them. Then, they each donned a holster, filled it with a gun and stuffed ammunition into their pockets.

Tom handed Susan his revolver so he could carry out one of the heavy ice chests. She looked at it as it sat in her hand. Tom moved up to her ear. "Just point and shoot." Susan nodded.

Mike and Tom picked up the loaded ice chests and walked out of the store, turning back in the direction they had come. Susan followed behind them, carefully balancing the revolver and trying not to point it at the men. The high-decibel alarm had succeeded in giving her a monstrous headache.

The whine of the bullet speeding past her ear took her by complete surprise. She dropped to the floor instantly. She yelled, but the men could not hear her over the alarm. They kept moving. She had to warn them somehow, so she fired the revolver into the air. Maybe that would also give their attackers something to think about.

Mike and Tom spun around at the sound of the revolver to see Susan crouched down on the floor ten feet behind them. She waved and pointed up and then at her gun. Dropping the ice chests, they scrambled back to Susan. She put her mouth near to Tom's ear and yelled, "Somebody's shooting at us! Get down!"

As Tom strained his eyes to get a glimpse of the shooter, the second bullet whizzed past him and ricocheted off the tile floor of the mall, shattering the glass of the nearby dress shop. Glass splinters flew in every direction. The three held up their arms to shield their faces from the tiny glass daggers.

"AHHH!" The pulsing blood rushing out of Susan's arm told Mike and Tom that she had caught some of the glass shrapnel in an artery.

"Hold on, Susan!" Mike yelled as he grabbed for the artery in the upper part of her arm to cut off the blood flow. The next bullet gave Tom a direction to aim at, and he began to fire back with the revolver that Susan had dropped.

"Come on!!!" he yelled. "We've got to get out of here!"

Mike put Susan's free hand to work holding the artery. Mike and Tom grabbed the ice chests and ran with them all the way out of the mall. They threw them into Mike and Tom's vehicles. Susan jumped into the passenger seat with Tom. Mike took the lead, screeching his tires as they left the mall parking lot.

They drove a few miles on the near-deserted loop before exiting to another parking lot. Mike stitched Susan's arm, as they discussed their plans.

"Now what?" Susan was trying to think of anything else besides what Mike was doing. She winced...not because it was hurting...it was just the thought of it all.

"First, we have to get you another vehicle. We've also got to pick up some other supplies. But, I think we should avoid any other malls. Too many places to hide," Mike smiled as he snipped the last stitch. "We have to decide which way we're going to go. Laura and Jason are broadcasting to the whole nation about our vaccine plan. Those people will be looking for us."

"Where do you want to go, Susan? You get first pick."

"I think I'd like the North East part. I know it better."

"Good point. I'll head to Texas and then north along the Western part of the country. Then, I can check on Emily and the kids. Tom, you should go to the central part."

Susan inspected the bandage that Mike was applying. "It's just so dangerous out there. I hate the thought of being alone."

"You're right. But maybe we can enlist some aid along the way. You know, get somebody to come along and help."

Susan looked all around them. "Yeah, but how do you know who to trust?"

IRAN

SATURDAY

"It has already begun!" Sadeq's raised voice echoed off the high ceiling of Nasser Ghane's office. "That Mexican woman died, but before she did, she managed to infect everyone on that plane. If you had stuck to the my original plan, this would not have happened!"

Nasser did his best to soothe the panicky Sadeq. "Malik has stepped up the vaccine production. It should be all right."

"I'm afraid you don't understand. Everyone who was on that plane is probably infected now. And they are infecting the whole Coalition population as we speak! It is too late for a vaccine. You don't even have a list of the passengers, do you?"

"Well, no, but we are working on it."

"It's too late. You'll never find them again. You better just get ready." Sadeq did not care that he was addressing the most powerful member of the Council. His grandson was in danger now because of the premature decision to move the attack date. "You Fools!! You have no idea what you have done!"

Nasser's steps became heavier and his eyes narrowed. This self-important man made his blood pressure go up. "It will not be a problem. Even as we speak, Phase Two is beginning."

H-HOUR + 0

"Geez, Sarah, I'm sorry to have to put you in this thing, but I don't know what else to do with you," General Herndon said breathing heavily. "I guess old age has finally got me...can't believe such a tiny woman like you could seem so heavy."

Herndon bent over, grasped his wife underneath her arms and continued to drag her toward the garage. He stopped dragging her when he reached the freezer and opened it.

"Good Lord, Woman. I thought you told me you were going to clean out all this junk. Frozen Zucchini, squash...we never eat any of this crap. Why in the hell are you always..." He stopped and looked down at his wife.

"I'm sorry, Sarah...I can't believe how I treat you. Even after you're dead, I'm raising Hell with you. I don't know how you put up with me all these years." The tears formed but they did not flow.

Sarah's battle with breast cancer had weakened her. Endless chemotherapy had left her vulnerable even to the early stages of the virus. He had tried to get her help. However, reaching any of her doctors by phone proved fruitless. TV and radio, in their increasingly infrequent broadcasts, had warned of the futility of trying to reach any medical facility.

Well Hell...call the office...see if any of those knuckleheads have any ideas. Herndon recalled the events of the past few days.

• • •

"General, Sir, how are you?" answered Captain Goodloe.

"Fine, Son...I need some help. Look, my wife has caught this crap going around and I can't get her any help. Does anybody there know anything?"

"Sir, are you aware that because of the epidemic the President has declared a State of Emergency?"

"Yeah? Well how reassuring...how can I get treatment for my wife?"

"General, Sir, they've set up hotlines...but, Sir, it's total chaos...all military medical centers are overwhelmed. General Hickson couldn't even get his son any kind of attention. My understanding is that they are giving treatment recommendations over the phone."

"Like what?...take aspirin and drink plenty of liquids?"

"Yes, Sir. I'm afraid that's about the size of it," Goodloe replied.

"Captain, tell me something...who's minding the store there?"

"Sir, to even say that there's a skeleton crew here is probably an exaggeration. I personally know people who have died from this stuff."

Herndon grew silent. He dropped his jaw as the truth came to him. He almost shouted out. "My God! I can't believe I haven't realized this before now! OK, Son, listen...we are under attack and we don't even know it."

240

"Well, Sir, I'll admit this flu or what ever it is does seem to be attacking everyone. "

"No, damn it! Listen to what I'm telling you. I should have seen this...this is not some kind of King Kong flu. It's a planned biological agent attack on us. This is what I want you to do. Get your butt down stairs and get one of our computer jocks to call up some numbers. How many of our flyboys are down with this crap? Is it everywhere? Are there any bases that have not been hit with the stuff? Get me any kind of numbers of this nature from every branch of service."

"Yes, Sir. I'll get right on it."

"OK. Call me as soon as you get anything. I've got to try to get Sarah some help."

"Sarah, Hon. We've got to at least try to get you to the hospital," he had told her. Sarah had been too weak to even argue with him. He had heard the reports of chaos and outright anarchy at all medical facilities, but had hoped that maybe his influence would be enough to wrangle her some kind of medical attention. He never got a chance. In fact, the best he could determine, he was never able to drive closer than five miles from the hospital. A complete jam of abandoned vehicles blocked every available access to the hospital for miles. He knew that Sarah would be too weak to walk that distance.

"Sarah, I'm going to walk to the hospital...get a wheel chair or something. I'll be back as quick as I can."

"No, don't leave me...take me home," Sarah said in a feeble voice.

"Keep the doors locked...it won't take long."

As he started walking through the residential area Herndon realized that his preoccupation with tending his ailing wife within the confines of his home over the past week had left him oblivious to how almost everything was breaking down. Most of the houses had a mountain of uncollected trash at the curb. It was easy for Herndon's logistics-oriented mind to translate the significance of mounds of garbage in an upscale neighborhood. *If we can't even get the damn trash picked up because everyone is sick...think about everything else*, Herndon thought as he hurried down the sidewalk. Continuing on about a quarter of mile, further evidence convinced him of the reality of the situation.

On the opposite side of the street, a man walked back from the direction of the hospital. He was a giant, powerfully built man carrying a young girl about ten years old in his arms. Her head hung down loosely over his arm. Bloody bruises covered her face and a dried stream of blood crusted from her mouth and ears down to her blond hairline. Her eyes stared, without blinking, toward the sky. The red color of her conjunctiva contrasted the blue of her irises. Her mouth was agape and one arm dangled down.

Herndon worked his way through the tangle of abandoned cars to intercept the man. As soon as he saw Herndon coming toward him, he laid the girl on the sidewalk and, in one sweeping upward motion, produced a pointed pistol. His expression left little doubt about the seriousness of his threat.

"Whoa, Son. Take it easy! I just need a little information," Herndon said, holding an open-palm hand out toward the man. "My wife...she's back in my car...she's very sick and..."

"You won't make it down this street without one of these." The man held his handgun up slightly higher. "It wouldn't matter...they can't help you...too many." Using his pistol to point in the direction of the hospital, he stuffed the gun into his belt, picked up the girl and walked in the direction where Herndon had left Sarah. The General stared at the man for a second as he strode away. He glanced back toward the hospital, which he could now see in the distance. He shook his head, knowing that the big man was right. For few steps, he followed behind the man. Then, a thought occurred to him.

It was reasonable to assume that the man had been at the hospital for some time in his futile attempt to get help for the girl, probably his daughter. In that case, his vehicle was most likely one of hundreds that was hopelessly entangled in the jumble of abandoned cars. If so, he looked desperate enough to try anything. Herndon had his doubts that the young girl he was carrying was even alive. Regardless, the General reasoned that his unencumbered vehicle might look enticing to the man. If he went straight to Sarah, it would be easy enough for the man to pull his pistol and hijack Herndon's car.

"What if he sees Sarah lying in her seat? He'll break in for sure...I should have taken her home like she wanted," Herndon spoke out loud to himself.

As he hurried, he tried to convince himself that he was just being paranoid. He thought he could see his car in the distance over the tops of the other vehicles. It looked like the big man was putting the girl in a car immediately in front of his car. Perhaps Herndon had the man totally blocked in. He moved as fast as he could. He thought he could see the man peering through the passenger side window, right where Sarah reclined in the seat. The man immediately went to and opened the trunk of his own car, producing a tire tool. He returned to the driver's side of Herndon's vehicle.

"Hey! Wait! I'm coming! I'll move it! I'll move it!" Herndon shouted as he ran at a surprising clip for a man of his years.

He stopped about twenty yards from the man. "Son, please wait. Don't...I'll move...drive you somewhere...whatever you want. "Herndon gasped for air after his short run. "Please don't bother her...she's very weak." Herndon edged toward the man.

"Let me look at her."

Herndon hesitated. The request was not what he had anticipated.

"Please let me examine her. I'm the Chief of Staff," the man said, nodding back toward the general direction of the hospital. Herndon stared at the hulk of a man. *Chief of Staff...more like a down lineman for the Packers...too young to be Chief of Staff...a pistol packing Chief of Staff at that,* thought Herndon.

"I'm sorry about pulling this thing," he said tapping the handgun. "If you had any idea what we've been going through...no security...*we* are the security. My sister's daughter...I promised...I promised my sister I wouldn't leave her in that pile of bodies at the hospital." He gestured toward the car where he had placed the girl.

Herndon stood at the open car door while the man examined his wife. The General could not help but notice the transformation in the man. He was no longer the menacing behemoth that had previously caused him so much concern. He handled Sarah with such care and gentleness that it was hard to believe that his previous behavior was anything but an act. The man

243

sighed as he pulled his massive shoulders together in order to extract himself from the car door opening.

"My advice is to take her home. Don't bother trying to get her to a hospital. Are you feeling ill?"

"I'm fine."

"Well, then you'll be able to give her better attention than she would receive anyplace else.

"She's a cancer patient."

"My friend, I have personally stacked people I have known for years in the halls. Take her home."

Herndon took his wife home. On the way, he stopped at the house of a doctor friend. He pounded on the door for several minutes. He knew that the chance of his friend being at home was slim. Radio and TV were constantly asking for all medical personnel to report to some emergency treatment center. If there was such a center, he had not been able to find any one who knew its location.

When they got back home he realized that Sarah was totally exhausted and turning for the worse. He figured he would try again in morning to get her into a doctor. She did not make it that long. Herndon had moved to the living room couch, hoping not to disturb her with his constant calls to Captain Goodloe. At 2:00 am Goodloe, called with a sketchy report of 'some kind of terrorist attack at several bases.'

"Sarah, Hon, there's been some kind of attack on several of our bases. I'm going to run up to the Pentagon...Sarah?...Sarah!"

Herndon had prepared himself mentally to lose his wife during her protracted struggle with breast cancer. Now, he would not even have the luxury of mourning her or giving her a proper burial.

• • •

Now, walking back from the garage, Herndon paused and looked back at the freezer. "Well Hon, I'll do better later...I'm pretty sure I won't have any better luck at getting you to a Funeral Home than I had getting you to a doctor. Anyway, I've got to get to the Pentagon. I think we're in big trouble. You should keep just fine...well, if they can keep the juice turned on, you will.

244

Maybe it was a good thing you didn't clean out all this stuff...with all that frozen Zucchini packed around you'll be..."

A flash of light, followed by a window-rattling boom, interrupted the General. Three or more explosions ensued. All the electricity went off. Herndon ran as fast as could into his house, locking the doors behind him. He knew from the general direction of the explosions what had been hit. He also knew what was going to happen next.

LAUGHLIN AIR FORCE BASE

SUNDAY AFTERNOON

Tony squinted his burning eyes again in an attempt to make out what he thought he was seeing. He had tried to call in sick that morning because his head was hurting and his back ached so bad that he could not find a way to make it stop. The phone had rung at least five times before somebody answered it. The voice on the other end was weak-sounding and totally unsympathetic to Tony's complaints. He had been told to report to the guard shack, anyway. Everybody else felt as bad as he did, or worse.

As he had driven to his post, there was no other traffic. The place was dead. This flu had taken everybody out. He had heard rumors that several people had died from it. Nothing could be done for it.

Still, why did he have to be here now? He just wanted to be left alone in bed. But no. Here he was, staring out into the damned scrub brush...and hallucinating. His eyes were telling him that a dark line was slowly rising at the edge of the horizon.

It was probably the effect of the setting sun in that direction. It hurt his eyes to keep looking into the sun that way, so he kept closing them and rubbing them to ease them some. He looked up again. The line had grown just a bit taller and was moving closer.

Sudden silence grabbed his attention as the lights and the heater in the shack went down. Oh, great, he thought. A power outage was just what he needed right now.

Tony closed his eyes. He had not meant to fall to sleep, but his eyes burned so he closed them...and took a lovely nap. Remembering his last concern, he jerked his head up to peer out of the window of the guard shack. He was sure he was hallucinating now. He thought he saw an army...only fifty feet away. He shook his head, trying to clear it. It was still there. He grabbed the walkie-talkie and put it up to his mouth. He was shot immediately.

Something told Steve that everything was not right. Maybe it was the fact that the phone at the security command post was too quiet. Only moments ago, it had been ringing incessantly and it seemed that everybody was having some sort of crisis. It made it really hard for him since he was the only one on duty that day. It was amazing what a little flu virus could do to a base. To make matters more mysterious, somebody had called in on a walkie-talkie a few minutes ago. Whoever it was failed to identify themselves and made no sense at all. What did he mean? An army had arrived. That was all he had said. It was complete nonsense, so turned his attention to more important things, like the power outage.

He picked up the phone to call the maintenance group. How strange. No dial tone.

Then, he heard the machine gun rounds. To add to his confusion, grenade blasts seemed to echo after the machine gun. He stepped out of the building to get a better view.

The piercing heat of the bullets helped him to understand. They really were under attack. Impossible. But then, why were his chest and arm bleeding? Then, he saw them. Soldiers in berets were advancing on each building, in succession, firing at anything that moved.

Black edges began to form around his eyesight. He slumped down and tried to brace himself with the brick wall behind him. To his surprise, he did not have the strength to stay upright. His body let his head land on the sidewalk. He could still hear the shooting. The sound of boots coming his way made him try to look in their direction. He could hear them yelling, but he could not understand them. At first, he thought they might be speaking Spanish, but then, he remembered that he understood Spanish. They were speaking something else when they came to him and finished the job.

RANDOLPH AIR FORCE BASE

SAN ANTONIO, TEXAS

"All units, all units. Respond to a situation at Randolph Air Force Base. Report to main entrance."

"All units...Ha! Yeah, right! Come on, man, get in. We gotta roll," yelled Officer Gonzales to his partner.

"What's up?"

"Don't know...they just called all units to the main entrance of Randolph. All units...whatta a joke. I bet we haven't got ten units operating in the whole city. Well, anyway, maybe a little action, huh?"

They turned into Randolph's main entrance. As they approached the main guard station, a young Air Force SP stepped out in front of their squad car, holding up his right hand. Another squad car waited in front of them.

"Officers, we are having terrorist activities on the flight line. I have been instructed to assemble all your units here. My CO is in route and will take you to the area we need help securing."

Even as they spoke, two more units pulled in behind their patrol car.

"Hey, Gonzales. What's the deal man? Have you heard from the head shed?"

"Naw, man I haven't been able to get a peep outta them since they sent us here," shouted Gonzales to the men in the patrol car behind him.

In short order, fourteen squad cars were lined up in front of the security station.

"Hey, Bud I think this is all there is. Where's your CO?" Gonzales shouted to the young SP. The young man held up his right hand to acknowledge Gonzales. He turned and walked into the security station, closing the door behind him. The security station building was bricked up to about four feet in height. Above this height, it was glassed in on all sides. The SP immediately put on a strange-looking helmet that was obviously equipped as a communications device. He adjusted the mouthpiece and nodded his head as he spoke into the receiver. He took a small device about the size of a roll of quarters out of his pocket and dropped to the floor. He curled up into a ball and depressed a button on top of the device he held in his hand.

The explosion lifted the car in front of Gonzales' car. The force blew the squad car up and backwards. It came crashing down on Gonzales' car, grinding metal as the top car slid down to the side, coming to rest with two side tires perched right above the top of the windows. A streak of fire sped toward the last squad car in the line. When the small missile exploded, pieces and parts of both men's bodies were blown out of the vehicle.

There was no escape. The destroyed front and rear vehicles boxed them in and prevented any flight, except for on foot. Two 50-caliber machine gun positions hosed the stunned men in the squad cars. One officer, whose left arm was only being held onto his body by a little skin and material from his blood-soaked uniform, survived the first pass of both guns. He managed to get out of his car and get off two rounds from his service handgun before both 50 caliber's focused backed in on him. Bloody intestines spilled out of his torso as it was nearly completely separated from the top part of his body. The whole attack lasted a maximum of fifteen seconds.

In the confusion, Gonzales realized that his partner's limp body and the chassis of the exploded car had shielded him from the machine-gun spray. He pulled himself from his seat belt, being careful not to put any pressure on his dislocated right shoulder. He used his left hand to force the car door open. Dropping to the ground, he let his body follow his legs into the slight ditch. From there, he was able to reach the line of bushes behind it. As silence crept back on the scene, he sat curled in a ball, hoping his escape had not been noticed. Crawling low on his belly, he crept along another ditch running along the periphery of the Base.

PENTAGON RUINS

H-HOUR + 7:00

"General?"

"Brian, Son...Thank God! I heard the blast from my house. I was sure you were dead. How bad is it there?"

"Sir, I really don't know. We can't get above. We've got the emergency juice up and the communication link up. The reports from the outside sound like there's not much left above. They really clobbered us. Sir, I need to warn you..."

"Save your breath son...do you have any reports...are we being hit in any other way."

"Yes Sir, we've got several reports... sketchy... commando-type attacks. Uhh, just a second, Sir. We're getting all kinds of..."

"Brian, talk to me. What's going on...Captain!" shouted Herndon into the phone.

"Oh God! General, we're getting reports from everywhere...it's like every base in the whole freaking country is under attack." Goodloe's voice betrayed his panic.

"It's OK, Son. Just talk to me. I need specifics, numbers...what kind of armaments do they have?"

"Yes, Sir. O.K., Sir...umm...umm," Goodloe stammered because of the mass of confusion surrounding him. The makeshift communications room had become a jumble of men yelling out the latest reports. It looked like a scene at the Chicago Mercantile Trading Floor.

"Brian, talk to me, damn it!"

"We are just getting so much coming in...Umm, O.K. So far, it seems to be at least just...everywhere just small arms-type fire fights. Umm, they seem to have hand-held type rocket launchers, some TOWs perhaps...grenades and satchel charges of some description...uh Stinger class missiles, maybe.... Yes, Yes we definitely can confirm Stinger types firing on our choppers at Hood."

"Fort Hood? What kind of numbers...How many?"

"Unknown Sir, but it's a strong force...probably the strongest attack. We even have a couple of reports of them gassing barracks with something. Also, there's a helluva lot of crap going on at the San Antonio bases."

"Iraqi-Iranian, right. How are we doing? Are our kids holding on? Do they have enough well, able-bodied men to mount a defense? Brian, now listen to me, Son, on the San Antonio Air Bases. Get them help now! Don't let the Coalition gain control of the flight lines. It's air cover...they're after air cover. They're after our own birds. If we lose those bases, we don't have enough well pilots to stop them.

SADEQ

IRAN

S adeq paced with his son in the hall outside his daughter-in-law's hospital room. "How long can it take to check this out?" He slowed his pace by the small slit of an opening to try to peek into the room. Just as he was able to see anything, the doctor mumbled something to the nurse and turned to go out the door. Sadeq had to take some fast steps backward to avoid being run over as the doctor came out.

"Well? How is the baby?" Sadeq blurted out.

The doctor took hold of Sadeq's shoulder and looked sympathetically into his eyes. "I'm so sorry. We have done all we can do. The heartbeat stopped a few minutes ago. I'm afraid that the child is dead."

"No! You just cannot hear it clearly. Surely, the child still lives."

"I wish I could make this easier for you. I'm sorry, but the child has died. We will have to remove him from his mother's womb. But I think the mother will live."

But Sadeq was not listening anymore. He really did not care about the woman. His grandson was dead...by a virus that he had released. The irony began to weigh on his head and he rubbed his temples to try to make it disappear. But, it stayed and only got heavier until he thought he would not be able to breathe much longer. He tore at his shirt and wailed as he ran out of the hospital, nearly falling several times because he could not see through the fog that had enveloped his mind. He knew that he would never be allowed to have another grandson. Look at what he had done to this one. His mind tortured him with visions of what the tiny victim looked like in the womb, with lesions covering his entire body. He knew too well what the virus did to a fetus.

He found himself sitting on a bench outside the building that housed his office. He did not know what time it was or how long he had been sitting there. He had no memory of the time. He was barely aware of someone sitting down on the bench beside him. He forced himself to look up to see who was calling his name. It was a familiar voice, but he could not place it with a face.

"Sadeq...Sadeq...Do you hear me?"

He was conscious of a pair of hands on the sides of his face, turning it towards their owner. It was Malik. Hated Malik. His worst accuser. Why did he have to see him now? The voices of the dying were doing plenty of accusing for Malik now. Sadeq was barely able to take it. Then, the picture of his mother sobbing began to form in his mind. He was sure he could hear her weeping. He put his hands up to his ears to try to stop it. It did not work. The sound grew even more intense.

"Sadeq, I heard about the child. I am so sorry for you. Is there anything I can do for you?"

Malik was torturing him with kind gestures. Sadeq knew that he did not deserve anything kind. He had killed his grandson...He had murdered millions of people. He did not deserve to be ranked with Hitler. Hitler was too kind. Sadeq had invented a new level of monstrosity. He had released a murderer intentionally. Even as he pondered the enormity of the fact, people all over the world were suffering and dying and they would continue to do so for a very long time. And he could not tolerate the pain of that knowledge anymore. Or the sound of his mother's weeping.

"Sadeq, are you all right? Do you hear me? Please try to talk to me." Malik could see the distant look in Sadeq's eyes. Sadness filled them all the way to his soul. His ripped shirt barely hung from his quivering shoulders as intermittent convulsions rocked through them, followed by short bursts of moaning.

True, Malik hated what Sadeq had done. But he never hated Sadeq. He would never understand why he had done this unspeakably horrible thing. His attention was drawn to the masses of people crowding the streets and sidewalks. They did not even suspect what was coming their way because of Sadeq's work. If they had, they would have fallen on him, en masse, and killed him. Malik was doing his best to spread the vaccine, but it was an impossible task, especially with the government officials denying a problem. The unsuspecting population was being thinned out, almost on purpose.

Sadeq had been an integral part of it all. But looking at the twisted form of his tortured friend, Malik had to feel some pity for the man. He had only done what he thought was right for his country. Malik had to get him home somehow.

"Come, Sadeq. You must go home now. I will take you." He took Sadeq by the arm and pulled him up off the bench. Sadeq did not even know where he was. Malik was leading a zombie. They got to the curb on the busy street where Malik had hastily parked his car when he spied Sadeq. Malik let go of Sadeq for a few seconds to unlock the car door.

The screeching of the tires announced Sadeq's sudden suicide.

PENTAGON

H-HOUR + 7:15

"Captain, who's the Senior Officer there?"

"Colonel Meyers, Sir."

"What brass have you got a hold of, Son? Who has reported in? Who did we lose above you? I've got to get a handle on who's running the show. What about Hickson...was he there?"

"No Sir, not Hickson. I'm not sure if he was above or not when we were hit. So far, the rescue teams working above haven't found anybody alive. Marlin... just a second, Sir...Marlin has been found. Sir, apparently General Marlin was in his car when we were hit. The body is badly burned, but they are pretty sure it's Marlin. A number were home sick, Sir. You are the only ranking Officer we've been able to contact so far. We are still trying...General, I'm fearful for your safety. We've received reports of assassin teams. The White House has made contact with us and even they have informed us about reports of assassins. We haven't been able to confirm any of this."

"Brian, I believe we will have to assume that most of our brass is dead. As far as the reports of assassin teams...they are true. Warn anybody you can. Any of our ranking brass is in grave danger. I'll explain how I know later. It's probably too late, but send armed teams to the homes. If they have a star, send a team to their house. I don't hold out much hope for any of them, but we've got to check it out."

"Do it." Goodloe snapped his fingers at a young man.

"Captain, until some other big dog shows up, I'm going to assume command. Put me on speaker. I want to make sure everyone hears this."

"Go ahead, Sir. I believe we can all hear you."

"Gentlemen, before the day is over, I'm afraid we will discover that our entire Pentagon Command structure has been decimated. Actually, we haven't got the whole day. Therefore, I'm assuming command. I'm giving Captain Goodloe a Field Promotion to Colonel. Goodloe, you're the CO now. Colonel Meyer, this is no reflection on you or your abilities. I just don't know you. Colonel Goodloe?"

"Yes Sir?"

"Colonel, I want you to scramble anything you can get in the air. Get it over San Antonio. Shoot down anything that flies over that city. I want a total stand down over that town. Civilian...everything. If it takes off or lands or flies over that town, it's a target. Get the word out. Have you got any relief to the San Antonio bases?"

Goodloe pointed to another man wearing a head set. "Do it. Sir, I have already scrambled Tomcat's from the Carrier Kitty Hawk."

"How many? How much time can they spend over San Antonio?"

"Six, Sir...maybe four to eight minutes. The carrier is pretty far out."

"No, no. We gotta have more. We need a constant umbrella over that town in case they take any of the flight lines."

"Sir, the best I can tell, our guys are doing a number on that bunch. The commandos are isolated on the flight line. It's just a matter of time until we gain control at some other base...Tinker...Oklahoma, right? OK, great. Sir, we're getting a good report at Tinker AFB. It looks like we will gain control of Tinker's Flight Line in short order. If we can scramble from there, we can put a hell of an umbrella over the San Antonio bases. Like I said, it's just a matter of time."

"Son, you haven't got time. The knock out punch is coming. It's probably coming at us right now. The genius Son of a Bitch who put this together didn't hit all our bases just to have his men get cut off and wither on the vine. Their job is to keep us penned down and confused and to buy time for the main show. Just like what we did to the Nazis with our paratroopers before the Normandy invasion. My guess is that the San Antonio bases, Randolph, Kelly, Lackland are the lynch pin of the whole operation. What else do you have besides the base attacks? Give me anything."

"Sir, we're getting a lot of weird reports...umm, increasingly we're finding that we've received a great deal of bogus reports. "

"What kind of bogus reports?"

"Well, for instance, all the Army bases in Virginia. Early on, we had reports of heavy Commando raids. I had a satellite video downlink with the CO's of Fort Monroe, Fort Story and also Fort Lee. Sir, I personally saw each one of those men giving me a live video account and there was fighting going on all around them and later..."

"I can't believe it! I told the whole lot of those ignorant Son-of a Bitch computer jerk-offs that this would happen. They said it couldn't happen...'Oh, General, Sir, we've got this safe guard, and that security...it would be impossible...' Kiss my ass! They got in...they tapped us, didn't they!"

"It would appear so, Sir."

"Now, we don't know what in the hell to believe. It's gonna be one big, wild-assed guessing game. O.K., what about Randolph? What can you confirm? How much of that is bogus bull-shit?"

"Randolph does appear to be a little different tactic. The CO...Uhh General Mickel gave me a video reporting that it's not much of an attack and that they should have it completely suppressed in a matter of minutes. Then, I got another report from a Colonel Iveson who says the CO is virtually on his deathbed with this bug and couldn't possibly have delivered such a report. Anyway, he stated that the whole issue was very much in doubt; and that he was up against a strong force and that he was in danger of losing control of the flight line. A few minutes later I got another video from General Mickel telling me it's all over. For quite a while, I was getting a running battle of words, each claiming the other's report to be a ruse. General Mickel insisted that the whole thing was meant to divert unneeded reinforcements from..."

"OK, OK! You decided that Iveson was the real deal...right?"

"Well, the General cursed me and told me he didn't have any idea what Barry Sanders, batting average was and I..."

254

"Ah geez," howled and snorted Herndon with laughter. "Brian, Son, you're not too original...plays football right? You get Iveson help?"

"We had of a couple of Apaches and somebody to put in them nearby at Fort Sam. They were at least able to help Colonel Iveson regain the flight line...that was our last report."

"OK, Son, but what I'm looking for is a major deal. Given time, we will figure out which attacks are real and which are cyber bullshit and we will mop up the commandos. They know this too. So, where is their main punch? It's got to be coming."

"Sir, like I said, so much...so much of it's hard to verify. We've got reports of commandos in rural towns that have no military significance... reports of demolition of everything from bridges to schools. It doesn't make any sense. I got reports of Iraqi oil tankers at several Texas ports...some small arms fire. Then, I get another report that said nothing like that was going on."

"Iraqi oil tankers?"

"Yes, Sir. That much we've been able to substantiate. They were due in port today."

"How many?"

"Twenty...is that right?...yes, twenty. That's right."

"Twenty tankers...that's gotta be it. No, that is it." Herndon stared up toward the ceiling. "My God, you showed me. When will I ever learn? Brian, when was the last report you got on those tankers? Which ports?"

"Let's see...Texas City, Galveston...maybe some of the smaller ports. I haven't heard anything back from there. It was one of the first reports we received after we got everything up and running again...maybe five hours ago. Nothing since then."

"Brian, get something over there to give you a good look...a chopper. That's got to be it. That brazen, genius bastard is just going to drive right up our own ports and off-load men and equipment."

"We're on it, Sir. Sir, I really must insist that we send you some kind of personal protection squad."

"I appreciate it, Son...trust me, I don't think it's going to be necessary. Call me back when you find out something about those tankers. Let me know when they get you dug out. When they get you uncovered, I'll take you

255

up on that squad. I'll probably need a pretty good escort to get to you. All right, Colonel, get after it. I've got a few things I need to take care of."

Herndon lay back on his bed and stared at the ceiling for several minutes. "I thought maybe you would like to hear me say this...Well, thanks for the dream. I damn sure would not have been ready for them."

He strained his head and neck in an attempt to see the bloody chunk missing out of his trapezius, slightly above where the collarbone joins the shoulder. He had been using a pillowcase to stop the blood. He looked at the blood-soaked embroidered pillowcase. "Damn, this would really piss off Sarah. What a mess."

He rolled over and picked up a small tape recorder. "Based on first hand experience, I would like to highly recommend—what the hell is this thing? Anyway, I would like to recommend the new Browning be given serious consideration to replace the M-16...umm, or at least be considered a viable candidate for a weapon to be included in the typical rifle squad...yeah, that's right...probably more in the role as a component in the typical rifle squad weaponry, rather than an outright replacement of the 16. Hell, this thing is more of a hand-held auto cannon than a rifle. Damn, can it lay down fire!"

Herndon sat up on the edge of his bed. He stared at what had been his bedroom wall and bedroom door, leading out into his hallway. It was now mostly a skeleton of splintered wall studs. Only a small amount of drywall material remained attached to the wall. The destroyed walls revealed two men lying in the hall near his bedroom door. At what would have been the beginning of the hallway lay a third member of the assassin team. His job would have been to complete whatever the first had not been able to complete. Beyond him, was yet another team member lying in the living room...further insurance that the job would be carried out.

They had been well protected with body armor, helmets and equipment resembling the type commonly used by non-military SWAT teams. The armor had not helped.

The one man in the living room was still living. He began to cry out one word. He repeated it several times. Even though it was in Arabic, the General knew what he was saying. He had been to enough battlefields where the wounded still lay.

"Crying for your mother, eh!—Well, she can't hear you—you murdering bastard."

RANDOLPH AFB
H-HOUR +7:30

olonel Iveson's courage and determination could not be questioned. The small bones of his left hand were exposed. His pinky and ring finger had been totally shot off. He had only stopped long enough to have his hand heavily wrapped in gauze. It now looked like a bloody, white boxing glove. It was his second wound of the day.

The first he received two hours earlier inside a hangar. Iveson had been leading a quick sweep of the hangars. The Colonel had almost casually entered one of the hangars while his men outside were engaged in a screaming, yelling firefight. He directed three Airmen to search the hangar. From the corner of his eye, he saw the three grenades rolled along the concrete floor by the cornered Commando. Iveson watched in slow motion as the explosions impacted two of the young Airmen, causing their arms and legs to fling back behind them in an unnatural, contorted position. He never even noticed the third Airman until the thud of the collision of the young man's body with his own vibrated his bones and teeth. The young Airman's body shielded the Colonel from the worst of the flesh-ripping impact of the grenade fragments.

The violent concussion from one of grenades had thrown the young man back into Iveson. The force of the Airman hitting the Colonel caused his head to slam against the concrete floor. Black spots melded together in Iveson's vision until he lost all consciousness. This undoubtedly saved his life.

The Commando quickly searched the scene after the grenades exploded. The only live target the Commando saw was the young Airman as he struggled to get off the top of his CO's body. His head, neck and limbs jerked and convulsed and would not obey any of his commands to function properly. He finally managed to get enough control to sit up. The commando

257

hit him cleanly in the throat with a single shot. As he edged to toward his fallen foes, he realized no further action was necessary. A quick glance toward the Colonel was enough to see that his head was lying in blood. The Commando hurled more grenades out of the hangar entrance. Even before they exploded, he ran out the hangar firing full auto.

For a few seconds, Iverson thought that maybe he should not move, just in case another Commando was hiding in the hangar. He tried to move and found he could not move his legs, so he assumed he was more seriously injured than he originally thought. He raised his head up and realized that the dead Airman sprawled across his legs was the reason for their immobility. He raised his hand to investigate the warm trickle on his jaw. A grenade fragment had penetrated his cheek on the right side of his face and exited at the corner of his lip on the left side of his face. The large slit on his left cheek exposed his teeth. It caused him to make a sort of flapping noise when he shouted orders.

Despite all his bravery, Iveson knew that his tactical knowledge was not going to win the day. He was a jet jockey, the CO of a Squadron of fighter pilots. Nothing in his training prepared him for what he now faced. Aerial combat technique was a subject he knew something about, not ground combat.

In spite of his lack of ground combat experience, he recognized that he was up against some warriors who did know what they were doing. At one point, the Commandos completely overran the flight line and set up a defensive perimeter. Iveson expected to see the rows of his F-16's start exploding in flames immediately. Instead, the Commandos did not even approach the war birds. The squad of Commandos nearest the jets set up defensive positions some three hundred yards out from the parked fighters.

Early on, it was apparent to Iveson that his Airmen were no match for their attackers. Iveson's men would fire wildly, often emptying entire magazines at a long-gone enemy or at a non-existing enemy. When they did have a target, most of the airmen were so excited that they missed badly enough to give their assailants a chance to seek cover. Many of his men were seriously ill. Even mustering the sick had left him with too few to fight off such well-trained, determined foes.

In contrast, the Commandos were efficient and lethal. Many of them fired their weapons on semi-automatic rather than full automatic, relying on sniper-like accuracy instead of spraying precious ammo. They fought coolly and worked as a team. If one of their group was injured to the point that he could longer fight, there was no attempt to stop and attend to his wounds. If one their members did stop over a downed comrade, it was merely to retrieve needed equipment, weapons or ammo.

Even when the Apache Attack Helicopters showed up, the commandos did not panic. They retreated in an orderly withdrawal from the F-16s and took cover by a berm on the beginning of the main runway.

"Pull back! Pull back!" Colonel Iveson commanded over a bullhorn as he leaned up against his staff car. *Let the Apache's take care of them. I'm not going let any more kids get killed fighting insane fanatics*, Iveson thought.

The Apaches were frightening, terrifying machines that bristled with multiple forms of death. It seemed almost unfair for any ground warrior to have to face such lopsided odds. Iveson actually caught himself admiring the commandos. It was one of those perverse kinds of feelings and thoughts that made him glad no one had the ability to peer into his mind. He chided himself. Here he was in the heat, confusion and whirl of battle and he was taking time out mentally to admire a group of remorseless, trained killers...a group of men who, because of their training, would not hesitate to slaughter school children if that had been part of their mission.

Still, he admired them because they did what they were created to do without hesitation. It was like watching the wildlife shows on TV where the African hunting dogs attacked their prey. It was bloody, without pity and efficient. They were performing according to their creation and function.

Now, Iveson found himself even feeling sorry for the commandos. They had fought with precision and ferocious, animalistic courage. As the two helicopters opened up with their chin guns, Iveson glassed the berm for signs of the Commandos' surrender. He hated to see brave men killed in a hopeless situation, but he knew that this type did not surrender. If they did surrender, a part of him would be disappointed.

Most of the Airmen came out from their cover to watch the show. They cheered wildly when the choppers started unleashing rounds from their rocket pods and ground burst erupted around the commandos' positions. Some of the Airmen fired rounds from their M-16s in the general direction of the commandos, even though the range was too great to be of much effect. This was compounded by the fact that dust and smoke began to obscure almost everything.

Iveson rested his elbows on top of his staff car and tried to scope the commandos with his binoculars. It was difficult to see anything. He initially thought that the firing from the choppers had caught the grassed area around the berm and landing strip on fire. He knew that a smoldering grass fire could really smoke things up, but it did not take him long to conclude that it was entirely too much smoke to be coming from the burning islands of grass between the tarmac. They had more than likely had laid down some kind of smoke screen.

"Colonel Iveson, it's the Pentagon, a Colonel Goodloe," Iveson's driver shouted, waving the phone from the car.

"Colonel Iveson here."

"Colonel we need an update."

"Well, we have them isolated on one end of the flight line away from the birds. The Apaches are finishing them off. Everything should be secure within the hour."

"Colonel, listen up. You are under direct orders from General Herndon to blow all aircraft on your flight line. Repeat, blow up, destroy, and render useless all aircraft, especially the F-16's on your flight line. You will be receiving a hard-line security coded transmittal of this order immediately. We have reason to believe that you are going to experience overwhelming force and we don't want to chance the birds falling into enemy hands."

"Listen you! I spent a great deal of time this morning trying to convince you that I was who I said I was, and you kept to telling me that you were getting bogus reports from my CO. I sent you hard-line security coded transmittals and you still would not believe me. Now, you want to me to believe your security transmittals. I've got...I don't know how many dead and wounded boys lying stacked in a hangar. They got that way trying to fight this bunch of crazies off our birds. I tell you the 16s are secure and now you're telling me to blow them to hell." Bloodstained spit collected at the corners of Iveson's mouth. The butterfly bandages that held his left cheek together strained at every shouted syllable.

"It's an order Colonel."

"I'll call you back!" Iveson shouted contorting his face so much that he tore loose the butterfly bandages holding his left cheek together.

Iveson glanced back at the rows of F-16s. He definitely felt like he was in one those 'Damned if you do and Damned if you don't' situations. He did not want to be the idiot who blew up billions of dollars worth of fighters because of some techno-cyber-ruse executed by a clever enemy. On the other hand, he did not want to disobey what might be a valid direct order. He had received enough reports to realize that hell was breaking out all over...it was possible.

Iveson bent his head down to speak to his driver. Airmen Gass had been his and General Mickel's driver for the past two years. While he was a competent driver, it had always amazed Iveson that Gass had managed to get into the Air Force, being as mentally slow as he was...not that you had to be a mental giant to enlist in the Air Force. Iveson's first attempt at telling Airmen Gass what he wanted him to do resulted in a mouth-open stare. Iveson repeated his instructions again slowly. "Get a hold of what ever his name was...that Colonel...I'm going to put the ball back in his court. I don't want to talk to him, though. Tell him...tell him I'm busy getting my ass shot off. Tell him we suspect a security breach in all communications. If it's a direct order from General Herndon, they're going to have to come up with some other way to verify such an unusual order. That will take them a while to figure out. Maybe, by then this will be over. When he calls back, say I'm not immediately available." Iveson reasoned that, if the issue were still in doubt, it would be different. But watching the Apaches at work gave him confidence. It was strangely frightening and comforting at same time.

Iveson to tried to peer into the gaps in the smoke with his binoculars, hoping to see something. He thought briefly about repositioning his men to make sure that none of the Commandos escaped from their present location on the side of landing strip. However, now the smoke virtually covered the entire landing strip. He thought better of it. That bunch could pop up anywhere along the smoke screen. The way they fought, any of his men in their path would get severely mauled. Besides, the area around the landing strip was wide open. Any commandos attempting to come out from under the smoke screen would get chewed up by the Apaches.

"Colonel." Airmen Gass held up the phone.

Iveson gestured with both his hands and mimed the words." I told you I didn't want to talk to them."

"I'm sorry, Sir. It's General Herndon...he said a lot of things about your mother...I told him you were busy getting your ass shot off. He said he wanted to talk to the part that hadn't been shot off...and if he didn't get to, he would personally see to it that my ass got shot off."

Iveson knew Herndon, at least by reputation. He held the phone down to his side and shook his head before holding it up to his ear.

"Colonel Iveson here."

"Look you ignorant..." The string of profanity did not stop for at least a minute. The words "court marshal your ass" were sprinkled about in the one-sided conversation.

Iveson held the phone away from his ear. "If he's not the real deal, he's good imitation." He moved the mouthpiece back to his face. "General, Sir. I hope you understand my concern with the apparent security breach we've experienced. If there were just some way I could confirm..."

"O.K., Son, I understand." Herndon spoke in an almost fatherly tone. "But there is no way we can do that now...and we have to act now. Think through this with me. Reports had it that they had overrun the flight line...they had the birds. Is this correct?"

"Yes, Sir. That's correct."

"They made no attempts to disable them, destroy them or anything, did they?"

Iveson paused for some time. Things had been happening so fast, kids being killed all around him. Maybe that grenade explosion had addled his brain and he had not been thinking too clearly, or maybe it had just been the fight for survival. "Maybe...maybe you're right. They did have the chance to do it."

"Maybe's ass...Now get to it. Call back when you've got it done."

Iveson sighed and began to formulate the best plan to disable the F-16s.

"Colonel!" Gass pointed over to a large open region that adjoined the landing strip proper.

"What the hell?" Iveson pulled the binoculars his to eyes. Moving at a high rate speed across the mowed field were at least twenty pick-up trucks. They had spread out and were heading straight toward Iveson and his men. Iveson focused his binoculars at something even further out. More vehicles were moving through a hole in the chain link perimeter fence.

A streak of light caused him to pull his eyes from his binoculars toward the nearest hovering Apache. The streak had come from the smoky area that concealed what was left of the Commandos. His eyes focused in on it just in time to witness its impact with the helicopter. His mind recorded it in slow motion. The explosion took out the helicopter engine. Still, the blades whirled. The pilot tried to control the craft and gain a flight attitude that might result in a survivable crash. The ground was too near; he crashed on the edge of the main landing strip. Fiery chunks rolled down the strip.

Immediately, the other Apache emptied all its remaining pod rockets in the direction from which the commandos had launched their missile. Another streak came out from the smoke. It came from much further down the smoke-covered strip. Iveson grimaced, awaiting the impact, but the missile went wide of the helicopter. The pilot arched the Apache in a sharp, banking turn. When it leveled out from its turn, it was facing the oncoming pick-ups. Two of their charging number had stopped. A flash came off the top of one the stopped pick-ups.

"TOWs!" Iveson shouted involuntarily. TOWs had the power to take out heavy tanks. The wire-guided missile hit the Apache flush. Flying debris from the helicopter reached as far as Iveson and his men.

Three pick-ups with mounted, heavy machine guns wheeled past the rows of F-16s. Iveson saw more flashes off the tops of the oncoming line of vehicles in the field. *Incoming TOWs.* The commandos had suckered them away from the war birds. They were surrounded. He shouted to his men to rally to him. He would see that he and his men did not die the cowards' death.

Phase Two

Iran

N asser sat down to begin the hastily called meeting of the Council. Silence crept over the group. He cleared his throat and replaced his glasses as he picked up the stack of papers before him.

"As you all know, the attack is proceeding as planned, despite the untimely death of Sadeq. He was a noble man in service of his country. We must all remember what he has done for us.

"On to other business. The second part of the attack is well under way. Our forces have succeeded in taking all of the military establishments in San Antonio. How are the air strikes progressing?"

The general sitting two seats away from him stood. "They are proceeding as scheduled. Our forces are approaching the coast of Texas to augment the attack on Fort Hood. Our pilots will be supplying air cover for them. There has been little resistance. The virus has done its job.

"Remember...quick timing is critical. The survivors of the virus will soon be recovering enough to give our plan some trouble. We must have the strategic locations taken by then. So far, the submarines and nuclear attack aircraft have not reacted. Just in case, the plan to evacuate our leaders from our major cities is under way."

The oil tankers loomed in the waters of the coast of Texas. They were not carrying oil. The second wave of Coalition soldiers filled them to capacity. These were the ones that would first take Fort Hood, then use American equipment to move north to all the strategic targets. The invasion would be complete within a week. By the time the American people began to recover, they would be under Coalition rule. The Great Satan would bow to the Coalition.

EXECUTION

"The Council is expecting me." Malik stood before the aide waiting for his reply.

"I will, of course, have to check with them. One moment, please." The young man straightened his back and rose from the desk chair. He disappeared through the ornate double doors and returned in a few minutes, holding one of the doors open for Malik.

"You may go in now."

"Thank-you." Malik walked past him and into the high-ceilinged room. His footsteps echoed as he walked across the huge spanse of terrazzo floor toward the small group of men at the other end of the room. They waited silently as he approached, as if they had just finished talking about him. Malik felt the tension in the group as they watched him.

He surveyed the group from a distance and saw Nasser Ghane sitting smugly in the chair at the head of the table. He knew that Nasser had orchestrated the entire war. Nasser leaned back in his chair, raised his hand to his mouth and stared directly at Malik. Malik's heart began to race as he felt a tug of panic. It was as if Nasser could see right through him. Malik's panic shifted to Yahya and his children. *Run Yahya!*

Nasser began in a low tone of voice.

"Well, Malik. It seems that you were finally successful." He paused as he stood and approached Malik, glaring the whole time. He paced a few steps in front of Malik, then turned and circled him. "You know it won't make any difference."

Malik locked eyes with Nasser as he came around to face him again.

"Successful at what?" He still hoped that he was simply being paranoid. How could anyone know that he had sent a warning? Nasser never blinked.

"Such a fool!...a traitorous, shortsighted fool! Did you think we weren't watching you? Of course you were going to try to warn your precious friends. You are not Iranian, Malik...you went over there and got sucked into the Evil until you could not even see that it was Evil. And you brought your blindness back with you to infect your entire family."

265

His eyes narrowed. "You will have the opportunity to witness their pain as they die before you...publicly, of course. You will serve as a mighty example for any other idiot in this nation who is tempted to go against us."

Malik squirmed against the sudden grip of the nearby guards. Then, he suddenly relaxed and hardened his jaw. Yes, they would kill him, but Yahya and children would be safe. They had already disappeared as planned, and Nasser would not be able to find them.

Nasser saw the defiance in Malik's face. The sides of his mouth began to curl into a sly smile. "Ah, so you're thinking they got away already." He turned and nodded to the guard at the room door.

Nausea poured over Malik as he heard Yahya's voice in the hall. "Let go of me now!" she growled at the men holding her arms and dragging her into the room. She turned and spat into the face of one of the men. He then jerked her hard and threw her to the ground, where she landed in a sobbing heap. When she looked up and saw Malik, she stopped weeping and wiped her bruised cheek with the back of her hand. The agonizing look in her eyes confirmed that she knew what was coming. And yet, he thought, she seemed victorious somehow. They had not found the children.

Nasser turned and smiled reassuringly to Malik. "Your children will soon be found and you can be together again as a family." He signaled to the guards and they led Malik and Yahya out the door.

Sitting on the floor in a squalid cell together, Malik and Yahya held on to each other, quietly hoping their children to safety. If all went well, they would find their way out of Iran and eventually to the United States, hopefully to find Mike. Hope was all they had left. Malik and Yahya would not live long enough to know the outcome of the war. They could only hope.

• • •

Sitting quietly at a small table in a dark corner of a café, Reza and his sister finished the lunch they shared. They had to use their money sparingly if it was to last. Reza unconsciously rolled and unrolled the small paper in his pocket that held Mike's address and phone number.

They looked at each other often to affirm their need to be unnoticed. Sibling quarrels had ended at the beginning of their harrowing escape. They were suddenly their only best friends and they had one goal...escape.

An old black and white TV droned at the front of the café, barely loud enough for them to hear. All the people in the café were talking and laughing when Reza's eyes both widened and sank at the same time and he nudged his sister sitting next to him, never letting his eyes leave the TV.

All of the young faces in the corner paled as they watched the scene on the screen before them. They had known the danger their parents faced, but it had not become real until now. They recognized Nasser as he addressed the crowd.

"On the eve of our victory over the Great Evil, we must purge ourselves of those who would spread its influence to our own noble people."

The camera zoomed in on the faces of Malik and Yahya as they stood waiting for their execution. The huddled children grabbed each other's hands under the table and blinked back their tears. The youngest muttered "Mother..." under her breath and the others squeezed her hands to silence her. If they drew attention now, they would be there next.

The guard pushed Yahya toward her death and she stumbled. Malik reacted, but could not reach her. She pulled herself up and gave Malik a look of fear mixed with determination. She took a deep breath as the executioner placed the noose over her head and lowered it to her neck. As she closed her eyes, a tear made its way down her cheek. It dripped off her chin just before the floor under her feet fell.

Malik dropped to his knees, sobbing. Then, he quieted himself, set his jaw and rose, glaring at Nasser.

"You are worse than the disease you spread."

Nasser backhanded him, sending his head to one side so hard that he nearly fell. He caught himself and walked defiantly up to his noose.

His children lowered their heads just in time to avoid watching their father die. The crowd cheered loudly as Malik died, and somewhere in the group, several people coughed.

They thought they were getting the flu.

WASHINGTON D.C.

H-HOUR + 7:30

This was Farid's favorite part. It was like playing a video game. Driving the van with the joy-stick was easy, except when making sharp turns. The image on the screen did not give enough peripheral field to aid in the turn, so it had taken a little practice to master the turns.

The only thing they had not practiced was the blast itself. However, as Kaveh had pointed out, the Oklahoma City explosion gave a pretty good sample of what one explosive-packed van could accomplish. Kaveh also insisted that, as near as he could determine, their vans packed a minimum of seventy-five percent more explosive power than the Oklahoma City van. Farid and his fellow operators controlled ten vans. At first, there was some concern that the Oklahoma City incident might make it difficult to obtain the materials necessary to make the explosives. As it turned out, there was no problem.

Kaveh's command center was well camouflaged. It looked like a dilapidated, old house because that was exactly what it was. It had been carefully selected for this reason and for its general proximity to the White House. Kaveh was the mission controller, and his headset linked him with another element of the mission. He had arranged the ten monitors in the living room. Each monitor allowed one man to control one van. The living room was relatively cramped, but that was fine as far as Kaveh was concerned. He wanted the monitors as close together as possible. This allowed him to pace back and forth behind the monitors and peer over the operators' shoulders.

Farid's van would lead the way. The others would hang back. Making the correct turns was the most critical part. If the operator missed a turn, it was often difficult to tell the van's location by looking at the image on the screen. The absence of traffic helped and there was no mistaking Pennsylvania Avenue.

As the procession began, Kaveh realized that the barricades on Pennsylvania were more numerous and placed farther away from the target than his information had indicated. Steel reinforced concrete barriers blocked the street, except for a small, guarded entrance. One soldier manned the entrance. Two hummers with mounted machine guns waited approximately one hundred yards beyond the entrance. The monitors plainly showed more guards and a tank behind the hummers.

"A tank...Nobody said anything about a tank. Our men...do they know of this, Kaveh? Maybe there is more," Farid shouted back at Kaveh.

Kaveh adjusted his headset and mouthpiece as he stared into Farid's monitor. "Yes...Yes, O.K." Kaveh replied to someone he was listening to over the headset. "Move forward, Farid."

"Kaveh, look!" Farid tapped the screen excitedly pointing to the tank. "Our men..."

"Farid, they are seeing exactly what you are seeing. We are prepared, trust us...move your van forward. The Pentagon is no more...you were expecting maybe a welcome mat? It probably just moved in. It will soon be moving out. I promise you," Kaveh said, scrutinizing Farid's screen.

Farid eased his van closer to the barricade entrance. The guard did not approach the van. Farid could see on his monitor that the guard had leveled his M-16 at the van. The screen turned to snow and Farid turned, giving Kaveh a questioning look.

"He shot it out...Now!" squealed Kaveh.

Farid slapped the detonation button.

The second van rolled up to the place where the barricade entrance had been. The whole region was still smoldering and smoking but it could be plainly seen on the monitor that the area was swept clean...no guards, no concrete barriers, no hummers. The tank had been moved and flipped up on its side. The second van simply drove past the tank. The White House lawn swarmed with soldiers.

A Cobra Helicopter swooped down on the van. One quick burst from its 20-mm cannon disabled the van and it crashed into the White House fence. The result was a white-hot explosion. The shock wave from the explosion blew the main rotor props and the tail section off the Cobra. The fuselage was then overtaken by the fireball and consumed.

Kaveh listened intently to someone over his headset and bobbed his head vigorously. "How many? Four! Allah be with us? Allah be with you. You're the ones they will be shooting at. We will keep them busy."

He pointed to the men at their respective monitors. "Decoy vans...that's you, you, you, you and you...Look at me...look up here." Kaveh excitedly tapped a large map of the immediate White House area of D.C. He explained the maneuvers he expected out of each of the five decoy vans.

"Number 6, you are here. You will turn here and then turn on Pennsylvania, then you will...Number 7, you are here and you will..."

Only four healthy Apache Crews...Incredible thought Major Franklin. Franklin had flown combat in Desert Storm and had led swarms of Apache Attack Helicopters, which had ravaged Saddam's Armored Units. It may have been cliche, but Franklin was one of those who had become "One with his machine." Cliche or not, it was a phenomenon that Aces and other aerial warriors of past conflicts had claimed. Most pilots guided their choppers through their maneuvers. Major Franklin mentally became part of the machine. It was like watching a talented running back weave through would-be tacklers. It was an art and an instinct that coaching, teaching and training could not impart.

Franklin almost resented that Apache's were two-man fighting machines. A gunner was seated in front and slightly lower than the pilot. He had romanticized about the old flying war machines, like the P-51 Mustang of WWII, in which the pilot was the driver, gunner, navigator...everything.

Franklin had just been radioed about the fate of the Cobra that had been taken out by the blast from the van. The first of the next group of vans was still several blocks away when he sited it.

"O.K. Here comes one. I got it. Don't get any closer than I am to it, or it will take you out," Major Franklin communicated to the other helicopter.

The Major had no intention of jacking around or taking chances. He cut loose with a Hellfire laser-guided missile for maximum range and safety. He actually missed the van by a good twenty feet, but the Hellfire was designed with the capability to take out the heaviest Soviet tank. A 'not-so-near' miss was more than enough to send the van rolling in flames. Franklin braced for the shock wave. When the van did not explode, he only shrugged.

"Geez, Major, they're everywhere...they're like mice!" a voice shouted over his headset.

He swung around and up to gain enough altitude to assess the situation. There were four vans close enough to take out with cannon fire. Several blocks further was a swarm composed mostly of vans, but several pick-up trucks and one tractor-trailer rig were also included. Men, clad in full combat gear, scrambled from the nearest of these vehicles.

"O.K., Boys, let's take care of business. Get these...we'll take care of that bunch in a minute." Franklin hoped his 'first things first' talk would prevent any panic, especially his own. It was a wasted order, as the three other choppers were already closing for shots.

"You're too close, back off...Use Hellfires," Franklin squawked over the radio as he saw one Apache chew up a van with 30mm cannon fire. Each round that impacted the van blew off entire sections of its body. The rear end came out from under the van, causing it to grind to a stop in a shower of sparks.

Franklin brought his Apache down low and fast, cutting across the White House lawn area.

"We've got help." Franklin heard the voice of his gunner and tried to locate what he was talking about. One UH-60 Blackhawk helicopter was emptying its load of troops near the White House perimeter fence. Three more were on a descent. Franklin turned his attention back to hunting the van.

"Major, we found a driver for a Hog and he's in route," came another voice over Franklin's headset. *A-10 Warthog...Hot damn!* The thought of the War Bird joining the fray, coupled with the landing of Airborne Troops bolstered him.

He saw one of his Apache's releasing a volley of pod rockets at a target that was not visible to the Major.

"That's the last of them, Sir."

The chase after the vans had drawn the four Apache's several minutes flight from the White House. Franklin had momentarily questioned his own decision to pursue the vans, but he saw no alternative with the potential of such devastating power being vented on the vulnerable ground forces at the White House.

He was in the lead of his Apache group and could see the fury of the firefight in the distance, as the tracer rounds made tracks in the air. He fought his instincts. He really wanted to charge in and visit the maximum amount of violence he could in the shortest amount of time—unleash everything—Hellfire missiles, pod rockets and cannon fire—in one massive blow. He realized that this would be a poor decision. *They've got too much cover...too many buildings...gotta pick and choose my targets.* His basic tactic would be something of a fire rotation. He did not want to expend his group's entire ordinance in one massive, undisciplined display of firepower. He knew that, with the forces massed against the White House, its defender could easily be overrun while his choppers returned to base for rearming.

He would have one Apache step up and lay down fire and rotate back to their home base in Maryland for rearming. There was one other factor. They could not expend all their rounds in case they had to fight at their home base. Franklin had already been sent radio reports of skirmishes at Fort Detrick and Fort Meade. *I hope that Pissed off Pig (A-10 Warthog) gets here soon. That would really help.*

"All right, Henson, you're up. Save a little of everything in case you gotta kick ass back home." Franklin looked down; the White House passed directly below.

Out of the corner of his eye, Franklin saw a flash. "MAJOR...GOING DOWN!"

"MY GOD!" To his right, Franklin saw that Henson's tail boom had been blown off. The loss of the tail rotor caused the helicopter body to spin wildly under the props. Over his right shoulder, he could see the snaking smoke trails and fire signature of missiles...maybe eight or more. They had to be Stinger type heat seekers the way they took out Henson. "MOVE!...GET OUTTA HERE!"

Franklin tipped the nose of the Apache straight toward the ground in an effort to pick up speed. Franklin's gunner thrashed left and then right trying to see what was on their tail.

"GO! GO! THERE'S TWO ON U.S." the gunner screamed after seeing the corkscrewing trail of the missiles. Franklin could tell by the look in his gunner eyes that he had seconds till impact. He resisted the urge to look back. Franklin was in a free fall toward the only escape and cover he saw. *TOO FAST...CAN'T MAKE THE TURN.*

He banked hard at the corner of the White House; his tail boom struck the ground. The first missile curved wide around the corner, following the heat trail of the Apache. It struck a tree. The explosion split the upper trunk. The second took a tighter path around the corner of the White House and exploded just beneath Franklin's craft. The force of the blast lifted the helicopter up and nearly had Franklin upside down before he gained control.

"MOTHER DUCK!...My God, stop...land this thing, Major" shouted the gunner.

"You hit?...What's the matter?"

"I wanna clean out my drawers...that's what's the matter!"

Franklin just smirked and hovered up to peek over the top of the White House. He saw the debris and burning shells of the three Apache's scattered across the White House lawn. To his left, he saw the telltale signature of a missile heading his way. He fired three pod rockets at the source of the signature and dropped back behind the White House for cover. The missile passed harmlessly overhead. He popped up again and his gunner let loose with cannon fire, decimating the squad that had been the source of the missile.

The A-10 Warthog came in blazing. It immediately fired three Hellfire missiles and its whirring cannon chewed up four vehicles. The Major could see the Warthog make a banking turn.

"NO, NO...KEEP GOING, DON'T LOOP OVER THEM," Franklin shouted.

He watched as the A-10 prepared to loop back for another strafing run. At the top of its banking loop, a missile streaked up from directly beneath it. The missile struck the Warthog in its right jet engine. The blast ripped the jet engine away from the fuselage. Despite the hole where the engine used to be, the warplane continued to fly. Franklin could see streams of tracer fire arching up toward the plane and thought he could see fragments and pieces being torn off the warbird. Still, it remained under power as it flew away, trailing black smoke.

"You moron...What an idiot," Franklin fumed over the A-10 pilot's stupidity or inexperience. If he had continued flying low and fast, it would have been doubtful that they would have been quick enough to ever get a heat seeker to lock on to him. When the pilot did his banking loop right above the commandos, they locked on to him easily.

"I think we're in deep tapioca," Franklin sighed as he rotated his chopper to watch the struggling Warthog.

Targets were becoming more difficult to find. It had become a contest. They shot and Franklin fired back and dropped behind the White House for cover. This would have been O.K. because Franklin was keeping them at bay until help arrived, but there was no help coming. Major firefights had erupted at all nearby bases. Franklin was down to a couple of pod rockets and some cannon rounds. He was getting low on fuel too. Fort Detrick had indicated that they almost had their situation in hand and had a crew for an Apache, if he could hold on. He doubted that he had enough fuel to make it to Fort Detrick.

Franklin popped back up above the White House for another round of 'shoot and duck'. He almost started trembling. *How did that thing get there?* The enemy was not anywhere in sight. The only thing he saw was a white van that had stopped in front of the main entrance of the White House, which had been blocked with vehicles for a makeshift barrier. Two presidential limos had even been added to the barricade. The White House defenders blazed away at the van. Franklin was frozen as to what action he should take.

The blast threw the vehicles and made giant shrapnel out of their parts. The shock wave threw bodies and body parts over a mile from the blast. The wave hit the White House, blowing out all the windows and doors. Franklin had dropped back down in time to be shielded from the shock wave and saw the fireball pass overhead.

He did not bother to hover up and look. He was nearly out of fuel and had almost no ordinance. He flew away low and fast, knowing that in a few minutes the happy victors would be firing weapons in celebration in front of the White House.

PENTAGON 7:45

"O.K., General. We got him through."

"Herndon here."

"General, well I must admit I am surprised to hear from you in such apparent good health," Ghane said flatly.

"Well, the sun does shine on a dog's ass every once in a while, Mr. Ghane...we've sort of got a little problem over here...would you mind getting to the point of this conversation?"

"Yes, I have several issues I would like to discuss. First, I would like to prevent further needless death and destruction in your country...Surrender and all hostility will halt immediately and..."

"My murderous friend, you can stick your surrender where the sun never shines."

"Well, I am very sorry to hear that, General. I am curious though...General, why have you not exercised any of your nuclear options."

"I think you know that already...I think you know that we can nuke you with our subs any time we want to...spit it out, I've been expecting to hear from you."

"Well, we both have nuclear cards to play. I propose that you carry out a thermonuclear strike on any one of our cities of you choosing. We, in turn, will demonstrate on one of your..."

"You haven't got that many to go swapping hits with us...I know how many you've got...I figured you'd get em over here.

"Well, General, let me spell it out for you...my cities are largely evacuated...your sick and dying populations are not...and can not. While it is true that we've been only able to procure a few nuclear devices of comparable strength to yours, we have been able to produce a multitude of more modest devices that we have..."

"Mr. Ghane, we have no more business to discuss...Brian, end this."

"Sir...he's off, Sir."

"Well, he achieved what he wanted there...a short term nuclear stand off. Figures he'll win or loose over here in seventy-two hours...a short-term nuke stalemate is all he needs. Hitting him over there resolves nothing

275

here...He wins here and holds the whole country hostage...wasn't bullshitting either...doesn't give a rats tail if we nuke 'em...just like Mr. Hitler...his whole country is expendable."

"That's incredible, Sir."

"He's a brazen genius...a genius who gets his guidance from the pit-o-hell...just where I plan to send him."

LARRY

SAN ANTONIO

The shrill bark of Ray's miniature Chihuahua pierced the silence. The dog really belonged to his wife, and Ray always made sure that everyone knew that. His dog was a hound. But now, both of them were announcing the presence of someone at the front door. Within a fraction of a second, the doorbell rang to confirm it.

Ray tried to hush the dogs as he peered through the tiny viewer in the door. Crazy Larry kept hitting the doorbell. Ray could see him talking to himself. He was obviously in a fit about something. Ray had never seen him like that before. He turned the dead bolt and pulled the door open.

"Hey, Larry! What? What's wrong?" Ray was about to open the door for Larry to come into the house, but Larry pushed it aside as if he was not opening it fast enough to suit him.

"Ray, you gotta listen to me...they're *here*!!"

Larry was always saying that *they* were coming. Ray did not know who *they* were. Larry was just very sure that they were coming. Ray had never heard him say that they were here before. He raised his graying eyebrows in surprise.

"Who's here, Larry?"

"Ray, you gotta listen. I tried to go over to the hospital at Lackland to get some medicine for my wife. They're here. They're all over the place."

"Larry, slow down. *Who's* here?"

"The Goddamn Camel Jockeys is who! They're talking in that gibberish and they're crawling all over the place."

Ray was perplexed. Larry had long ago earned his Crazy Larry nickname, but now he was going overboard. "Larry are you feeling O.K.?"

Larry began jumping in little circles and his voice raised about three levels. "Hell Yes, I'm feeling O.K. I tell you I saw them with my own eyes. They would not let me onto the Base so I sneaked around to the side and saw them. They're crawling all over *our* aircraft! And I didn't see one American. They've taken over! Listen to me, Ray!"

Ray dropped his eyes. He did not want Larry to see what he was thinking. Poor Larry had finally lost it. After all these years of being a veteran, all the stress of the epidemic must have pushed him right over the edge.

But Larry saw what Ray was thinking, anyway. "You don't believe me, do you?"

"Well, Larry, it is a little hard to..."

"Hell, come with me and see for yourself!"

Despite feeling a little sick, he smiled at Larry. "O.K., Larry. We'll go check it out." Maybe he could convince Larry that everything was as it should be.

HOME

SAN ANTONIO

The sign announced to Mike that he was only ninety miles from San Antonio. The long drive had been broken up by the many stops he made to vaccinate people he saw. It took a good bit of time because he had to explain that they were to vaccinate others from their vaccinations. All of them were glad to see him. Some had even heard Laura's broadcasts telling about the vaccination campaign.

But, most of them were hesitant when Mike explained the required procedure to them. He could only hope the recipients would actually comply with his instructions.

Finally, he turned onto the nearly abandoned Loop 410. It would only be a few minutes before he could hold Emily and his kids again. With all he had been through, it was a pleasant surprise that he was even going to get to see them again.

Driving down the streets of the suburb, Mike could see the effects of the epidemic. Bodies wrapped in old sheets sat unattended along the streets. Mike watched as two teenagers hauled a bundle from their home. Their shocked expressions brought Mike's stomach to his throat. The head of the victim became uncovered as they struggled with the weight, revealing a gray perm. This must have been their mother.

Mike slowed and rolled down his window. "Where is your father?"

The two pulled themselves out of their blank stares, looked at each other, then pointed to another bundle by the street. The girl's chest began to convulse as she sobbed bitter tears and dropped her half of her mother. The boy put down his half and went to hold her as Mike slowly drove on. He had seen plenty of sights just like this one. He had to keep going.

The smell of death permeated the cab of his vehicle. Yet, there was nobody to deal with the bodies that lined the curb. Mike could tell which corpses had been there for a few days because their sheets oozed fluids onto the sidewalks.

He could not look at it any longer. He knew that this gruesome scene was the same all over the United States. He was doing all he could do about it. He closed his eyes to rid himself of the sight and turned his head in horror.

The streets of his neighborhood were quiet and deserted...except for the area immediately surrounding his house. Cars of every description were parked all along the street, and all the driveways for several houses up the street were filled.

Mike growled to himself. What did they think they were doing? He had sent specific instructions with Luke that they were not to be in contact with anyone. Yet, it looked like they were having a damned party! He drove his four-wheel drive vehicle up onto a lawn and slammed the door as he got out of it.

As he stormed up to his front door, he noticed that a large percentage of the cars parked there boasted license plates given only to veterans who had earned the Purple Heart. But he did not have time to worry about that.

As he passed the front door to his next door neighbor's house, Mike thought he heard Luke's voice talking loudly to someone. He slowed and walked up the sidewalk to the house. Grasping the door handle, he flung it open. A room full of older men turned to see who had opened the door so unexpectedly.

Luke stopped his speech. "Mike! How did you get here? We didn't think..."

Mike did not let him finish. "What the Hell is going on here?!! I told you to stay isolated!"

"It's not what you think, Mike. We had to meet somewhere. The Small-pox is just the tip of the iceberg. Come in and let us explain."

Mike scowled as he surveyed the scene. "Well... start explaining..."

RMI

SAN ANTONIO

Luke brought Mike into the strange group of men gathered in the family room. Chairs had been moved from every room in the house to seat the crowd, but most of the men were standing on the periphery of the room, leaning on the paneling and furniture. Others were sitting towards the center of the room so that the men behind them could see and hear clearly.

All the eyes in the room followed Mike as he entered. Mike could see plainly that several of the men in the room were sick. They squinted at him through red eyes and looked feverish and flushed. He had no doubt that they had the virus. But these were older men who had been vaccinated at an early age. They would get sick, but not as sick as people without any protection.

Luke pulled him to the front of the group. "This is Dr. Mike Thompson. He's the one I told you about. I didn't think he'd make it here this fast. Mike, these are the members of the Retired Military Intelligence. We were having a meeting about what we can do."

Mike looked quizzically at Luke. "There's not much that we can do, besides what I told you about with the vaccines."

"No, Mike. You don't get it. There's more to it than you know."

"What do you mean?"

"The virus was just the first phase of the attack. Some of our men, here, say that the Coalition forces have taken over the military bases, right here in San Antonio."

Mike's mouth fell slightly open. Then, he crossed his brows. "Are you sure? How do you know?"

Ray stood up. Mike thought he had seen him somewhere before, but he could not place where. "We've seen them. They're all over the bases. They're flying the jets off with bombs and coming back without them."

"How do you know they're Coalition forces?"

Another RMI member answered this question. "Believe us. We know Coalition forces when we see them. It used to be our job to know them."

Luke tried to help Mike understand who these men were. He had found Ray and Larry in his vaccination trek. "These men worked in military intelligence before they retired, Mike. They know their stuff. Besides, didn't you say that it was the Coalition forces that sent over the virus?"

Mike had to admit. "O.K. I guess it makes sense. But what are they doing?"

Anger burned in the eyes of the next member to jump up. "They're bombing us with our own bombs in our own jets, By God!"

A murmur grew as it passed through the group. Passion turned to rage on the faces of the men. Luke waved his hand into the air to get their attention. "O.K. But remember, we're here to come up with some sort of a plan." The rumble began to fade. "Does anybody have any ideas?"

Crazy Larry stood up from his place on the floor. "I think I have something you can use. I always told you I was ready."

Ray closed his eyes and winced. So far, he had kept Larry under control. He stood up next to him and took him by the shoulders. "Uh, Larry. Sit down." Now, Mike remembered seeing the two men at the grocery store before the trip to Mexico.

Larry shoved him away like some sort of aggravating fly. The other men, who knew Larry's problem, were embarrassed for him. They tried not to look at him. But he insisted on getting their attention. Just before Ray could get his grip on Larry's arm, Larry pulled a small paper bag out of its hiding place under his shirt and emptied its contents into his hand. He held it high in the air.

"*This* is what you need! And I've got plenty of it!"

The men in the front of the group reacted immediately. Shocked expressions covered their faces as they vacated their proximities to the stash of C4 plastic explosive in Crazy Larry's hand.

MIKE'S HOUSE

Mike burst through the door and latched onto Emily, slowly closing his eyes in relief.

"Mike! When did you get in?"

"Just a while ago...I can't stay...gotta go...."

Emily scowled. "I was so worried about you!"

Mike looked at her. "Sorry, Emily. It's just that I have to hurry." A sudden look came over his face as he hugged her. "Emily...you're what we need right now."

"What?...What are you talking about? Tell me what you're doing."

"Look, it's a long story. All this Smallpox is just the beginning. The Coalition has attacked us. We have to fight back."

"What? How do you know?"

"Look, they've overrun the bases and they're using our own aircraft to bomb us. We've got to stop them somehow."

"Who is 'We'?"

"The men next door. It's a group of veterans and others. We are the only ones left. Now, look, Emily...here's what I need you to do. Get on the phone. Call everybody you know. Find out how many are still out there and not too sick. Tell them to be at the gym at the high school in two hours, but not to park in the parking lot. We don't want to draw attention...just yet. We plan to ask them to create a diversion while we do what we can to stop the bastards."

"Right."

"Oh, and get Jacob to call his friends. I bet they can help."

Jacob jumped into action. The virus had forced him to stay in the house for far more time than he had spent there in the last year. His fingers almost twitched in excitement as he dialed.

The sound of his friend's voice thrilled him because he knew that Schiller would be really good at this. It was exactly what Schiller did best. Jacob had always known that Schiller would use his talents well...he was just too good at them. For the last four years, Jacob and Schiller had arranged and practiced explosions of every possible type in the back yard, or out in the woods if they were too big.

Schiller's vast computer skills had opened a myriad of doors to opportunity. Schiller navigated the web to obtain the knowledge and materials they needed for their little projects. They had no actual plans to blow anything up. They were simply fascinated by the explosion itself, like a flame captivates a moth.

If Jacob's father had only known, he would have locked him in a cage and never let him out. Mike had always liked Schiller. Behind those sharp blue eyes, the brain of a young genius stayed perpetually in motion.

Jacob knew now why they had gotten away with all the stunts they had performed. They had been practicing...preparing for this without even knowing it. Now, they were going to use all of their skills for something important.

"Schiller! Get your stuff...let's go!"

"What? Are you crazy, Dude? We can't go do that now."

"No, Schiller. You don't get it. This Rules! My *parents* told me to call you. Can you believe it, Man? They *want* us to bring our stuff...you know, to blow stuff up...on purpose."

"What do you mean? They want me to blow stuff up? That Rules!"

"Yeah, Dude. We need some of those bombs. You still have some of that thermite?"

"Why, Dude?"

"Cuz my parents are leading an attack...on the people who did this."

Jacob could almost see Schiller's face drop as he remembered what he was trying to forget. In the quiet on the line, Jacob could hear Schiller's breathing become harder. He had just lost his sister and he was not sure if his parents were going to make it. He had not caught it. He figured he was just too mean. He had not known that 'someone' was responsible for it.

"What do you mean 'the people who did this'?"

"It was the Iranian Coalition...they sent it over here on some post-cards. Anyway, their men are over here trying to take over. We're gonna help stop them."

Schiller felt his ears and face begin to burn as the anger swelled in his mind. He glared off at nothing in particular. He set his jaw.

"What do they need?" he asked in a quiet tone.

"Like I said...get your crap and get over here. We have to create a diversion for them."

Schiller smiled his broad smile...the one he had forgotten all about in the last few days.

"That Rules!"

MACARTHUR HIGH SCHOOL GYM

SAN ANTONIO

The scene in front of the gym gave no indication that people were meeting inside. All the cars had been parked randomly down the streets, even in driveways, to avoid the appearance of a meeting. People walked toward the school a few at a time, as requested.

The ragtag group of survivors included every segment of society. Mike's family's calls had resulted in an increasing number of calls. Anyone who knew of any other nearby survivors called them in return. The result was a mixed group of exhausted, frightened people, freshly robbed of loved ones. Many were sick themselves and they arrived at the meeting under newly found power of anger as they realized that 'someone' was responsible.

So, as Mike stood on the gym floor, he felt the restlessness of the group around him in the stands. He looked at his notes and stared out into the crowd. It was a huge gym. He was not sure about anything. He was not nervous even though speaking before a group of any size used to make his voice, hands, and legs shake. He stood up before the mass.

He was bothered by what he did not feel. He wanted to feel something...anger, sadness, hate... anything, but not just numbness. *Maybe this is like a traumatized patient. The body just goes into shock and feels nothing. The mind...emotions...maybe they do the same thing...maybe I just can't believe what I'm asking these people to do.*

"Help me...help us," Mike whispered as he waited for the reverberating murmuring to die down. As he introduced himself quietly, the crowd grew quiet also.

"A few short days ago, something happened that none of us could even imagine. We've lived through things we never thought we'd witness. I don't know if we were simply caught napping...I don't know if we just grew complacent...I don't know why...I don't know exactly how it happened...but it HAS happened. This much I do know...when evil strikes...and evil always strikes sooner or later...good men, good women...brave men, brave women will be called on to stop it. They will be called on to sacrifice. That's what is being asked of you today. If you join this fight, some of you...maybe many of you...all of you...I just don't know...we all could be killed. I also believe that if we don't act...if we don't attack...if we don't prevail...death and horrors will continue to be visited upon us...and after us, the rest of the world."

"We have a plan." Mike nodded and a projector came on, lighting up a screen behind him. "They have their hands on these." He pointed to the rows of F16 fighters. "Our information is that every base in the country is under siege. We can't expect much help, but if we can destroy these aircraft HERE in San Antonio, it will remove their air cover.'

"If we destroy these...then...*THEN THEY WILL KNOW THAT THEY HAVE NOT DEFEATED US!* They will know that we will keep attacking them until they are *ALL DEAD OR TUCKING THEIR TAILS ALL THE WAY HOME!* Any of you want any part of this?"

Total silence followed for what seemed to Mike like an eternity. The only noise coming from the auditorium was a few scattered coughs. The rejection seemed to choke Mike. *How can this be?...What has happened to us!...Help me! Help me! Oh, my God...help me!*

Mike drew a deep breath and raised his eyes to gaze out over the crowd. At the very back of the auditorium, Mike thought he saw a fight taking place. He rubbed his eyes, but the fighting figures still looked shadowy. To make matters more confusing, the crowd seemed completely indifferent to

284

the melee, as if nobody but Mike saw it. The brawl became totally obscured by the standing throng at the back of the auditorium.

Somewhere from the back, near the fight, Mike saw a single man shoot a clinched fist in the air. Mike could see the man's mouth and face move like he was shouting something, but he could hear no words. Several people near the man began to work their arms in the air in slow motion. Their mouths moved but no sounds came out. In the same slow motion manner, the whole crowd rose. Many jumped up onto their seats.

It reminded Mike of what happens when the audio goes out on the TV and the volume control is turned up. Suddenly, the audio returns and the blast from the full volume TV almost makes you jump. The noise was almost overwhelming.

Mike took several quick steps backwards. He almost started to laugh. He wanted to laugh hysterically. The realization and the absurdity of what he had just touched off made him visibly shake. "My God, what am I doing?"

San Antonio—Thursday evening

"Bè still!" Doreen was having a hard enough time without Ray moving all around. She focused her attention on the spot she had missed. The camouflage paint she was spreading on Ray's face was dark-colored, so Ray's white skin shone through the places she missed. It made it easy to notice and fix. Her full attention was fixed on her task because she did not want to think about what it meant. In a few minutes her husband would be joining his fellow veterans in a raid on a heavily guarded Air Base.

After all these years, she thought she would never have to face these fears again. After all, her husband was retired from the military. He had even retired again from his days as a private eye. She had thought that she would never have to fear his going off to dangerous assignments again. But, here he was, getting ready with all the resolve of his earlier years. Never mind that he was sixty-seven years old.

"Ray, are you sure that this is a good idea? Why can't somebody else go?"

"Doreen, we've been over this before. There isn't anybody else. It's up to us. We don't know what they're bombing, but it has to be stopped...not to mention the virus...Doreen, just think about the bodies. Now, come on and let's get this done. I'm almost late." He looked into her eyes and saw that they were moist with tears. "I'll be all right. Haven't I always come back to you? Even from Viet Nam? Don't worry, I'll be O.K." He stood up and held her tight. She had always been so brave when he left, even for a year at a time.

Mike watched as the men returned to the meeting house in the dark. He had been next door at his own house getting all of his gear ready. His face matched the faces of the returning men, as did his camos and combat boots. He scanned the scene and had to smile. He did not know how much good they could accomplish, but anything they did would be far better than just letting it happen around them. Retribution for this attack was dependent on this ragtag group. The handful of retired veterans had just recently lost their benefits from the government in the last budget cuts, yet these men had answered the call to duty, just as they had in their youth. It made him proud to be associated with them.

He did not know how much good they could do, but he knew that whatever hell they could give the Coalition forces would help something. Maybe, there were other resistance groups operating in other places. Maybe, together, it would make some sort of difference. He did not know. He only knew that they had to do what they could.

Crazy Larry had arrived early with his stash of explosive. How the man had been able to get hold of such a supply was beyond understanding. But, so was the whole disaster. At least, this was one turn of events in their favor.

They checked their weapons and ammunition and coordinated their locations on the maps. Timing was going to be critical. The enemy would have anticipated such a civilian attack.

THE BATTLE

"Well it is a plan...a suicide plan," mused Mike to himself. "The Plan" was pretty basic. Military minds would call it a massive frontal assault with a smaller coordinate flanking assault. The big rigs, the eighteen wheelers, would lead the first wave. They would be used to plow through the outer perimeter fences and other barriers. Behind them would come a menagerie of vehicles of every description.

It was decided that pickup trucks would be the follow-up assault vehicle of choice, as much as possible. Pickups allowed the occupants standing behind the cab in the bed of the truck, to have unobstructed forward firing. Most had been fitted with at least some makeshift, homemade armor plating. Many had various versions of battering rams welded on the front. Others had what amounted to a heavily built up bumper. At least one carried what appeared to be the blade of a bulldozer. Someone had come up with the bright idea that they could disable the grounded jets by ramming them. No one wanted to think about the chances of any of them ever making it close enough to carry out such a feat.

"Correle vauto...Vamos, man, we gotta go, primo!" Caesar DeLeon demanded.

"Caya' te hombre, I gotta fix this good por los pindajos, man...unless you wanna get you ass shot off by them, man!" Mimo Montalvo shouted as he raised his welding hood. "Hand me another pinche welding rod, primo." Mimo flipped his hood back down and welding sparks started spraying again.

"Listo Pisto, that's it...we're ready man, Muy fine!" Mimo said as he banged his creation with his fist. It looked something like a king-sized snowplow assembled on an extreme machine monster type pickup. On the vertical apex of the plow, he had created what looked like a huge serrated knife. A small slit remained in the otherwise plated over windshield. Armor plating rose up from the bed of the pickup to about shoulder-height of a standing man.

"Come on primo, no querre' tarde por la party... we're late man, get in," Caesar shouted, as he cranked up what was now hardly recognizable as a

287

pickup. Mimo climbed into the back and promptly sprawled over a pile of assorted firearms. Caesar had the back loaded with a smorgasbord of weaponry, some homemade, some commercial. This included pipe bombs, pipe bombs strapped to butane tanks and Molotov fire bombs.

"Stop this thing, man...we got too much caca back here, man...I can't move around." Mimo bawled as he took a kick at some offending object.

"Lo seinto, primo...can't stop...we muy late hombre...we gonna need it all," Caesar shouted back through the missing rear window. The truth was they were late.

The big rigs were gathering speed, pouring out more black diesel smoke with each gearshift. As planned, they rolled toward Randolph AFB from as many different routes as possible. The hope was to disguise vehicle movement as being something other than an attack. It was also assumed that nice straight, long columns of trucks would make efficient targets for the constant umbrella of F-16s and other craft over the airbase. Therefore, each "attack group" was typically comprised of just two tractor-trailer rigs, followed closely by three or more rigged assault vehicles.

One of the final waves would be composed primarily of motorcycles. The thought was that they were too unprotected for the initial wave. They could be easily be cut down by small arms fire and could carry only a limited amount of firepower. Still, they might prove effective later if the battlefield became clogged with destroyed vehicles.

Mimo pounded on the cab and pointed to the rigs moving on the highway. "Meda lo primo, that's our bunch."

Even at the distance of approximately half a mile, he recognized the rigs of the "attack group" they had been assigned to. When Mimo and Caesar failed to meet at the coordinated attack time, there was no waiting for them.

"Dale' gas, that's them...up the highway, man," pointed Mimo.

Caesar closed the gap considerably when the big trucks slowed down to take an exit ramp. They were now within five miles of Randolph AFB. The two eighteen-wheelers made wide swings as they turned left on an overpass.

The white flash erupted behind the first rig and in front of the second rig. The overpass collapsed, along with the fiery remnants of both tractor-trailers. High above, almost invisible to the naked eye, a Coalition pilot congratulated himself on his accuracy with the laser guided "smart bomb."

Mimo and Caesar both instinctively ducked down in the truck as chunks of concrete and other debris rocked their vehicle. Neither could quite grasp what had happened, and Caesar stopped the truck in frozen amazement. The vehicle that had been following closely behind the big rigs was now a burning hulk, resting on top of what left of the destroyed overpass.

Mimo and Caesar continued to sit and watch in dumbfounded amazement as the three occupants of the one unscathed pickup leaped out of their vehicle. They were too slow. A missile traveling on a corkscrewing path arched down from an unseen aircraft. The unfortunates were blown to three separate directions. One of their flopping bodies landed within ten feet of Mimo and Caesar.

Mimo tried to make his arms move in order to beat on the cab and tell Caesar to move, but they would not respond. He tried to yell, but he just kept making little squeaky noises. Finally, he got his arms working to the point where he looked like he was flapping wings, but his voice would only make louder squeaks. To his relief, Caesar had the tires on the truck smoking as they fishtailed in acceleration.

Mimo was thrown to the bed of the truck. Loose pipe bombs and other weaponry flew around. He struggled to get to his feet, but Caesar was making such wild turns that Mimo was rattling around just like their homemade weapons. He managed to get a handhold on the side plate armor to pull himself to his feet.

Spray from a heavy-caliber machine gun kicked up chunks of pavement parallel to the path of the truck. Caesar turned violently, again throwing Mimo up against the armor plated sides. More strafing fire ripped to their left. Mimo had not even located what was firing on them, but by now he had figured that they were being pummeled from above.

This was not the way he had visualized it. Even though they had been briefed on the likelihood of suffering heavy loses from jet and helicopter gun-ship attack, it just was not reality to him that their entire attack group could be wiped out before they even got close to the airbase. He had mentally prepared himself for the fearless charge across the open expanse of the airfield, in the face of constant fire. He never thought they might die while running for their lives, miles from their objective. He knew that it would probably be just a matter of a few seconds until the pilot gunning for them made a successful pass.

Mimo managed to pull himself up again. They were racing down a side road at a speed that blew tears out of his eyes. It looked like they were passing between rows of warehouses. He felt an intense heat as something fast streaked past his head. The missile detonated directly in front of them. Caesar slammed the truck into a sliding stop and ground the gears as he peeled in reverse.

Mimo had regained enough of his voice to squeak out, "You loco, andelante! They get us for sure, man." He frantically pointed straight ahead.

"Keep you head down, primo," was all that Caesar would allow. He slammed on the brakes and made a hard left turn. Mimo raised up just enough to see why Caesar wanted him to keep his head down. The truck crashed through a chain-link fence and headed straight up a concrete ramp toward the closed sliding bay door of a warehouse. The doors scarcely slowed the truck as they skidded to a stop in the darkness of the warehouse.

From above, their hunter banked his aircraft. He pinpointed the warehouse with his laser site. The bomb hit the huge warehouse squarely. The fireball that ensued from the explosion quickly consumed the structure as the building collapsed in on itself. The black smoke went up, joining other smoke to form a layer over San Antonio. Many burning wrecks were already adding to the cloud over the city

PENTAGON

"Yes, Sir, a very reliable report, a detailed report. Sir! It appears there is a sustained, heavy counter-attack against the Randolph insurgents. This could be the break we're looking for, Sir. They are requesting any support...especially air cover. Apparently they are really getting clobbered by.... It's a civilian attack, Sir... That's right, Sir." Goodloe snapped in uncharacteristic curtness.

"*Civilian!*...Well, I'll be a son of a...O.K., O.K., maybe...maybe. Now listen to me, you're right. This may be our one chance, but *you gotta make this...I repeat, you have to make this clear to everyone!* It doesn't sound like we've got enough fighters and pilots available to take them on straight up...not right now, anyway. They are going to keep their defensive umbrella over Randolph and Ft. Hood. pretty damn tight. Get as many fighters as you can muster. Put anything you can find up in the air. We gotta make it look like as big of an attack as we can...*when they move to engage us, bug out. Get the hell outta there.* That should take some of the heat off of our civvy friends. Our boys are not to engage them...no deep penetrations yet. We can't afford to lose anybody. Have our boys keep the heat on though...have 'em keep flying, poking arou nd the edges of their umbrella. If our civvies really begin to take it to the enemy, they'll pull down most of their fighters to give close-in support to their ground troops. *That's what you're looking for, son.* If that happens, swoop in on 'em with everything you got...kick them hard square in the ass and don't let up. You might get some penetration...do some real damage. All right, Brian...get after it son!" Herndon slammed the phone without even waiting for a reply.

San Antonio

"Pinche pindajo, you can't hit *schit*! I gonna kick you ass! Just you wait, man," Mimo yelled out, throwing his fist in the air at their departing adversary.

Caesar peaked out cautiously behind his friend. He shared none of his friend's newly found bravado. He knew they had been lucky that he kept on moving and that somehow they had not been seen as they smashed into the adjacent warehouse. He looked at the burning heap of what had been a gigantic building. "Gracias Jesus Cristo!" he whispered as he watched Mimo's continued antics.

"Beso me culo." Mimo shouted, spanking his now naked behind.

Mimo was on a real roll now and Caesar knew it would take his amigo quite a while to finish his repertoire of displays and insults. He had seen what he thought was a roof hatch and thought he might be able figure a way up to see what he could see.

"Hey, Primo venga se, get up here. You need to see this, man," Caesar called down to Mimo.

In short order, Mimo emerged out of the hatch on the roof with Caesar. As he carefully straightened up to balance himself on the steep sloping roof, he looked in the direction he saw his friend staring.

"Chengus Domingus!" gasped Mimo.

They were much closer to Randolph Airbase than Caesar had guessed. He could clearly see rows of fighters in the distance. Even as they watched, an F-16 lifted off the runway. He could also see countless plumes of dark smoke some distance from the landing strip. There was a heavy *whump,* followed by a fireball. Caesar figured it was at least two miles away. He heard several quick successive *whump*s at a greater distance, but he could not locate their source.

He noticed vapor trails in the sky that were so numerous that it looked like some giant had gone wild scribbling on the big, blue ceiling with a white marker. There was a quick pinprick of a flash high among the white trails. It was easy for his mind to interpret that as an exploding aircraft of some sort.

"Meda." Mimo pointed to a vehicle that came from an area of the landing strip that was not visible to them from their vantage point. Two other vehicles followed it, but it was hard to discern exactly what kind of vehicles because of the distance.

They were heading straight for the upper end of the strip. It appeared that they were getting near the tarmac, but Caesar knew that, because of the distance and the angle, the vehicles were probably actually much further from the runway than they appeared.

"All right! Way to go, chacho...get 'em boys. It's our guys, man!" Mimo cheered with such vigorous body language that he nearly lost his balance on the roof.

Caesar was pretty sure he was right. "Go...go... gooo!" He urged through gritted teeth. He saw a flaming white streak go over the top of the lead vehicle, followed by an explosion several vehicle lengths behind it. Just as it reached the tarmac, a huge orange ball erupted under it, causing it to summersault in the air. The next vehicle was already on the runway and suddenly it veered off the pavement, stopping for no readily detectable reason. The third vehicle halted considerably short of the runway. A thin slip of barely noticeable dark fumes began rising from it. Through the increasing haze it appeared that a figure got out of the smoking vehicle, but if it went very far, Caesar could not see it. He thought he saw the figure go to the ground, but he was not sure.

Mimo turned to Caesar. "You know primo, I don't think we're doing so good, man."

They both watched and listened to the sound of the distance battle for several minutes. First, letting out a long and slow whistling breath, Caesar made an unannounced exit down the roof hatch.

"Hey! Where you going, man," Mimo shouted down to Caesar who was already standing on the floor of the warehouse.

"Gonna take care of those jets, man."

"Oh me Cristo-Santa Maria...you loco, man. You saw what they doing over there, man. They ain't nobody making it, man."

"I thought I just heard you say you're gonna kick their ass."

"Oh, I gonna kick their ass man –you know – I just didn't mean I was gonna kick their ass today!

Caesar disappeared from Mimo's view and the loud, rumbling roar of their pickup told Mimo where he had gone.

"You coming or no, man?" shouted Caesar.

Mimo banged his head on the roof. "Me madre! Me madre! Me madre!"

• • •

Mike and Luke's small task force had selected the tallest building they could find that gave them a respectable field of view of Randolph's runway. Mike especially wanted a clear view, if possible, of the far end of the runway. The major frontal attacks were to begin on that end of the airbase; essentially this was the opposite side of the base from the task force's proposed infiltration point. What he was seeing through his binocular did not increase his level of confidence.

There was not a genius, military planner in the bunch. With all the haggling and planning by committee, settling on one concrete plan of attack made Mike's stomach churn, but he was their leader-apparent. It did seem to make sense to him at the time. Surely the Coalition troops would have to rally to the far end of the airbase to repel a serious threat.

It did not take a military genius, or great in-depth and analytic assessment, to reach the same conclusion that Mimo drew-"I don't think we're doing so good..."

The sun would set in less than half a hour. From everything Mike could see, the frontal the assault had fizzled. Explosions rocked the area, but most were nowhere near the base. F-16's constantly landed and took off. The smoky haze and Mike's lack of expertise in military hardware kept him from identifying some other aircraft.

He did recognize the Apache Helicopters. Those things really worried him.

Mike's group had brought several two-way radios, but they were to observe strict radio silence on all channels. Termination of the attack constituted the only reason for their use. Abundance of radio chatter might tip off the Coalition Forces about the impending attack. Mike thought that watching too many old movies had inspired the "radio silence" and much of the stuff that everyone was suggesting. Radio silence sure did not make any to sense him once the main assault commenced.

Apparently, many of the members of the main assault agreed with Mike, because they carried a continuous dialogue on all monitored channels. Disaster dominated everything Mike heard. He could hear more of the battle than he could see. Occasionally, a fireball rose up from somewhere in the city, followed by its heavy report. However, the explosion frequency decreased. He did see one fireball go up near the far end of the runway, and he thought he could see a burning wreck.

Darkness extended over the area. Mike turned to Luke. "What do you think?"

Luke just sucked his lower lip under his teeth, gave a shrug and slightly nodded his head. Nobody had any discussion to add.

• • •

Counting himself and Luke, the task force included ten men. Weapons, packs containing extra ammunition, explosives and other items weighed down each of the men.

Getting past Randolph's perimeter fence with relative ease had encouraged Mike. They had remained under cover for at least fifteen minutes, checking things out with some sort of night vision device before making any kind of move. Mike felt certain that getting on the flight line would be another matter.

To his surprise, this side of the huge airbase lacked the expected enemy activity. Still, they made slow progress because they frequently stopped to let Luke scan with his night vision device.

When they reached the flight line perimeter fence, they were supposed to find a large culvert. Luke served as navigator and scout. Thanks to his global position unit they wasted few steps, and Luke lead them straight to the pipe exactly where their maps had indicated it would be.

They went under the fence, through the large metal culvert. It forced them to do a full bend at the waist and a half squat, but they moved quickly down the pipe until they reached the far end. They knew there would be grating over the culvert's end, and had brought bolt cutters. However they had not counted on the large clog of sticks, logs, trash and other debris that had washed and stacked up on the grate.

The bolt cutters pinched easily through the bars, but getting past the clog would present a bigger problem. The huge mass of the clog prevented them from muscling it forward, especially since the culvert's size allowed only one man to work on the pile. The only solution was to pass it stick by stick and log by log to the next person.

Mike had just pulled on the first big limb when he saw something move in the pile. Darkness prevented him from making out what It was. He wanted to shine a light on whatever it was, but he knew he did not dare. He stuck his head slightly into the pile and simultaneously lifted up a tangle of limbs and trash.

It instantly leaped out onto Mike's head. He crashed backwards into Luke, involuntarily screaming and flailing wildly at the beast. Mike knocked the creature back behind Luke, where it promptly exhibited gravity-defying abilities by running a complete loop inside the culvert. Seeing only more people past Luke, the creature reversed its course and ran back past Luke. He ran straight for Mike's leg, and scampered up on the back of his neck and head. Mike could not help himself. He yelled at the top of his lungs. Every time he swatted at the creature, it nimbly avoided Mike's hand and ran part of the way down his back. He tried to hit it as it moved down to the small of his back, and it scampered back to Mike's neck and head. To Mike, this activity seemed to go on forever, and he could not understand why Luke was not coming to his aid. In reality, the event did not last fifteen seconds. Eventually, the animal grew weary of the sport and leaped off of Mike, escaping out of the culvert.

"What was that thing!" Mike was gasping at a full yell.

Luke grabbed Mike around the neck, clapped his hand over Mike's mouth and whispered harshly and slowly into his ear, "A...little...furry... ANIMAL!" A creature known to many as a Ring-tailed Cat had accosted Mike, and Luke was in no mood to give him a lesson in the fauna of the Southwestern U.S.

As the panic drained from Mike, he realized the reason for Luke's anger. Embarrassment bathed over him...so much at stake, and he had screamed his head off like some frightened schoolgirl.

Mike wanted to apologize to everyone.

Mike started to whisper "I guess..."

"Shhh, listen."

Voices amplified. Then a light hit the rubble in front of the culvert, piercing inside. The light swept away. Two distinct voices conversed. The sound of car door slammed, and more voices followed. The light swept back, and stopped again on the pile in front of the culvert. The chain link fence sang that distinctive *scheennn* sound it makes when someone strikes it or gives it a good shake.

Mike looked up as if he could some how see through the pipe and the thick layer of soil covering it. He heard and felt the vibrations of steps above them. The first step on the bare, uncovered end of corrugated metal culvert made a ping. Mike felt Luke ease the muzzle of his weapon around him and point it generally toward the pipe opening. Mike heard the faint click of Luke taking his weapon off safety. He copied Luke's actions. The pinging steps continued very slowly. They stopped.

296

Mike could feel himself shaking. He told himself to take his finger off the trigger of his Mini-14. He did not want to cause anymore foul-ups. He breathed deeply through his nose and slowly exhaled out his mouth, thinking that it might help control his trembling.

They heard two more slow steps. Whoever it was had obviously reached the lip of the pipe. It sounded like he must have gravel or something adhering to his shoes or boots, from the grating noise it made on the metal pipe.

The unseen soldier shouted something and it made Mike jump with a start. A light much more intense than the previous light hit the pile of refuse at the mouth of the pipe. Even shining through the clog, it made enough light for Mike to see the expression on Luke's face. For some reason, Luke laid down, almost hugging the floor of the pipe. All the men copied Luke except Mike. Luke grabbed Mike by the leg and motioned him down.

"Aahhhh!...Aahhhh! The noise echoed through pipe and startled Mike so badly that he nearly let out another yell himself.

Mike raised his head slightly and saw the silhouette of a man standing outside at the other end of the pipe. The man pointed a rifle toward the inside of the pipe.

More shouts ensued, but Mike did not understand them. The man standing on the lip of the pipe yelled something in response. Mike noticed that the silhouette of the individual at the opposite end of the pipe no longer appeared to be pointing a weapon. Instead, he had straightened up so that Mike no longer saw his head. The soldier shouted something to someone else. The silhouette disappeared.

A loud, clanging noise rattled down from the far end of the pipe.

"*Grenade!*" was the only thought that came to Mike's mind. He made himself as flat possible. Something made more clanging and rattling down the pipeline. Mike raised his head enough to spy the silhouette again, as it made a throwing motion. Whatever it threw made one clang on the side of the pipe, then struck Mike on the right side of the head on his ear. Mike grabbed his ear and resisted the urge to yell out.

Rocks?

The silhouette sustained the barrage for at least a minute, then shouted something and vanished. The light shifted off of the pile. The sound of someone climbing over the chain link fence came next and the light extinguished.

They strained to hear more talking and a vehicle door slamming. The vehicle drove off.

Mike's stomach, which had been resting just under one swallow, rebelled now, and Mike abruptly got up on his hands and heaved. Nothing came out of his gaping mouth. He heaved again loudly and a large volume shot out, splashing against the sides of the pipe and rebounding back to Luke behind him.

Mike straightened up to his knees, using his rifle for support. He looked around while still gasping. From outside the pipe in front of him, an upside down head peered at Mike. It turned slightly from side to side as if it could see nothing.

Firing erupted. Multiple rounds flashed out of the muzzle of his rifle before Mike realized he was the one doing the shooting. Luke's weapon, on full auto, began flashing also and tearing holes in the corrugated metal.

The dead soldier at the front of the pipe slid sideways off the pipe and limply crashed down on the pile below. Distant shouts reached them and Luke did not hesitate. He clambered right over Mike. The impassable tangle of a few moments ago now barely slowed Luke down. He crashed over and through it.

Mike followed Luke's lead, but with less success. Luke's first move had been an athletic, headfirst leap. He still had not cleared the entire pile, but he managed to get his legs under him and kept them moving. He did not falter much.

Mike's youthful mind forgot about the fact that his body had survived a few more years than Luke's body. His attempt to copy Luke resulted in more of a swimming motion out on top of the pile. This did not prove to be a very effective technique. Shouts and the rumble of an approaching vehicle preceded a spotlight that quickly swept to Mike as he thrashed around trying to free himself. The spotlight blinded Mike as he heard the angry bee sound of projectiles flying past him. At first, he did not understand, but then he realized that they were shooting at him.

Mike saw his situation as hopeless and he raised his hands in surrender. When he did this, his now streamlined body crashed down through the brush pile. This instantly landed him at the bottom of the drainage ditch that lead to the culvert. More importantly, the spotlight no longer found him and he temporarily escaped the enemy's line of fire.

Muzzle flashes exploded from above the culvert and behind the fence, but they were not firing at Mike or Luke. Mike's men had backed out of the culvert and now laid down fire from behind the fence. Mike spotted Luke motioning for him. He crawled on his belly towards Luke.

"Now's our chance, lets go!" Luke whispered.

Mike hesitated. Headlights of numerous vehicles drew near. Luke grabbed him roughly and repeated, "Let's go!"

They followed the drainage ditch virtually at a trot. The depth of the drainage ditch prevented them from seeing out over its banks. They stopped once so Luke could read his GPS unit. The sound of a much heavier caliber automatic weapon let Mike know that, even though they saw no further signs of the firefight, it still continued.

Luke grabbed him, pointed at his GPS and motioned that they needed to climb up the bank of the drainage ditch. They both raised up to look over the bank.

There they were!

The nearest fighter rested only a few hundred yards away. Up until now, Mike did not have a clue about their distance from the fighters, though he had every confidence in Luke's ability to find them.

Mike had not known what to expect. In his mind's eye, he thought that a whole gaggle of "Hup-two-three-four type" guards secured the well-lit area where the F-16's sat all in a row. Instead, darkness surrounded the aircraft and it lacked defenders. Out on the runway itself, constant activity abounded as the aircraft landed and took off. *This part might not be so tough after all.*

Luke worked slowly with his night vision scanner. He stopped and lowered his head in obvious dejection. Mike strained his eye in an attempt to see what had so affected Luke. A vehicle, minus its lights, drove up and stopped halfway between them and the nearest fighter. Someone got out of the passenger's side and blared a message over a bullhorn. A loud, whooping alarm bellowed.

It appeared to Mike that they raised straight up out of the pavement, two of them within fifty yards of Mike and Luke. The Coalition soldiers got up from wherever they had been lying, and ran in place until all their steps synchronized. They trotted off, all in step.

Luke growled fiercely into Mike's ear, "Do what I do!"

He jumped up in the darkness and started mimicking the same run-in-place cadence. Once in step, he trotted off at the same slow pace. Mike skipped the run-in-place thing. This proved to be a mistake because he never quite fell into step, but he did not want to fall too far behind Luke.

As they rounded past the tail of the first fighter, Mike comprehended that the group they followed trotted past the rows of parked F-16's. One fighter blazed down the runway preparing for takeoff. An explosion ripped somewhere out in the dark, well off the end of the runway. A helicopter flew directly over head. Mike recognized it as an Apache. It had not traveled very far from them before it fired three pod rockets, and then opened up with its chin gun in the general direction of the explosion. A large, white streak passed over the top of the helicopter, while a host of smaller white streaks arched up to the helicopter from a multitude of directions out in the darkness.

Mike finally realized the situation. The assault still had a little life left in it.

Luke made a left-hand turn, and simply jogged into the row of fighters. He stopped, kneeling down under the wing of one of the jets. Pulled off his pack, he motioned for Mike's pack also.

"You cover me...I'll plant."

Mike knew that Luke meant that he had seen enough of Mike's bungling, and had no intention of letting him blow both of them up after making it this far. Luke intended to work his way back down the row of fighters, setting charges as they went. They had lost many of their charges when they had gotten separated from the other men and their packs.

They no longer mimicked the Coalition cadence. Mike and Luke raced in a dead run to each jet.

"Three more," Mike gasped, indicating the number of charges they had remaining.

Mike heard the angry bee sound again. This time he knew exactly what it meant, but he could not locate the source of the firing.

Luke collapsed.

Confusion clouded Mike's brain. Somewhere in the fog, he realized that Luke had been hit, but it barely registered. Mike's right leg quit working, but he did not have time to figure out why.

A muzzle flashed out of the dark.

He emptied Luke's M-16 at the flashes.

"How much time?" He asked as he fumbled in Luke's pack, searching for another clip.

Luke did not reply. He just moved his lips and blinked his eyes.

WOOSH-WHUMP.

The first fighter went up.

The light of burning jet fuel clearly illuminated Luke's weakening face.

Another explosion...five jets blazed...Mike could feel the heat already.

Luke gave a vacant look and he muttered, "We better leave."

Mike struggled to get up to drag Luke.

His right leg still refused to function.

He glanced down at his leg. Blood covered the entire leg. A gaping hole penetrated the leg about four inches above his kneecap.

He grabbed Luke by the collar. Pushing off the best he could with his left leg, he dragged him towards a hangar.

First the concussion wave...then the heat...

...another explosion...

The world tilted...

It went black...

Explosions...

Firing...

Men running past...

Daylight...

A strange-looking vehicle stopped near him. It revved its engine and plowed into a fighter's wing. It swerved around and clipped another one.

"What 't hell you think you doing, man. We done kick their asses, man. These are OUR planes now, primo. I knew better than let you drive."

"Oh." Mimo grinned.

"Back up some, man, I wanna see something," Caesar demanded.

Mimo backed to where Caesar indicated.

Caesar looked down.

"Hey, primo...these are some of our boys-I think they're alive man."

WASHINGTON, D.C.

"Yes, Brian...that is great news...Wonderful...great, great... Wonderful. No, I can hardly believe it myself, son.... Did we loose many?...outstanding. You did great job, son. No...no.... It won't assure us victory, son.... I agree...Their momentum is gone."

The General closed his eyes. The pungent smell of burning flesh that had haunted him since the beginning of his dreams had suddenly left.

He breathed in deep.

Fresh air...the smell of hope.

For we wrestle not against flesh and blood, but against principalities, against powers, against the rulers of the darkness of this world, against spiritual wickedness in high places.

Ephesians 6:12

For ordering information, call Purple Sage Publishing at 800-839-8234.